THE ECONOMICS OF TRANSPARENCY IN POLITICS

The Economics of Transparency in Politics

Edited by

ALBERT BRETON
University of Toronto

GIANLUIGI GALEOTTI
Università di Roma (La Sapienza)

PIERRE SALMON
Université de Bourgogne

RONALD WINTROBE
University of Western Ontario

Routledge
Taylor & Francis Group
LONDON AND NEW YORK

First published 2007 by Ashgate Publishing

2 Park Square, Milton Park, Abingdon, Oxon OX14 4RN
711 Third Avenue, New York, NY 10017, USA

Routledge is an imprint of the Taylor & Francis Group, an informa business

First issued in paperback 2017

British Library Cataloguing in Publication Data
The economics of transparency in politics
1. Transparency in government - Economic aspects
2. Political culture - Economic aspects 3. Freedom of
information 4. Democracy 5. International relations
6. Political corruption
I. Breton, Albert
306.2

Library of Congress Cataloging-in-Publication Data
The economics of transparency in politics / edited by Albert Breton ... [et al.].
p. cm.
Includes index.
ISBN-13: 978-0-7546-4933-5
1. transparency in government. 2. Government information. 3. Disclosure of information. 4. Freedom of information. I. Breton, Albert.

JC598.E26 2006
352.3'8--dc22

2006031442

ISBN 978-0-7546-4933-5 (hbk)
ISBN 978-1-138-27766-3 (pbk)

Contents

List of Figures

List of Tables

List of Contributors

Albert Breton, Department of Economics, University of Toronto

Giorgio Brosio, Dipartimento di Economia, Università di Torino

Federico Etro, Dipartimento di Economia, Università degli Studi di Milano

Gianluigi Galeotti, Facoltà di Giurisprudenza, Università di Roma (La Sapienza)

Piero Giarda, Facoltà di Economia, Università Cattolica di Milano

Russell Hardin, New York and Stanford Universities

Manfred J. Holler, Institute of SocioEconomics, University of Hamburg

Louis M. Imbeau, Département de Science Politique, Université Laval

Glenn P. Jenkins, Department of Economics, Queen's University and Department of Economics, Eastern Mediterranean University

Chun-Yan Kuo, John Deutsch Institute, Queen's University

Johann Lambsdorff, Department of Economics, University of Passau

Pierre Salmon, LEG-CNRS, Université de Bourgogne

Ronald Wintrobe, Department of Economics, University of Western Ontario

Alain Wolfelsperger, Institut d'Etudes Politiques de Paris

Introduction

Albert Breton, Gianluigi Galeotti, Pierre Salmon, and Ronald Wintrobe

The view is widespread that more transparency in institutions leads to better outcomes. That, however, is surely too enthusiastic a view. To illustrate, a *sine qua non* of popular democracy is the secret ballot – the suppression of transparency. To appreciate one of the central virtues of secret balloting, consider the fact that in a number of organizations, the leadership, for obvious reasons, insists that the preferences and opinions of the rank and file be revealed through a hand count instead of a secret ballot. Transparency, in that case, is a way of controlling the membership.

Other examples where transparency appears to lead to worse outcomes than secrecy include the refereeing of papers submitted for publication to scientific journals and the refereeing, through letters of recommendation, of the value of candidates to be hired or promoted. It appears that the reports are more objective when, in the first case, papers sent to referees have been anonymized and, in the second case, when the names of referees are not revealed to candidates. In both cases, secrecy trumps transparency.

Still, there are many areas of activity in which transparency would appear to be the superior alternative. The purpose of the 10th Villa Colombella Seminar was to provide an occasion for the formulation and discussion of positive (as distinguished from normative) rational choice models of the advantages and costs of transparency in select areas of public sector activity or, to put it differently, to analyze what is, in effect, the social level of obfuscation in politics that results from rational behaviour.

Some examples of specific topics which we hoped would be addressed are:

The effects of political competition on transparency: It seems that it would be easier for an organization (or an individual) to obfuscate – to be less transparent – when it is the only agency in possession or in control of particular pieces of information. One question that this raises is whether political competition (among political parties, centres of power in compound governments, and among governments in decentralized governmental systems) reduces the capacity to obfuscate – increases transparency. If the answer to this question is yes, follow-up questions include: how does competition achieve this result? under what conditions? are there exceptions?

The effects of transparency on political competition: If political competition is conceived as a force inducing political actors and political agencies to do as well or better than actors or agencies with whom they interact, will that incitation be more powerful if the costs of obfuscation are increased – if more transparency is allowed? In what way does that incentive operate? Is the mechanism different in governments than the one at work in markets?

The IMF, the WTO, Seattle and transparency: Among the grievances expressed in Seattle, Genoa, and elsewhere against the process of globalization and the structures that rule it such as the IMF, the WTO, the World Bank, the European Council of Ministers and central banks, surely one of the most significant is the demand for more "openness" or transparency. It is said that most of the leaders of these organizations are unelected and, moreover, that when they create dispute settlement tribunals these operate too much in secret. Would outcomes be better or worse if decision-making processes were more transparent? How could that be done? Would greater transparency lead to more democracy? Would it lead to more efficiency? Is there a conflict between democracy and efficiency in the operation of these structures and if so, how can it be resolved?

New communication technologies, politics, and transparency: In *Nineteen Eighty Four* George Orwell (1949) predicted that advances in communication technologies would permit a new level of political domination by a dictator affectionately called Big Brother. Even though modern TV and the Hollywood machine have made propaganda more pervasive than ever, it is not always pro-government. "Horizontal" media like the Internet and fax machines appear to have fostered liberty rather than repression by dramatically diminishing the possibilities for the governments to deceive the population, to suppress information, and to keep secrets from the people. Moreover, these technologies seem to have enlarged the possibilities for citizens to communicate directly with each other and to organize against governments via Internet, e-mail campaigns and so forth. Yet, where there is so much information, others might argue that transparency is reduced, a result of information overload and noise, a process encouraged as many individuals increasingly turn to visual technologies for information, "instant news", and so forth rather than more in-depth sources such as newspapers and books. So, do these new technologies produce more transparency or less? Do they improve the political process?

Contracts, asymmetric information, and transparency: George Akerlof (1970) showed that when information is asymmetrically distributed between buyers and sellers and when iron-clad guarantees to consumers are not possible, sellers have an incentive to obfuscate the quality level of their products. Since consumers cannot easily detect differences in quality, one result is that they refuse to buy and one equilibrium is that no market exists. A large literature on possible solutions ensued. We do not wish to deal with these private sector problems here, but are interested in whether analogous solutions to the obfuscation problem can be found for the public sector.

Redistribution and transparency: Transparency is a particularly sensitive issue in matters pertaining to income distribution or redistribution. Obfuscation is pervasive in this area. Some questions which seemed clearly worth pursuing concern the direct effects of variation in the degree of transparency about incomes and transfers on redistribution efforts and outcomes. Other interesting questions relate to the effect of transparency, or absence thereof, on the relative saliency of redistribution issues compared to other issues on political agendas and in political debates. Attention might also be given to the effects of this relative saliency of distributive issues on other matters such as the satisfaction of citizens, civil peace, the avoidance of unstable or cycling democratic decision-making, or even, albeit this time as an indirect effect, redistribution itself. It must be stressed that redistribution should be understood quite broadly, so as to include important and topical questions such as the modes of equalization among local jurisdictions or the form taken by support to, say, farmers.

Corruption and transparency: That a lack of transparency in decision-making processes is, in one way or another, a necessary condition for corruption to develop need not be stressed. The question arises, however, of whether there may not also be circumstances or settings in which more transparency is either conducive to more corruption or, at least, to corruption taking forms that are more detrimental to efficiency or equity. Along this line, could one not argue that, in some settings, the requirement of more transparency would lead to greater efforts devoted to obfuscation, and eventually to the generation of more waste? This is analogous to the argument that direct bribes are relatively efficient compared to the dissipation of rents involved in rent-seeking, and that more round-about ways of granting rents are much more wasteful than direct transfers of money.

Bureaucracy and transparency: Again, it hardly needs stressing that a lack of transparency in decision-making is, in one way or another, a needed condition for the development, in bureaucracies, of some generally condemned tendencies. The question arises whether this is incompatible with the observation that a degree of opacity or obfuscation is indispensable for efficiency in bureaucratic settings. For example, in models of bureaucracy which stress the importance of informal networks as essential to efficiency, it would seem that informal payments must necessarily be given in secrecy. In parliamentary systems, budgetary secrecy is usually held to be necessary if the process of making the budget is not to be corrupted. Can these two viewpoints be reconciled? Or can it be shown that more transparency is always better or always worse?

Many of the problems we had identified were addressed in the papers presented at the Seminar. As well, a number we had not thought about were mentioned. One phenomenon of singular importance – the advent of "embedded" journalism to report not only on war but also on peaceful domestic popular manifestations (as happened in Miami in November 2003) – was unknown in the years and months preceding the Seminar and so was not discussed when we convened in Beaune in

2002. Though there is material in some of the chapters of this volume that can be used to shed light on this new reality, the question 'did the embedding of journalists make the conduct of the Iraq war more or less transparent' was not addressed. The research of Amartya Sen (1981) and of Jean Drèze and Sen (in Drèze, Sen, and Hussein, 1999) has documented the crucial role of a free press in the prevention of famines. Though at first sight, embeddedness taints the impartiality of the political media, more research is needed to establish whether it adversely affects what is to be expected of a free press in times of war.

Many of the papers and the discussion they generated during the Seminar in Beaune made clear that neither transparency nor obfuscation are all-or-nothing realities. If we postulate the existence of a metric (t), varying between zero and one, along which we could measure the degree of transparency, t would never be equal to zero or to one. For example, if we define transparency as the availability of all data and information on a particular matter, the consequent information overload that will generally result means that it is possible to have full transparency on the supply side of the equation as it were and less, possibly much less, than full transparency on the demand side of the same equation.

The problem is, however, still more complicated than the above signals. One author (Brosio) suggests that transparency exists when all parties to an event have access to exactly the same information; in the absence of this strong symmetry, some degree of obfuscation obtains. This seems to be a reasonable proposition. However, when combined with the information overload problem just noted, it would appear that full transparency is not easily, if ever, achieved on either side of the equation. In a rational choice perspective in which it is necessary to assume that observation of the real world is not inordinately expensive, it seems reasonable to suppose that the average person is aware that full transparency is always lacking. That would go a long way in explaining what appears to be the existence of a surrogate demand for secrecy and obfuscation on the part of various groups in society. For some authors (Salmon and Wolfelsperger), there are players who manipulate the degree of saliency of issues as a way of altering the degree of obfuscation. We note that this task is made easier by the existence of a latent surrogate demand for secrecy and obfuscation.

There are further definitional problems and approaches. To illustrate, some chapters (Brosio, Etro and Giarda, and Imbeau) rationalize a lack of transparency by assuming that information is asymmetrically distributed between the parties engaged in an activity or game. Their analysis makes it clear that asymmetry can be "technical" – a given of nature or of the institutional context – but also that it can be manipulated by some of the players in ways that are advantageous to them.

A seminar focused on transparency and obfuscation had to pay attention to the interconnections between transparency and corruption. Though virtually all the chapters can be read as having something to say on the subject, four of them (Breton, Jenkins and Chun-Yan, Lambsdorff, and Wintrobe) pay particular attention to the consequences of corruption. Attention is also paid to the possibly more difficult question of whether corruption is possible in a world of transparency. One answer is that if transparency is defined as the availability of all data and information, the consequent information overload implies that corruption and transparency can co-exist.

If the costs of corruption are greater than its benefits (measured, say, in terms of accelerated economic growth, as in Wintrobe's chapter), an important theoretical and practical question is that of the optimal degree of transparency or, put differently, the optimal volume of information that on relevant matters should be made available to the public. This proposition, in turn, raises the further question of how the notion of 'public' should be defined.

We note that the various problems associated with transparency and obfuscation are possibly more severe in the private sector – corporate enterprises (Enron, Parmalat, and others), not-for-profit organizations, and so on – than they are in the public sector as there are fewer journalistic inquiries and news out of the former. The fact that most chapters in the volume focus on the public sector is not a denial of this possibility.

The chapters are assembled in four parts. Those in Part 1 are mostly concerned with the manifestations of transparency and obfuscation in domestic democratic settings. Those in Part 2, with the same realities but in an international context. The chapters of Part 3 look at corruption; and those of Part 4 at some of the implications of transparency and obfuscation for the working of governments and the formulation of public policies.

In Chapter 1, Pierre Salmon and Alain Wolfelsperger argue that many policies are opaque to the general public or to voters with regard to the means used by governments to implement them and to the real objectives of these policies. To the authors, it is not very surprising that some agents – politicians or governments – try to hide or distort the information provided. However, in democratic settings in which there is considerable political competition and entrepreneurship, it is somewhat puzzling that these agents succeed, often over long periods of time. As a complement or as an alternative to other explanations, Salmon and Wolfelsperger explore the reasons why some voters could prefer not to be better informed about a particular government policy even if the information were offered them at no cost. In the second part of their chapter, the authors examine, in this light, two case studies of policies in which opacity or obfuscation has played an essential role, to wit law enforcement or crime control and price support in agriculture. In both cases, the authors argue, the apparent victims of obfuscation have had good reasons to acquiesce to it.

In the second chapter, Russell Hardin argues on the basis of documented historical cases that obfuscation – deceit on the part of public officials – is sometimes in the public interest and sometimes opposed to the welfare of the population. Among the former is secrecy in the conduct of war and in efforts to apprehend criminals or fugitives. In the same group of cases are effective vaccination programs against, say, poliomyelitis which would be jeopardized if the details pertaining to the risks of contacting the disease through vaccination were known. In the second group of cases is the use of deceitful procedures in the pursuit of certain objectives, for example, changing the rules in favour of certain groups such as high-income taxpayers, that are detrimental to the interests of the citizenry at large.

Hardin's chapter also argues that in circumstances such as the writing of constitutions, too much transparency may be harmful. He contrasts the openness of the debates in Paris in 1789 to draw up a constitution with the secrecy of the debates in Philadelphia in 1787 aimed at a similar outcome. His point is that when expert knowledge is needed, secrecy will often be superior to openness in allowing that expert knowledge to be effectively used.

In the last chapter of Part 1, Albert Breton reviews three bodies of literature – on bureaucracy, on regulatory capture in a context in which private individuals police their own professional activities, and on decentralization of governmental systems – and argues that, except for self-policing and capture when transparency always generates more efficient outcomes, transparency can have both positive and negative consequences. In the case of bureaucracy, the formal and informal structures that are essential components of all organizations – whether public, private (corporate enterprises), or non-governmental – will be more efficient if some behaviours and activities inside the structures are transparent, while others are not. The same is true of decentralization in which yardstick competition works more efficiently the more transparent the behaviour of benchmark governments, and less efficiently in the reassignment of powers, the more transparent the constitution because the latter then acts as a barrier to successful reassignments.

In Chapter 4, Manfred Holler provides an analysis of the struggle or contest between the conflicting principles of liberalism and populism in the context of Cold War cultural policy. That policy was jointly designed by the cultural Ivy League elite represented by Nelson Rockefeller's Museum of Modern Art and the Central Intelligence Agency. The architects of the policy succeeded in making Abstract Expressionist painting the dominant Western aesthetic culture despite substantial resistance by United States politicians and unfriendly comments from behind the Iron Curtain. In the pursuit of the objective and the achievement of the goals, government policy was secondary because of successful private initiatives, secret action, and obfuscation.

Ronald Wintrobe, in the chapter that follows, remarks that transparency is the new *desiderata* of institutions. He goes on to note that the word transparency has, however, many meanings. His analysis focuses on one context, that of transparency in the system of political economy or political and corporate governance. He then looks at this issue through the lens of Benjamin Barber's analysis of globalization in his 1995 book: *Jihad vs McWorld.* In this context, transparency, now identified as the forces of McWorld, is pitted against another powerful force, jihad. But McWorld also stimulates jihad, as Barber asserts. Wintrobe provides a simple explanation of this in terms of rational choice. Wintrobe then identifies two broad systems, the shareholder and stakeholder systems, and suggests that while the shareholder system is superior in terms of transparency, the stakeholder system is better at generating and promoting solidarity and thus holding the forces of jihad in check. However, it is often suggested that the solidarity system is inimical to economic growth and prone to corruption. He presents some evidence and commentary on this point, particularly with respect to the Korean and Chinese systems, in which there has been spectacular growth along with substantial corruption. He argues that this raises a number of questions: if growth is what is desired, is corruption necessary for that growth, especially in the stakeholder system? Is this price worth paying? and is the American system, on the surface so transparent, free from this flaw?

Part 3 pays particular attention to the relationship between transparency and corruption. In the first chapter of this section Johann Lambsdorff suggests that transparency generally prevents corruption in government and therefore is productive of positive welfare effects. However, depending on the underlying model one chooses, the adverse welfare effects of corruption can differ substantially. He develops four different models. In the first, corrupt agents generate welfare losses because principals are unable to write contracts based on honest dealings. In a second model, a corrupt principal is unable to credibly commit to policies that are respectful of sunk investments. Thirdly, a contested principal may be constrained to serve the public, but competition can be wasteful. And finally, a powerful and corrupt agent is likely to bring about x-inefficiency, while the principal's self-serving purpose leads to allocative inefficiency.

In Chapter 7, Glenn Jenkins and Chun-Yan Kuo note that there has been a growing emphasis in many developing countries on export-led growth policies that attract both domestic and foreign investment into activities for the expansion of manufacturing exports and that often the actual outcome of the policies has been different from what had been intended, because investors often face foreign exchange controls, tariffs on imported inputs, and a costly system for the exemption or refund of sales taxes and tariffs on inputs used to produce exports. These factors have frequently bred corruption. The authors address two issues related to the design and information requirements for the administration of some of the fiscal provisions that affect the competitiveness of a country in the production of manufactured exports. The first relates to the fact that under a system of VAT taxation, the refunds that would insure that exports are tax free are often either not paid in a timely fashion or are fraudulently overstated in the claims made by exporters. The second issue is how to relieve exporters from the burden of taxes levied on imported inputs. The authors argue that all the mechanisms that would permit a removal of these impediments to exports have serious limitations and many of them provide fertile ground for administrative corruption.

In Chapter 8, Giorgio Brosio discusses several arguments proposed in the literature or by office-holders to justify a degree of obfuscation in the ways intergovernmental transfers (in a single country) take place. He acknowledges the possible relevance of some of these arguments under a certain political perspective but he focuses on a detailed analysis of some of their ill-effects in terms of efficiency and of the accountability of governments. In the simplest case, a lack of transparency regarding the sums transferred from a higher level government distorts the comparative assessments of performance voters engage in. In more complex settings, obfuscation distorts the assessments by voters of alternatives available with regard to intergovernmental redistribution or equalization.

In Chapter 9, Louis Imbeau proposes a theory of budgeting based on the principal-agent theoretical framework. He first offers a description of the delegation structure and information asymmetry in a public university, as a prototype of the institutional framework he uses to articulate his argument. He then explores the dynamics of a simple principal-agent relationship where both actors can be either transparent or opaque regarding the budget information each controls. Imbeau shows that the outcome of the game varies with the presence or absence of built-in incentives aimed at modifying the agent's preferences. He proceeds to develop a more complex model where the principal delegates part of his or her responsibilities to a supervisor and shows that the budget outcome depends on the supervisor's collusive behaviour which in turn varies with the incentive structure in place. In the last section of the chapter, he discusses several normative and positive implications of the model.

In the final chapter of the volume, Federico Etro and Piero Giarda examine the trade-off between the transparency of rules and efficiency in a model of constitutional choice pertaining to the federal organization of a state. In such a context, the basic trade-off translates into one between decentralization and redistribution, where the former is associated with transparency and the latter with efficient fiscal policy. The authors compare a centralized and a decentralized system in a two-regions model with income inequality and the supply of local public goods. The centralized system leads to an optimal income redistribution with an inefficient allocation of local public goods across the regions, while the decentralized system generates limited redistribution and a tendency to the overprovision of local public goods. This leads them to a first result which is that decentralization is preferred to centralization when inequality is great. Two other conclusions also suggest a rationale for the trade-off between decentralization and redistribution: first, a transition from centralization to decentralization will be supported by the regions if and only if the central government accepts incomplete redistribution; second, a fiscal federalism with a House of Regions, where regions bargain on redistributive transfers, induces efficient policies but produces only partial redistribution.

We are grateful to Massimo Bordignon, Basudeb Chaudhuri, Valeria De Bonis, David Hojman, Grégoire Rota Graziosi, Bengt-Arne Wickström, and to Bernhard Winkler for acting as discussants. We are also grateful to the Italian Ministry of Education (National Research Grants, 2000) for its financial assistance.

References

Akerlof, G. (1970), 'The Market for "Lemons": Quality Uncertainty and the Market Mechanism', *Quarterly Journal of Economics*, 84:3, 488-500.

Drèze, J., Sen, A. and Hussein, A. (eds.) (1999), *The Political Economy of Hunger: Selected Essays* (New Delhi: Vedams).

Orwell, G. (1949), *Nineteen Eighty Four* (New York: Harcourt, Brace).

Sen, A. (1981), *Poverty and Famines. An Essay on Entitlement and Deprivation* (Oxford: Clarendon).

PART 1
In Democratic Contexts

Chapter 1

Acquiescence to Opacity

Pierre Salmon and Alain Wolfelsperger[1]

Introduction

Many policies are opaque, at least along some dimensions. Opacity may affect both the means used to implement policies and the real objectives that they pursue. Our concern with opacity is limited to the cases when it is the result of obfuscation, that is, of some effort on the part of governments or other public bodies (central banks or international organisations, for instance) to hide or misrepresent their choices. Some authors have noted that obfuscation seems often to entail inefficiency. When office-holders endeavour to hide some aspects of their actions or true motivation, they may be compelled to choose policies, or modalities thereof, that are not the most efficient given their true goals. Typically in that case, it seems that more direct policies would serve these goals better and at a smaller cost.

Although, in any given context, the precise reasons why politicians or bureaucrats may want to hide or distort information are more complex and not as well understood as often thought, the existence of a general incentive to deceive in that way is not really surprising. It fits with the general vision of democratic politics that political economists have elaborated over the last fifty years or so. A more intriguing question, thus, is why, or how, obfuscation so often succeeds – even over long periods of time, and even when, as just noted, it seems to be associated with inefficiency.

The rational ignorance of voters, along the line initiated by Downs (1957), might seem to be the obvious solution and, in fact, it plays a central role in some much-quoted analyses (for example Magee, Brock and Young 1989). The argument is well known. Because no individual vote can have a significant influence on electoral outcomes, it is irrational for a voter to spend resources to get information for the purpose of voting 'better'. This may allow many kinds of government misbehaviour. But does that include obfuscation? In fact, there are serious objections to the application of the reasoning to obfuscation. Under some extreme assumptions about the context in which the rational ignorance mechanism operates, voters are completely and universally uninformed. They know nothing and, of course, because they are rational, they know that they know nothing. But then obfuscation becomes

1 We are grateful for the very useful comments made on an earlier version by Alain Marciano and by the participants in the 10th Villa Colombella Seminar, in particular by our discussant, Bengt-Arne Wickström.

pointless and policies can be expected to be fully transparent. For obfuscation to make sense, some information must be assumed to be able to filter through and reach the rationally ignorant voters. If this is the case, it must then be acknowledged that, at least in democratic settings – in which there is a lot of political competition and entrepreneurship – there are many channels through which voters will be supplied for free with a lot of information of a kind that may make them detect existing, and especially enduring, obfuscation. Sources of supply that come to mind in this context include political parties, unions, associations, interest groups, the media, and academia. In such an assumed world, rational voters will also be able to rely on processes of information transmission based on signalling (Austen-Smith 1991). The foregoing reasoning does not necessarily lead to a complete rejection of voter ignorance as a permissive cause of enduring obfuscation but it suggests that exclusive reliance on it leads to a view of the matter which is not very plausible. At the minimum, ignorance cannot be the whole story, so to speak.

In the literature more directly concerned with accounting for inefficient policies, there are now models in which opacity plays no significant role. In these models, the inefficient policies are preferred by politicians precisely because they are inefficient.[2] If only because here we are concerned primarily with opacity rather than with inefficiency, we prefer to share with the rational ignorance approach the view that the attitude of citizens or voters with regard to information is a key element in the understanding of policies that are apparently inefficient and are in any case clearly opaque. Contrary to the standard theory of rational ignorance, however, we consider situations in which at least some voters would prefer not to be better informed about a government policy even if this information were offered them at no cost – or even, at the limit, if they had to make an effort (that is, assume a cost) to remain uninformed. Put differently, what we want to do is to find why and how apparent victims of obfuscation may not be real victims at all and may in fact prefer, or at any rate accept, to remain uninformed or misinformed. A disclaimer is needed here. Such behaviour on the part of the 'victims', when it applies, does not preclude other causes of opacity operating at the same time. The other causes may pertain in particular to the motivations of politicians, to the activities of interest groups, or even to the cost voters would have to assume to get the relevant information. In a second-best and uncertain world, there is nothing impossible in the opacity of a policy suiting at the same time voters, politicians and lobbies.

In the first part of the chapter we explore, in a simplified way, a number of mechanisms that account for or lead to the phenomenon we are interested in - that is, voters preferring a policy to be opaque rather than transparent. In the second part of the chapter, we discuss two policies (law enforcement and price support in agriculture) in which opacity plays an essential role, albeit in a different way. Concluding remarks are offered in the last section.

---

2 See Rodrik (1995, 1471-73) and the references therein. An alternative hypothesis is that inefficient policies may be preferred by interest groups concerned with the size of their membership (Acemoglu and Robinson 2001).

Mechanisms of acquiescence to opacity

The specificity of information yielded by transparency

Transparency implies information equally available to everybody. Making things transparent eliminates information asymmetry by providing information to those who did not have full access to it. It seems obvious that individuals who now have full access to information whereas previously they did not should always welcome the change. This, however, assumes two things. The first is that information is always, in this context of transparency as in other settings, a *good* – that is, something whose utility to everybody is positive and increases with the quantity available. The second is that the collective consumption dimension of information does not matter. Under these two assumptions, people should always be pleased to get more *free* information, which is what transparency usually offers.

Both assumptions, however, can be questioned. Let us begin with the second. The question is not whether information has a collective consumption dimension – in the case of transparency it always has – but whether this dimension has an effect on the utility that individuals derive from it. Often, the collective dimension does not matter. Then, individuals, even when they make up a very large group (a whole electorate for instance), consider a piece of information provided to all exactly as they would view the same piece of information made available to themselves only. But quite often also, this is not so. The fact that information is provided to others as well as to oneself does make a difference.

The other assumption (that additional transparency, providing additional information, is always a good) is also far from being always true. Let us use the distinction just made. When people disregard the collective dimension of transparency, the information they get from increased transparency is similar to information they would receive privately. One is inclined to think that this type of information always yields positive utility. But this may not be so. Even in that case as we will see, there are situations in which individuals derive zero or even negative utility from more information. When, on the contrary, individuals do consider the collective dimension of transparency as important, it may be the case that they derive at the same time positive utility from the information provided to them personally by an improvement in transparency and negative utility from the information provided at the same time to others so that the sum of the two is negative. In that case, individuals will prefer opacity to transparency. They would have liked being better informed if they had been the only ones to receive additional information, but they do not like the others, or some others, to receive it also, and this second consideration pre-empts the first.[3]

3 Transparency in our analysis is a property of something produced by an institution like government. The question we address is whether individuals concerned by this output welcome that property. The question of their own opacity or transparency is irrelevant. This implies that we do not discuss the case of individuals who detain some private information about themselves at the same time as they would derive utility from getting some of the private information detained by others. Establishing generalised transparency would give them access

Exclusive reliance on outcomes

When the collective dimension of transparency is not a central consideration, why would individuals accept or prefer opacity? In other words, how is it possible that the information that transparency provides yields no positive utility? As a rule, for this to happen, the additional information that more transparency would provide must be useless. When this is not so, additional information will have an effect on decisions to be made, and standard conceptions of rational decision-making dictate that individuals should assign positive utility to it. We discuss two different reasons why information may be useless. The reason we consider in this subsection is when the nature of the information is such that those who receive that information cannot exploit it. This consideration may underlie among others the oft-asserted hypothesis that voters consider only policy outcomes.[4]

Information asymmetry is a major characteristic of the relationship between the great majority of citizens or voters, on the one hand, and the whole set of individuals constituting "the state" or "government", on the other hand. There is lot of information used within government to which the citizens do not have access. One natural way to address the situation which that creates is by using one variant or another of the principal-agent model.[5] In many versions of this model, the principal is the whole citizenry or electorate, considered as homogeneous, whereas the agent is either the party in power or the whole set of institutions and their personnel (that is, all the politicians and bureaucrats), making up 'the state' or 'government', considered as a unitary actor. For convenience, let us adopt the second interpretation. Citizens, acting as a single principal, entrust the state with the pursuit, constrained by some rules, of their interests. The problem on which the literature focuses is the likelihood that the agent will "shirk", that is, make decisions contrary to the interests of the principal. This is made possible by the information asymmetry already mentioned combined with the fact that the interests of the principal and those of the agent are not fully aligned or convergent. Thus, if citizens could share more of the information detained by the state, this would necessarily be a good thing, mitigating somewhat the problem of shirking.

---

to the private information detained by others but at the same time compel them to provide access to information they may prefer keeping to themselves. In that case, as a consequence, transparency is often not wanted and even disallowed by rules such as those protecting *privacy* – or possibly also *secrecy* (as practiced in various professions or administrations).

4 Arguments in favour of considering only outcomes can be found or discussed in various strands of the literature – the theory of retrospective voting, of course; Albert Breton's theory of competitive supply of governmental goods and services (Breton 1996); many years ago, Max Weber's analogy between the people and a buyer 'who may know how the shoe pinches – but never how to make a better shoe' (cited in Slagstad 1988, 125); or, in the context of the current debates on the European Union, reliance on 'output-oriented' legitimacy (Scharpf 1999).

5 See in particular Barro 1973; Ferejohn 1986; Persson and Tabellini 2000, chapter 4; and Przeworski et al. 1999.

Although it is adopted by many authors, this approach to representative democracy is not fully convincing because it reduces this system of government to a second best arrangement, direct democracy being implicitly assumed to be always the first best solution. Citizens do not see their delegation of powers to representatives in this light, that is, as a consequence of one kind or other of fairly practical or matter-of-fact difficulties which they would encounter if they had to decide themselves. They see this as an implication of the very different nature of the information which they, on the one hand, and the government, on the other hand, possess.[6] Both sides have an incentive to build up or acquire background knowledge, a form of capital without which they could not understand and process new information. However the background knowledge which they are induced to build up is very different. It is specialised, that is, adapted to the different needs or tasks citizens and the personnel making up the state must be familiar with. It must also be noted that, because background knowledge is a form of (specific) capital, accumulated over time, it cannot be made instantly suitable to process information of a type foreign to the specialised needs or tasks it has been shaped over time to satisfy or perform.

In such a situation, it seems reasonable to expect that citizens will be mostly concerned with the results of governments activities whose assessment does not require a form of background knowledge, that is, of specific capital, which they do not possess. This will generally mean that their attention will concentrate on outcomes that have a direct, at the limit measurable, impact on their welfare. Because they have no means to judge, they will tend to be inattentive to the means employed by government, and also to the question of whether these means are the most appropriate to produce the outcomes they are concerned with. In elections, this will lead them to discount electoral platforms and to give precedence to an assessment of the performance of the incumbent team. In other words, they will tend to vote retrospectively.

One implication for our purpose is that information provided about the means used by government will generally not be 'consumed' by citizens: as a consequence of lifelong specialisation, they do not possess the processing equipment which is a necessary complement to the information (that is, without which it is useless). This points to a form of rational ignorance which is not the result, as usual, of each voter having a negligible influence on outcomes, but of the nature of the information available, which is such that it cannot be used.

---

6 Implications different from the one in the text can be drawn from the defence of representative democracy as a first best solution when voters are fully aware of their informational inferiority (in some matters). In particular, this view of representative democracy may lead to stress the importance, in the choice of voters, of the personal characteristics of the candidates. For an informal case along that line (see for example: Salmon 1993; and Brennan and Hamlin 2000). For a more theoretical analysis – in the context of a discussion about opacity and transparency – of how voters try to gain information about the types of politicians (see in particular: Coate and Morris 1995; Lohmann 1998; and Bordignon and Minelli 2001).

Another implication is that citizens cannot be expected to take into account, at least to a sufficient extent, the possibility that the different goals which the state pursues in their name, and to which they are attached, may not be fully compatible – and thus the policies which aim at meeting them simultaneously feasible – given the existing constraints (budgetary or technical, namely). It can be the case, in particular, that nothing can be done to satisfy a need expressed by citizens, even when that need is increasing. Should the government make fully transparent the incompatibility among goals, or the impossibility to satisfy a given need? This would come down again to assuming the existence of a type of specialized background knowledge among citizens that they do not possess. Obfuscating the goal or the need itself may be a more promising strategy and one which may in the end be accepted by citizens, as we will see in the section on crime control policy.

With regard to the exclusive reliance on outcomes, where it is justified, we should perhaps speak of acquiescence to ignorance rather than to opacity. Additional information about anything other than outcomes brings zero, not negative utility. Under the assumption (to which we stick for the moment) that the collective consumption dimensions of transparency do not matter, to find a mechanism that yields negative utility it seems necessary to turn to psychology. This is still somewhat unorthodox but rapidly becoming acceptable in economics.

Freedom to think about something else

Suppose that voter X has decided that she definitely supports policy P, which has several characteristics, among which K – an inseparable attribute of P. K may pertain to the means employed to implement P, to the objectives of P, or to its implications or effects. We do not have to go into the reasons why X's decision to support P is final. Perhaps the decision cannot be reversed. Perhaps it could be reversed but X has a particular reason (a norm for instance) to support P whatever the information about it. Perhaps X's support for P is only very strong.

Now suppose that X does not like K. Thus thinking about K causes her some discomfort whereas it cannot induce her to change her decision or opinion favourable to P. Thinking about something else increases X's well-being at no cost. This will be achieved if P is designed in such a way that K is as hidden or inconspicuous as possible. Making P more transparent, by disclosing the content of K, serves, as perceived from the standpoint of X, no purpose but decreases her utility.

As explained elsewhere (Salmon 2001), thinking about something else is perfectly compatible with rationality. It is a very widespread and major phenomenon (once we have decided to eat *foie gras* or lobster, most of us prefer and manage not to think about the details of the over-feeding and boiling-alive processes the animals have experienced), and a phenomenon which is even more significant when public, collective, decisions rather than private, individual ones are concerned. It is a bit surprising to economists because there is no tradition in that discipline to consider 'the mind as a consuming organ' (Schelling 1984) – that is, as something subject, on par with the body, to utility-providing or utility-depriving flows – but is compatible with a rational choice approach nonetheless.

Self-deception, a better known phenomenon, is another matter. Its compatibility with rationality is a moot point. In our example, self-deception, in the form of wishful thinking, would appear if X went one step further and formed the belief that K does not exist, a more palatable K' existing in its place (geese enjoying being over-fed, in the example above). Thinking about something else involves no false belief whereas self-deception does. Anyhow, both can lead voters to prefer opacity to transparency. There is probably more scope for utility-increasing self-deception in the context of forming one's opinion about public issues, or in that of voting, than in the setting of private activities because, in the first case, decisions are more remote and their stakes lower.

Acquiescence to opacity when the collective dimension of transparency is essential

Let us consider the same individual X but suppose now that X is very influenced in her assessment of transparency by the fact that it is information available to every one. We assume also that X supports P but, contrary to the foregoing discussion, that she is not certain not to change her mind. Consequently, X always assigns positive utility to being better informed about all the properties or characteristics of P, including K. However, X is less sure about more information to others. As a strong supporter of P, she may think that, if there were more information available about that policy, she would personally have a low probability of changing her mind whereas there would be a higher probability that at least some of the other supporters of policy P would change their minds.

Suppose that N individuals support policy P, whose characteristic K is opaque, and that, for some reason, all N individuals must support P for it to be decided. Each individual has the same probability π to change his or her mind about P if K becomes transparent, but their criteria or preferences are not the same. The probabilities to change one's mind are not perfectly correlated; for convenience, assume them to be independent. How does each individual evaluate the prospect of K becoming transparent? For any of the individuals, the probability that he or she will gain from it is equal to the probability π of changing his or her mind. The probability that he or she will lose from the transparency of K is equal to the probability of not changing his or her mind while somebody else does. It is equal to $[(1 - \pi) - (1 - \pi)^N]$. For $\pi < 1/2$, and N not too small, the probability of losing from transparency is larger than the probability of gaining.[7] This result also obtains when the probabilities are (imperfectly) correlated (N will simply have to be somewhat larger).

7 In the setting assumed here, risk-averse individuals may prefer transparency not to be increased even though they are more likely to gain than to lose from it. To introduce neutrality in a simple way, assume that, under perfect information (transparency of K), the loss of utility involved in getting a policy one dislikes and the loss of utility involved in not

The mechanism illustrated here is fairly general. Thus, we could assume that individuals know only their own valuation and have subjective probabilities. If most voters are pretty sure that more transparency would not make them change their owns minds about the policy they support, but are uncertain about what would be the case of other supporters, again this should lead to a preference for opacity rather than for transparency. Also, instead of P being a policy, it can be a politician, a political party, a regime, a system, etc. As for K, it can be any kind of negative fact about P.

Various extensions of the analysis can be elaborated. One is vote-trading. Individual X dislikes A and likes B whereas individual Y likes A and dislikes B. They exchange votes and both support A and B. Now suppose there is some prospect of getting negative information about A. X may fear that, while this is unlikely to make her change her mind about the log-rolling agreement (she did not like A anyway), it might change Y's interest in having A adopted, which in turn may make Y change his mind about the agreement and thus about supporting B. As a consequence X may prefer the negative information to be withheld.

Obfuscation by the manipulation of salience

There are cases in which all the information about a policy is freely available to all, and even fully reported in the media, and, nonetheless, the policy smacks of opacity – or, rather here, of obfuscation. Obfuscation works, not by hiding anything, but in the way the policy and especially its objectives are formulated or framed. In particular, it may operate by manipulation of salience.

Salience refers to differential weight. It is an important variable in the spatial theory of voting (see for example: Enelow and Hinich 1984, chapter 2), and it also plays a role in other research areas. One such area is that which Peyton Young (1994) calls the 'positive theory of equity' (that is, the study of how people decide what solutions are equitable). In the theory of voting, a policy issue is more salient than another if the weight given to it is larger. In Young's analysis, when, in a specific context, a yardstick, a norm, or some characteristic of the claimants is more salient than another, it will 'count more'.

The extension of our reasoning to the case of obfuscation by manipulation of salience is worth pursuing given its pervasiveness in reality, but it requires some care. The problem to address is that the benchmark used to judge whether or not there is obfuscation is less clear-cut in the case of salience than it is in the case of transparency. Admittedly, in many concrete settings, the question of whether a policy is transparent or opaque is not that simple.[8] However, when discussing transparency

getting a policy one likes are both equal, and equal to u. Then, in our example, expected utility from transparency, E(U) is equal to:

$$E(U) = \pi u - [(1 - \pi) - (1 - \pi)^N] u = [2\pi - 1 + (1 - \pi)^N] u$$

When N gets large, this tends toward $(2\pi - 1) u$.

8 Inspired himself by the terminology of somebody else, Ottmar Issing (1999, 506) makes a distinction between accountability and transparency which we do not use in our

in general, a simple context can be assumed, allowing transparency, opacity, and thus obfuscation, to be treated as more or less objective or unambiguous facts. At the limit, the question discussed comes down to whether a feature A of a policy (or situation) P is or is not disclosed publicly. If it is not, P is not transparent. If the government is deliberately responsible for this, there is obfuscation. And, for reasons explained above, it may be the case that the public, or some subset thereof, accepts it. In the case of salience, to get, especially in a context in which there is acquiescence, a benchmark as relatively clear as that used for transparency, one must assume, independently of existing salience, something like 'objective', 'natural' or 'intrinsic' salience (or the salience that it is legitimate or logical to expect). The mechanism we have in mind will thus take this form:

1. The public debate focuses on various features of policy or situation P rather than on feature B. In that sense, feature B is not salient.
2. Given its intrinsic characteristics, B ought to be salient. The fact that it is not is unnatural.
3. The government is, in part, deliberately or voluntarily responsible for B not being salient. In that sense, there is manipulation of the salience, and obfuscation of the true nature of policy P (which, by assumption, is that B is a major aspect).
4. Individuals X are logically related with B in such a way that for them B should be salient (for example, B is the fact that they are seriously harmed by P).
5. Individuals X have the capacity to ensure that the debate focuses on B, which would thus become salient.
6. They do nothing of the sort – which we interpret as meaning that they acquiesce to the contrived low salience of B. This is puzzling.
7. One possible explanation is that making B salient would not change policy or situation P but would unnecessarily generate discomfort (disutility) among individuals X (who are aware of this).
8. Another possible explanation is that individuals X fear that B becoming more salient would lead to a new political equilibrium in which policy or situation P would be replaced by policy or situation R, which is less favourable to them. If individuals X are risk-averse, even a small probability that this may happen may be enough for them to prefer relative salience to remain as it is.

This mechanism or sequence is central to the case study of The Common Agricultural Policy below. For the moment, we simply argue, without providing

---

chapter but which is nonetheless interesting for our purpose: "accountability is linked essentially to 'deeds', i.e. observable and verifiable actions, whereas transparency refers primarily to 'words', i.e. attempts to convey explanations and the thinking behind the actions." The transparency of a policy may be lacking simply because the "explanations and the thinking behind the actions" are not provided, even though nothing substantial is hidden. See also Winkler (2000).

support or illustration, that, in many if not most circumstances, manipulation of salience is unlikely to succeed without some degree of acceptance, and even rational acceptance, on the part of the apparent victims. The reason is that the relative weights given by society to the various aspects of something cannot be decided by fiat. They can be influenced but not decided by government.[9] Politicians often want to turn the attention of the public or the focus of public debate from one aspect of a policy to another one, but, in democratic settings, they succeed seldom if there is no substantial subset of the media or the public having some reason to concur.

A second remark is that distribution issues are particularly prone to be addressed by the apparent victims in the way suggested above. People are more or less aware that criteria of justice or even equity are to a large extent contradictory, and that decision-making in the area of income redistribution is likely to be instable (doomed to 'cycling', in the vocabulary of the spatial theory of voting). They may have also other consequences to fear from a focus on redistribution (the public disclosure or claim that, under some criteria, they deserve their unfavoured fate, for instance). But if an issue becomes framed in terms of redistribution, that is, if its distributive implications become salient, this more or less compels everybody to engage in the distributive fight, if nothing else for defensive purposes. Thus many may prefer the distributive implications of policies not to be made too explicit. There are various ways to achieve this. One typically used by governments is to stress the universality of the protective role of the state, under a long-term perspective and over a whole array of policies. Thus if a major characteristic of a given policy P is to benefit only a small group, whose claims to be favoured would generally be judged as unjustified, the salience of this bias can be much reduced, with the acquiescence of many if not all, by an emphasis on other characteristics of policy P, or on the embedding of P in a larger set of policies benefiting in turn many different categories of citizens.[10]

Aggregate acquiescence: a combination of motives

As soon as we face a concrete situation involving many people, all the foregoing forms of behaviour can be active at the same time, and disentangling their contributions is often both difficult and unnecessary. Some individuals are wary of transparency and salience because they want to think about something else. Simultaneously, other individuals or the same are afraid of the effects of transparency on the decisions made or the positions adopted by others. Some are perfectly informed but prefer the matter

9 What Young (1994, 126) says of the salience of standards of comparison is worth quoting here: '...the salience of a standard of comparison is a function of three factors: rational argument, authority, and precedent. Each of these factors lends credibility to a given way of framing the problem, and solidifies the players' belief about what the outcome is likely to be.'

10 Similar ways to deal with distributive issues are found within organisations and groups. A trade union for instance, even if it devotes unequal attention to its members, may insist on a goal that serves the interests of all, and many of the members who are less well treated may also wish their fate to be glossed over so that the union avoids internal feud.

to be framed in a way which lowers the weight of some considerations. Others, who could be informed about means, have no use for such information and look only at outcomes. There might even be significant minorities who do not acquiesce at all to opacity or obfuscation. All these attitudes and behaviours can be aggregated so as to make up a global attitude of public opinion consisting of disregard for some possibilities of increased transparency, or even consisting of a positive preference for opacity or low salience. Some application of this point will be found in the two case studies to which we turn now.

Opacity in crime control policy

Providing safety to persons and to their belongings has always been one of the main responsibilities of the state. Citizens expect their demand on this point to be satisfied but they do not know how that is to be achieved. They have some idea of the means available to government but no knowledge of their aggregate or relative efficiency. Now, it has happened in France (we concentrate on that country) that crime (except homicide) has increased considerably over the last decades, that people have been aware of this increase and displeased by it, but that government, whatever the shade of the party in power, has seemed (until recently) to respond very placidly if at all. In a democracy, inaction in the presence of an explicit demand for action is puzzling (but see Cadot and Sinclair-Desgagné 1992; Howitt and Wintrobe 1995). It seems particularly puzzling when the issue is something as close to the concrete concerns of individuals as is insecurity.[11]

The solution to the puzzle which we will offer here is based on the idea that government knows, as a form of private information, that, given various constraints, it has in fact no means at its disposal to obtain a significant diminution of insecurity. Why this impotence? Simplifying somewhat, there are three main types of public decisions that might have an effect on crime. Let us consider them in turn. The first is an increase in the financial resources allocated to law enforcement in general, to the police in particular. The results of empirical studies about the latter are very uncertain.[12] They do however suggest that, to get significant results, the increase in the financial resources allocated to repression – or for that matter, prevention (see Donohue and Siegelman 1998) – must be considerable. Increases in public spending of the required magnitude are hardly thinkable given the other needs of citizens

11 Because, in France at least, there is no very significant difference between right-winged and left-winged office-holders on this issue of security, we do not share the view formulated by Algalarrondo (2002) among others that the reason for the relative inaction on the part of government observable in matters of security is mostly ideological.

12 For instance, according to Eide (1998, 363), 'many of these studies show that police activity has a negligible, and sometimes positive, effects on crime.' The level of crime can be both the consequence of the level of police activities and its cause. Studies, such as Levitt (1997), which take into account this identification problem generally conclude that police activities do have a negative, albeit modest, effect on crime.

the government has to care of.[13] Under such conditions, it is understandable that any government – even if exclusively concerned with satisfying the demands of citizens, as we assume – will find spending on policies other than strengthening law enforcement more productive.

A second conceivable way to act on crime would be to change (at constant financial cost this time) the methods employed in the law enforcement system. What we have in mind here is not technical progress, from which not much can be expected in the short or medium term, but the lifting of a number of constraints and restrictions imposed on the behaviour of the police and the judges. These constraints and restrictions aim at protecting the freedom and privacy of citizens, minimising the risk of errors in verdicts, preventing police officers from using violence, mitigating the severity of sentencing, promoting the rehabilitation of prisoners, and so on. Making them lighter or more flexible might have a non-negligible effect on crime, albeit at a very high cost in terms of violation of rights constitutionally entrenched or values to which many citizens are strongly attached. It could even end up replacing one form of crime by another, ominously committed by the personnel in charge of fighting crime, that is, the police and the judiciary.

Lastly, it seems established that the level of crime is related to economic conditions and income distribution. A third way to act on crime could therefore be the implementation of a macroeconomic policy and a policy of redistribution more directly targeted than they may be now at reducing unemployment and providing incentives to engage in legal productive activities. But, again, what would be required for an impact on incentives to be perceptible is a change in the said policies of an order of magnitude that is in fact precluded by the importance of the other objectives and considerations that constrain them.[14]

Statistical information on crime is complex and difficult to interpret. In this, it is quite different from statistics on inflation or unemployment, which are circulated regularly and attract considerable attention. For the public to notice a change in the level of crime, and thus in the level of insecurity it feels exposed to, that change will have to be very substantial indeed. Little variations will remain unnoticed. But, as the foregoing discussion suggests, policies that would change the situation to the extent required are not really feasible. The question, then is why cannot the government make the reasons for its impotence completely transparent? In the previous section,

---

13 Some successful aspects of the policies recently adopted in the United States (e.g., zero tolerance) are sometimes suggested as a possible source of inspiration for the new policies contemplated in France. The underlying conditions are quite different in the two countries and comparisons therefore hazardous. Still, it should be stressed that the number of people under bars is over two millions in the United States (700 per 100,000) whereas it is somewhat over 50,000 in France (85 per 100,000). See *The Economist*, 10 August 2002, p.37, and *Le Monde*, 16 August 2002, p.4. The financial cost of a policy *à l'américaine* would be considered exorbitant by all sectors of political opinion.

14 In their study of the case of New York, Corman and Mocan (2002) conclude that the contribution of economic factors in the reduction of criminal activities has been relatively small.

when referring to representative democracy and the principal-agent relationship, we explained that there is a type of information which the public cannot make good use of. This, however, should not prevent government to address citizens in these simple terms: "increasing insecurity is an inevitable ill, against which nothing can be done if public spending on law enforcement is not increased to an unsustainable level or if methods are not allowed that are incompatible with the fundamental principles under which our society operates".

Such a message is most unlikely to be understood by the citizenry for several reasons. Confessions of impotence are generally detrimental to the image of itself any government wants to convey. But here, because of the impossibility of presenting in detail its justification, the message would probably be completely disbelieved and interpreted as reflecting pure cynicism. Such interpreted attitude would be resented as being particularly shocking when concerning a responsibility as essential to the nature of the state as the provision of security to citizens. It would undermine trust in government overall. In addition, in a setting of political competition, such language would almost certainly raise a public good or prisoners' dilemma problem. Even though it would be of the interest of both the party in office and its serious contenders that such a message were accepted as true by voters, it is likely that contenders would not resist the temptation to free ride, abstaining thus to confirm the truth of the message – when not contributing further to its disbelief. The existence of various populist or extremist parties and candidates obviously aggravates the danger of misinterpretation and reject, whereas that of pressure groups cannot be relied on to mitigate it. Only pressure groups systematically hostile to repression *per se* might express some support or understanding but this would probably prove counterproductive.

Because the strategy just discussed of 'telling the people the truth (albeit without explaining it)' seems doomed to fail, the strategy a government will find most natural to use consists in deliberately ignoring the problem, that is, doing its possible for it not to be included in the political agenda, while continuing to deal with insecurity as it has always used to deal. With regard to substance, the policy is the same as above, but it is now associated with complete opacity rather than with the maximum of transparency compatible with the information processing capacity of the public. Because the problem cannot be solved as the citizens would like, the best policy for the government is thus to do as if the problem did not exist. This eliminates or mitigates all the problems that the transparent message discussed above would raise, and ensures that there will be no confession of impotence, no loss of trust, no loss of credibility, and greater likelihood of tacit support by political competitors (who, except populist parties and candidates, have no interest in endowing with perhaps lasting salience an issue they also will be unable to solve when in office).

This strategy of opacity has another advantage. It can rely on the objective support of a majority among experts. In France at least, most of the individuals who are considered as experts in the area of crime and insecurity belong to, or are very much influenced by schools of sociology which seek the main explanation of individual behaviour in various kinds of social and economic determinism. This leads them to share with the government the view that the problem of increased insecurity cannot be solved. If it exists, which they may not concede, it is the consequence of a deeper disorder in the functioning or in the basic structures of society. If a remedy must be sought, it should be at the level of the disorder not at that of the symptom. But specialists often doubt that the phenomenon exists at all. They prefer to acknowledge the growth – at the limit deemed somewhat hysterical, probably contrived, and in any case groundless – of a simple 'feeling of insecurity'. They may also contest the reliability or interpretation of statistics, or suggest that attention should be focussed on more important topics, such as traffic accidents. At best, they may advocate reliance on an improvement in economic conditions, possibly but not necessarily dependent on the change in macroeconomic policies mentioned earlier. All this suits perfectly, though in principle fortuitously, the interests of the government. It provides, if need be, an effective substitute to the detailed justification of its position that the government finds impossible to make known.

Before turning more directly to the question of acquiescence to the strategy of opacity summarised above, we must address a possible objection. It can be observed that citizens are not simply desirous to get more security but often demand that some particular measures be taken. Does that imply that we have been wrong to assume that citizens know their own incompetence about how means relate to outcomes? Or, rather, should not the implication be that citizens have preferences not only about outcomes but also about means, which in a sense makes these means something akin to ends? Indeed, this should be expected to be the case if, as it seems, many citizens subscribe, at least in part, to a retributive conception of justice. Under that conception, repression is first of all 'punishment', and the necessity to punish does not derive from its expected consequences in terms of dissuasion or prevention, but from its non-consequential capacity to constitute by itself a compensation for the deeds committed and the violation of rights they involve. What counts is that *justice has been done*.

If, at least in part, citizens reason in this way, as is certainly the case, this is a fact which government must take into account. This explains that it engages in actions whose rationale, from the usual perspective of dissuasion or prevention, seems dubious. It is tempting to see in such actions, typically heavily symbolic, an attempt to trump the public in making it wrongly believe that the government acts with energy against insecurity. But this may be quite unfair. The government faces two different demands from the citizenry. In the matter of security, the best response, as we have tried to show, consists of doing nothing but making the reason for that opaque. To satisfy the desire for retributive justice, however, the necessary strategy is to engage in some repressive action and make that transparent. The apparent vacillations of government between what looks as excessive tolerance and what is apparently inefficient repression may thus reflect the duality of the criteria that voters use to assess its performance.

In what sense can we speak of the acquiescence of citizens to the opacity of the policy followed by government with regard to security? We assume that the reasons why the government chooses to do nothing are compelling. Then, when behaving as if the problem itself did not exist the government does exactly what the citizens would do if they had the same information. As argued in our earlier discussion of the mechanism of acquiescence to opacity, thinking about something else is the best attitude one can adopt when facing a problem that cannot be solved. Citizens may be inclined to feel that the problem of increased insecurity exists and should be heeded but they observe government behaving resolutely as if the problem did not exist and required no special attention. In behaving in that way, the government sends citizens the implicit message that if they were better informed they would know that they are mistaken, that no attention is warranted, and that they had better forget about insecurity. Because they trust government, many citizens tacitly accept that argument and, for the main, do think about something else. Normally these citizens constitute a majority. But, notably under the pressure of populist parties and candidates, uninterested in the short run in holding office, the issue of insecurity may become salient for a while both in the public debate and in the minds of a majority of voters. The question then for the party in power, and normally also for its contenders, is to make the problem disappear again from the political agenda.[15]

Finally, let us mention an additional reason for citizens to acquiesce to opacity in the policy area of security. This time, the motivation stems from the discomfort generated by the use of some means – some of the methods used by the police, or living conditions in prisons, for instance. On the one hand, people are clearly aware that they cannot judge whether a means is particularly cost efficient or is the only instrument available to achieve some objective they agree with and find important. On the other hand, as was the case with retributive justice, they have preferences intrinsic to the means, which they treat thus as ends. Consequently, if much information, or information of a vivid kind, is provided on the means just mentioned with reference to the police or to life in prison, this may, for moral or other reasons, generate painful emotions in many people. In turn, the awareness that there are two sides to the matter (two conflicting objectives), whereas, as simple citizens, they lack the knowledge that would be necessary to address the trade-off between the two, is potentially the source of some discomfort, akin to cognitive dissonance. This may be very much relieved or alleviated by information about means being severely curtailed. Citizens may be grateful for the ensuing opacity because they are wary of the effects of transparency on themselves (and preferring, in that case, government-made opacity to self-made self-deception, so to speak) or on others.[16]

15 In France, the issue of crime did become salient in the presidential election of 2002, and, already to a lesser degree, in the legislative elections that followed. Our expectation is that, because the reasons for its impotence in that policy area are still there, the new majority which came out of these elections will eventually succeed in inducing most voters to 'think about something else'.

16 Inasmuch as insecurity is especially intense in certain areas, administratively referred to in France as 'zones difficiles' thinking about something else might prove difficult to achieve for those who live in these areas. Whether this will influence the behaviour of the vast majority of the population who do not inhabit there will depend on the capacity of those who do to influence the political agenda in general.

Opacity in the Common Agricultural Policy

Many economists probably agreed with *The Economist* when, in 1990, it characterised the Common Agricultural Policy as 'the single most idiotic system of economic mismanagement that the rich western countries have ever devised'.[17] To many, the fundamental flaw in the Common Agricultural Policy (CAP) was its reliance on price support (a reliance made less exclusive by the 1992 and 1999 reforms), entailing (given the size and ownership distribution of farms) a huge transfer from consumers of food to large farms. At a more technical level, elementary diagrams were used to show that the simple substitution of deficiency payments to price support, even though it would bring no remedy to the flaw above (both instruments make support to each farm proportional to its output and thus to its size), would at least eliminate one source of waste (one deadweight loss). How could such a policy have been implemented in the first place, and then tolerated over such a long period of time? The answer seemed obvious: the policy would not have been accepted at all if it had been transparent. Thus opacity was from the start one of its major characteristics.

We agree with that statement but not with the implications usually drawn from it. In this instance, existing explanations do not pay sufficient attention to the underlying puzzle: why have not the constituencies that seem to have been the victims of opacity or obfuscation been mobilised by political parties or entrepreneurs so that more transparency and perhaps different policies would have come out? To address that question, we will:

- first, try to identify what exactly was opaque in the CAP;
- second, argue that the policy did achieve something extremely important;
- third, that alternative, more transparent policies would probably have been unsustainable or inadequate;
- and, fourth, that the apparent victims of opacity were not irrational in accepting it.

We must stress that our analysis does not concern the CAP as it stands now (it seems clear, anyhow, that a completely different policy is in the making). We try to understand the matter as it could have been assessed by the actors concerned when that policy (or, in fact, any of the national price support policies that preceded it) was started – and until it began to change substantially, about a decade ago.

The nature of opacity

This is really a case of obfuscation by salience, along the line suggested above. Nothing important about the CAP was really hidden but it was opaque nonetheless – not so much, as often claimed, by the burden falling on consumers rather than on taxpayers – but by the way its objectives were defined, and then made accepted by

17 *The Economist*, 29 September 1990, cited in Rieger (2000, 182).

all. This is also true of the national policies pursued before the CAP in the countries which were to start it. In both cases, obfuscation of intrinsically essential aspects of the policies came from the focus put on concepts such as 'parity', 'equity' or 'fairness' *interpreted in aggregate terms*. In Germany, according to the Agriculture Law of 5 September 1955 (the 'Green Law'), 'the "social situation" of people working in agriculture was to be brought up to the same level as that of "comparable professional groups"' (Milward 1992, 241).[18] In France, the first clause of the Law of 5 August 1961 reads: 'The purpose of the law on the orientation of French agriculture is to establish parity between agriculture and other economic activities in the framework of economic and social policy' (id., 248). In the Treaty of Rome, article 39 specified five objectives for the future Common Agricultural Policy: 1) increasing agricultural productivity, 2) ensuring a fair standard of living for the agricultural community, 3) stabilizing markets, 4) ensuring the availability of supplies, and 5) ensuring that supplies reach consumers at reasonable price.

What is interesting in this article 39 is also the things that it does not say. It would be an anachronism to blame it for not mentioning topics that surfaced later, such as the quality of food, respect for the environment, or the effect of the policy on the agriculture of developing countries. It is understandable that the diminution of employment in agriculture remained somewhat tacit as a possible effect or condition of increased productivity. The most telling silence is thus the one about distribution within the agricultural sector. Who, among farmers should benefit most from support, or how should the income distribution among farmers evolve, are questions that could have been addressed in the Treaty but were eschewed. In Article 39, the second objective was formulated in a way which directed the mind or centred the debates on the parity between a 'community' of farmers (tacitly, in activity) and the rest of the economy. It allowed its interpretation for operational purposes as a relation between two aggregate statistics, the average income of farmers ('real farming income', or 'net value added in agriculture per worker', in the language of the Commission) and GDP or GNP per capita.[19] As a consequence, the expression of distributional

18 The continuity between the CAP and the agricultural policies that preceded it in several of the member countries must be kept in mind. Even though France has been a major beneficiary and supporter of the CAP, some of the characteristics of the latter, in particular the fixation of a high reference price for support, responded to a demand from German rather than French agriculture.

19 Some claimed that parity meant full per capita income equality between the agricultural and the non-agricultural sectors. But the consensus meaning which emerged was only constant ratio between the per capita incomes, or equality between their respective rates of growth. A rough calculation suggests that, if the ratio has remained relatively stable in France over a period of almost 50 years, this has not been the case in all the other countries. In 1949, the share of agriculture in GDP was equal to 12 percent in France, 11 percent in West Germany, and 28 percent in Italy. If we divide these figures by those given in the text concerning the share in employment, we can estimate income per capita in agriculture to be in France and Germany a little above 40 percent of income per capita in the country as a whole, and almost 70 percent in Italy. In 1997, the share of agriculture in GDP was equal to 1.9 percent in

concerns if any was, to a large extent, channelled or encapsulated in the monitoring of the evolution of that single ratio (or an equivalent ratio between two growth rates). Distributional concerns thus did not expose the main way the policy worked, which, simplifying, was *a huge transfer from consumers, mostly low-income, to a minority of relatively affluent farmers.*[20]

The main achievement

To summarise the main achievement of the CAP, it would be difficult to find more appropriate words than those which Alan Milward (1992, 257) employed in his discussion not of the CAP but of its purely national predecessors after the second world war (policies also based on price support and protectionism). Referring thus to these predecessors, he concedes that, in the late 1950s, it was possible to argue "that a human management of the problem by the state had succeeded in transferring labour while improving productivity and avoiding unemployment, genuine hardship and social unrest." This applies also perfectly to the CAP.

For a fair assessment, however, awareness of the magnitude of the phenomena involved is essential. In 1949, the share of agriculture in total employment was equal to 29 percent in France, 25 percent in West Germany and 41 per cent in Italy. In 1960, the respective figures were still 22 percent, 14 percent and 33 percent; in 1997, they had fallen to 4.6 percent, 2.9 percent and 6.5 percent.[21] That such a transformation, involving also a momentous process of urbanization and intra-country migrations, could take place smoothly, without serious disruption, must be put to the credit of agricultural policies, even if it was facilitated by rapid overall economic growth until the early 1970s. The 'farm problem' was a considerable one in the 1950s and 1960s. It has more or less vanished today (at least, with regard to the European Union before enlargement), in spite of what the concerned actors find convenient to claim.[22]

France, 0.8 percent in West Germany, and 2.5 percent in Italy. Dividing by the 1997 figures for employment given in the text, suggests that the ratio has remained exactly the same in France (parity has been achieved in a relative sense), but has fallen in Germany and in Italy. This might be an effect of East Germany, if the figures for Germany have not been corrected for it, which we do not know, and of the Mezzogiorno. In any case, because of the importance of part-time farming and non-farm incomes, this type of calculations seriously underestimates nowadays the average total incomes of farmers (see Pelkmans 1997, 177).

20 '80 percent of benefits obtained by 20 percent of the farmers' (Pelkmans 1997, 180).

21 Only 4 percent in 2000 in France, according to the recent census.

22 A policy adapted to a very small fraction of the population can be quite different from the one which imposed itself when a third or a fourth of the population were farmers. We will argue that a major obstacle to deficiency payments of a large magnitude is their budgetary cost, which is related to the size of the population of farmers. Employment in agriculture in the United Kingdom was a mere 5 percent of total employment in 1949 (when it was still, as we saw, equal or superior to 25 percent in France and Germany and about 40 percent in Italy). This explains that the UK could use deficiency payments rather than price support prior to its entry in the Common Market.

The inadequacy of alternative policies (a counterfactual exercise)

Though recommended by most economists, alternative policies would probably not have worked. One policy, making more transparent the income transfer to farming, would have been to substitute deficiency payments for price support. This would have been a clear case of Pareto improvement, the theory suggests. To be such a thing, one condition is that large farmers should have been given at least the same support in real terms that they received under price support. This would have required an increase in tax revenue of about 10 percent in Germany and France and 20 percent in Italy (see Zobbe 2001, 15-6).[23] Would have taxes of such magnitude, 80 percent of which now much more transparently for the benefit of large farmers, been acceptable to parliaments and public opinion? Distributional considerations would certainly have become salient. The political debate would have focussed on them. Most probably, the outcome would have been a combination of much less total support for agriculture and of a distribution of that support much less unequal.

But, in fact, this means that the first alternative policy, based on a paretian justification of recourse to deficiency payments, would have been found politically unfeasible and replaced by a second alternative policy, consisting again of direct subsidies to farmers but independent from, or much less related to, the output or size of the farm. Such a policy is in fact the one considered the most natural, and recommended directly, by the many economists who impute support to farmers to considerations of redistribution and justice. If this is indeed the main concern underlying farm policies, the theory of optimal assignment of instruments will also recommend using means-tested direct income payments. But if, as argued above, the main policy objective of the CAP and its predecessors was a smooth transition from an economy in which the agricultural sector was, at least in terms of employment, a major sector to an economy in which it would become very small, then a policy of support to the small farmers would have been completely inadequate.

At best, if not too contested and eroded by the claims of other components of the population, it would have succeeded to channel funds mostly to the small farms. As a consequence, it would have tended, if not to ossify completely the inefficient structures of European agriculture, at least to slow down considerably their adaptation.[24] With direct payments to the small farmers only, or (which comes

---

23 Zobbe's (rather simple) calculation is as follows. In 1967, support represented about half of the value of production in the countries concerned by the CAP. The share of agriculture in GDP in Germany was about 5 percent and in France and Italy about 8 percent. Thus, under deficiency payments, the fiscal transfer to farmers should have been equal to about 2.5 percent of GDP in Germany, and 4 percent in France and Italy. Hence the required increases in budgets indicated in the text.

24 Again, the magnitude of the change which did take place is important. In 1955, in France, 52 percent of the farms had a surface of less that 10 hectares (see Averyt 1977, 23). The 5 percent of farms having a surface of more than 50 hectares had 25 percent of the total surface used by agriculture. In 2000, farms of more than 50 hectares employ 77 percent of the surface, and those of more than 100 hectares 50 per cent. Farms of less than 20 hectares still

almost to the same) with payments independent of output and surface, we would still be facing 'the farm problem'. At worst, the rest of the population would have balked at the prospect of maintaining over time so substantial a socially-motivated transfer to so large a fraction of the population (say, 10 or 15 percent).

As a consequence, a third alternative policy would have emerged, close to laissez-faire (somewhat mitigated, however, by the existence, in the welfare state, of various kinds of safety nets). A large number of farmers would have had to leave their farms at short notice and seek occupations in the industry, often at long distance from where they lived. The welfare-oriented political personnel holding office in post-war Western Europe, still highly influenced by the experience of the inter-war period, could not accept such a prospect and the risk of serious political instability that it entailed.

Acquiescence of the 'victims'

Abstracting from constituencies abroad, the two main categories of "victims" were the buyers of food, especially low-income families, and the small farmers. It is worth observing that neither category protested with a minimum of vigour or continuity against the policy. Consider first the consumers. The consumer organisations in Europe are still relatively weak and they were almost inexistent in the first decades of the period we are concerned with. But the trade unions and the political parties of the Left were the natural representatives of low-income consumers. They did not protest either. Where the Left was in power, it did nothing to change the policy.[25] Before concluding from that observation that obfuscation had succeeded in misleading consumers into acquiescence to a policy that harmed them, the question must be raised of whether the policy did harm them, or, if it did, of how seriously.

There are two points to be made here. First, it must be observed that under the CAP agricultural producer prices declined rapidly (although less than world market prices) – for instance, at a rate of 3.7 percent annually over the period 1979-91 (Pelkmans 1997, 178). Given the fantastic modernisation of food-retailing which took place at the same time, the price of food paid by consumers probably declined even more rapidly. This result is largely the consequence of gains of productivity, themselves closely related to support being heavily biased in favour of the largest, most efficient farms. Under direct income payments, assuredly fairer to small farmers, productivity gains would have been smaller, and either (without protectionism and

---

constitute about 49 percent of the total number of farms, but they occupy only 6 percent of the surface (Bourgeois 2001).

25 Incidentally, protests by political parties or governments against the CAP, and attempts at reforming it, were always stimulated by concerns about the growth of its budgetary cost, as if there was no burden to the consumers. For year 1988 though, the estimated cost to consumers of the transfers to farmers was 64.6 billions ECU (the euro replaced the ECU one to one), whereas the net budgetary cost, assumed by taxpayers, was "only" 37.8 billions, making a total of 102.4 billions (that is, 320 ECU paid on average by each household so that each full-time farmer could receive on average 11600 ECU). See Pelkmans (1997, 178).

with a declining world price) the support policy would have been increasingly costly (in the end to consumers also, as taxpayers) or (with some protectionism) prices would not have declined as much.[26] The second point is that, as we saw, the alternative policies were probably not feasible. But if we, from our standpoint as observers, can judge these policies implausible, why would not the consumers and their representatives have come, if not exactly to the same opinion, at least to a feeling of high uncertainty about policy change?

The majority of small farmers also failed to criticise the price support policy. Most of them remained faithful to the main farmer organisations which defended vehemently that policy. Were they mistaken? The question, similar to the one just raised with regard to consumers, is whether that policy really caused them some harm, and if it did, to what extent. Here an essential consideration is that of who owns the land. The theory suggests that support proportional to output, and particularly price support, first of all raises the remuneration or market value of fixed factors, that is here mainly of land. When the owner of land and the farmer who exploits it are different persons, price support thus benefits the landowner and not the farmer (another common criticism of output-based support policies). However, in the countries concerned by the CAP, and especially in France, most small farmers have always been and still are the owners of the land they exploit. This meant that farmers leaving the farm could sell their land to remaining neighbours at a higher price under price support than they would have done under, say, direct income payments.

Small farmers could understand as well as we do that they should have no confidence in the possibility of implementing an alternative policy under which their fare would have been durably better. They knew also that they would have vehemently protested against the first alternative mentioned above, entailing grossly unequal deficiency payments. They could anticipate that a policy of direct income payments of a sufficiently large magnitude would not have been durably supported by voters or public opinion. And they feared most of all the complete renunciation to support for agriculture that such a policy could have brought about. Thus, at the minimum, it was not clearly irrational for them to concur in the defence of aggregate 'parity' and not to oppose the CAP.

We have argued that price support was a policy that was not irrational for consumers and small farmers to accept. Opacity was a basic characteristic of that policy: the basic mechanism underlying the policy – subsidising the rich and gently pushing outside the poor – could not be made salient without the policy becoming unfeasible. It was also rational consequently for these categories to accept opacity in this sense. They could not logically accept the policy and not the obfuscation. This may seem somewhat strange because opacity was to a large extent designed with their reaction in mind. We think that the analysis of the mechanism of acquiescence to opacity suggested above offers a way to solve this puzzle. Most small farmers may

26 As to the third alternative policy mentioned earlier in the text (laissez-faire, more or less), how could consumers, this time as also citizens, have welcomed the social disruptions that it would have implied?

have been persuaded at the same time that, taking into account political feasibility, the policy was the less bad one and that, nonetheless, displaying or stressing its true main characteristics, which were largely related to income distribution and justice, would have opened up a debate whose ultimate outcome was likely to be unfavourable.

Conclusion

Many public policies are opaque to the general public or to voters with regard to the means used by governments to implement them and/or to the real objectives these policies pursue. It is not extremely surprising that some agents – politicians or governments in particular – try to hide or distort information provided to others. But, in democratic settings, in which there is usually a lot of political competition and entrepreneurship, it may be considered as puzzling that they succeed – often over long periods of time. As a complement or an alternative to other explanations, we have explored the reasons why some voters could prefer not to be better informed about a government policy even if this additional information were offered them at no cost. Thus, voters may be aware of their inability to judge some aspects of policies and consequently accept that these aspects remain opaque. Knowing that some kinds of information will be both useless and likely to generate some discomfort, individuals may even express an active preference for remaining uninformed. Another mechanism is based on the fact that transparency is information made available to all. As a consequence of this characteristic, even if one, personally, derives utility from additional transparency, one may at the same time derive negative utility from the fact that the same information is provided to others. This may lead to prefer opacity. Finally, opacity may take the form, not of any feature of a policy being hidden, but of the way the policy is framed and the relative salience of its various aspects distorted.

In a given setting, several or all these mechanisms may operate simultaneously, not only on different individuals but also, probably to a lesser extent, on the same ones. For many purposes, it is not really necessary to disentangle the respective influence of the mechanisms. It is enough that they generate, at the aggregate level, acceptance of – and sometimes preference for – opacity.

Admittedly, we stressed different mechanisms in the two case studies that followed the more abstract analysis. Thus, to explain why, in a context of rising insecurity, the general citizenry has acquiesced to a public policy consisting not only in devoting no particular effort to improve crime control but also in obfuscating any basis to do so, the mechanism we assumed to play the main role was citizens' awareness of their inability to gauge the overall situation by themselves. We suggested also that the uselessness of the additional information provided by increased transparency may well have been compounded, from the perspective of citizens, by the expected discomfort associated with this information. In the interpretation of the European Common Agricultural Policy that we offered in the second case study, opacity, or obfuscation, took the form of the real objective and modus operandi of the policy being made as little salient as possible, the stress being put instead on a misleading concept of 'parity', suggestive of a concern with justice in reality absent. We ascribed the acquiescence of the apparent victims of the distortion to the fear that full transparency of the policy, displaying in a fair way all its characteristics, would have fostered a kind of public debate whose outcome they could legitimately fear to be unfavourable.

The fact, however, that in each of the two stories, we stressed only some of the mechanisms does not mean that in reality the other mechanisms do not or did not also play a role. Thus among the individuals who accept to be told that increased security is not really a problem, or who accept that it be considered as a minor issue, many probably are above all fearful of the effect that more information or greater salience could have on others. In the case of price support, it is likely that, in fact, many small farmers felt unqualified to question public pronouncements and/or preferred not to think too much about their, or their children's, fate.

References

Acemoglu, D. and Robinson, J. (2001), 'Inefficient Redistribution', *American Political Science Review* 95:3, 649-61.

Algalarrondo, H. (2002), *Sécurité: la gauche contre le peuple.* (Paris: Robert Laffont).

Austen-Smith, D. (1991), 'Rational consumers and irrational voters', *Economics and Politics* 3:1, 73-92.

Averyt, W. (1977), *Agropolitics in the European Community: Interest Groups and the Common Agricultural Policy.* (New York and London: Praeger).

Barro, R. (1973), 'The Control of Politicians: An Economic Model', *Public Choice*, 14, 19-42.

Bordignon, M. and Minelli, E. (2001), 'Rules Transparency and Political Accountability', *Journal of Public Economics* 80, 73-98.

Bourgeois, L. (2001),'Recensement de l'agriculture 2000: restructuration à marche forcée dans la décennie quatre-vingt-dix', *Paysans* 270, Reprinted in *Problèmes Economiques* 2750 (27 February 2002), 14-6.

Brennan, G. and Hamlin, A. (2000), *Democratic Devices and Desires.* (Cambridge and New York: Cambridge University Press).

Breton, A. (1996), *Competitive Governments. An Economic Theory of Politics and Public Finance.* (Cambridge and New York: Cambridge University Press).

Breton, A., Galeotti, G., Salmon, P. and Wintrobe, R. (eds.) (1993), *Preferences and Democracy.* (Dordrecht and Boston: Kluwer).

Cadot, O. and Sinclair-Desgagné, B. (1992), 'Prudence and Success in Politics' *Economics and Politics*, 4, 171-89.

Coate, S. and Morris, S. (1995), 'On the Form of Transfers to Special Interests', *Journal of Political Economy*, 103:6,1210-35.

Corman, H. and Mocan, N. (2002), 'Carrots, Sticks and Broken Windows', *Working Paper No. 9061* (Cambridge, MA: National Bureau of Economic Research).
Donohue, J.III and Siegelman, P. (1998), 'Allocating Resources Among Prisons and Social Programs in the Battle Against Crime', *Journal of Legal Studies*, 27, 1-43.
Downs, A. (1957), *An Economic Theory of Democracy.* (New York: Harper and Row).
Eide, E. (1998), 'Economics of Criminal Behavior' in: Bockaert, B. and de Geest, G. (eds.) *Encyclopedia of Law and Economics.* (Aldershot: Edward Elgar).
Elster, J. and Slagstad, R. (eds.) (1988), *Constitutional Democracy.* (Cambridge and New York: Cambridge University Press).
Ferejohn, J. (1986), 'Incumbent Performance and Electoral Control' *Public Choice*, 50, 5-26.
Grémy, J-P. (1998), *Les aspirations des Français en matière de sécurité: Leur évolution entre 1990 et 1998 selon les enquêtes du CREDOC.* (Paris: Institut des Hautes Etudes de Sécurité Intérieure).
Howitt, P. and Wintrobe, R. (1995), 'The Political Economy of Inaction', *Journal of Public Economics*, 56, 329-53.
Issing, O. (1999), 'The Eurosystem: Transparent and Accountable or "Willem in Euroland"', *Journal of Common Market Studies*, 37:3, 503-19.
Levitt, S. (1997), 'Using Electoral Cycles in Police Hiring to Estimate the Effects of Police on Crime', *American Economic Review*, 87, 270-90.
Lohmann, S. (1998), 'An Information Rationale for the Power of Special Interests' *American Political Science Review*, 92:4, 809-27.
Magee, S., Brock, W. and Young, L. (1989), *Black Holes Tariffs and Endogenous Policy Theory.* (Cambridge and New York: Cambridge University Press).
Milward, A. (1992), *The European Rescue of the Nation-State.* (Berkeley and Los Angeles: University of California Press).
Pelkmans, J. (1997), *European Integration: Methods and Economic Analysis.* (Harlow: Addison Wesley Longman).
Persson, T. and Tabellini, G. (2000), *Political Economics, Explaining Economic Policy.* (Cambridge, MA. and London, UK: The MIT Press).
Przeworski, A., Stokes, S. and Manin, B. (eds.) (1999), *Democracy, Accountability, and Representation.* (Cambridge and New York: Cambridge University Press).
Rieger, E. (2000), 'The Common Agricultural Policy: Politics Against Markets', in: Wallace, H. and Wallace, W. (eds.), *Policy-Making in the European Union*, 4th Edition. (Oxford: Oxford University Press), 179-210.
Rodrik, D. (1995), 'Political Economy of Trade Policy', in Grossman, G.M. and Rogoff, K. (eds.), *Handbook of International Economics*, Vol. III, (Amsterdam: Elsevier), 1457-94.
Salmon, P. (1993), 'Unpopular Policies and the Theory of Representative Democracy', in Breton, A. et al. (eds.), 13-39.
Salmon, P. (2001), 'Thinking About Something Else: A Rationality-Compatible Mechanism with Macroscopic Consequences', *Kyklos*, 54:2/3, 453-64.

Scharpf, F. (1999), *Governing in Europe: Effective and Democratic?* (Oxford: Oxford University Press).
Schelling, T. (1984), 'The Mind as a Consuming Organ', in *Choice and Consequence: Perspectives from an Errant Economist.* (Cambridge, MA. and London, UK: Harvard University Press).
Slagstad, R. (1988), 'Liberal Constitutionalism and its Critics: Carl Schmitt and Max Weber', in: Elster, J. and Slagstad, R. (eds.).
Winkler, B. (2000), 'Which Kind of Transparency: On the Need for Clarity in Monetary Policy-Making', *Working Paper No. 26* (European Central Bank).
Young, H. (1994), *Equity in Theory and Practice.* (Princeton: Princeton University Press).
Zobbe, H. (2001), 'The Economic and Historical Foundation of the Common Agricultural Policy in Europe' (Paper Presented at the 4th European Historical Economics Society, Oxford: Merton College).

Chapter 2

Citizens' Knowledge, Politicians' Duplicity

Russell Hardin

By what license does an official in a democratic government act through subterfuge toward citizens? It is part of the vision of democracy that it, more than other forms of government, requires truthfulness and transparency if it is to succeed, that is, to fulfil its own vision. Democracy, like justice, must not merely be done, it must be seen to be done. The simple argument is that if citizens are to decide who should govern, then they must know what the governors do or might do. Hence mendacity on the part of politicians and officials is especially harmful. If this is true, then in a system that gets its strength from truth, lies might be all the more effective and destructive (Campbell 2001, 16).

Nevertheless, politicians in democracies often lie and keep secrets about public business, and citizens seem to license them to do so in some cases. License could come from the answer to the question: Do I want to know X if the price of my knowing it is to let all or at least many others know it as well? Suppose it is widely agreed that there are some things which, under particular circumstances, we would want kept secret from ourselves in order to keep them secret from certain others; and suppose that secrecy often seemingly requires lying to keep the truth hidden. This category of official decisions calls into question any conception of democracy that is purely procedural. It inherently includes some concern with outcomes and their 'democratic' effect. It is very unlikely that we could adopt a constitutional or legal provision that would spell out when it is okay or even required for officials to lie to us. Hence we can expect officials to decide for themselves, ad hoc, when they can or should lie. At most, we the citizens can hold them accountable only after the fact, through retrospective voting or through political action of some other kind.

A more general principle, if we can devise it, is that their actions should conform to a role morality for elected officials. Such a principle should subsume cases of our preferring that officials be secretive or even lie is that their actions should conform to the role morality of elected officials. If we devise such a role morality, we can conceive it on analogy with professional ethics. In general, a professions' ethics are a function of what its mandate is. We go to doctors in order to protect our health and to lawyers to defend us against suit or for beneficial legal advice. If the mandate of elected officials is to represent us, this mandate entails particular constraints on their behaviour. We generally expect them to represent us in working for our interests or our commitments. In particular then, officials should not do what would violate our interests.

An obvious complication here that runs against an easy analogy with professional ethics is that our elected representatives might be governed by several possible theories of representation and, hence, different theories of agency. Before considering this complication, however, let us suppose that the agency relation of our elected officials is simple and let us focus on lying and secrecy. The minimal criterion these must meet if they are to be justified is that they serve the interests of the relevant representative's constituency.

Immediately, it follows that actions that involve a conflict between a constituency's and its elected official's interests seem to violate the role or professional morality of the official. If you are a public official, your rewards – mostly salary and the usual benefits – are established by law. You should not use the power of your office to extract even greater rewards in the form of bribes, gifts, jobs for relatives, and so forth. Hence you should avoid conflicts of interest. For example, you should not help to award a government contract to your spouse's construction firm, law firm, travel agency, consulting firm, or whatever. Ed Meese arranged government jobs for people who loaned him money when his credit rating was very bad. Alaska's Senator Frank Murkowski, elected governor in 2002, appointed his own daughter to finish his Senate term. Historically, preferment of one's family members was common; indeed, it was a principle of aristocratic government. Very early, the preferment of party supporters was standard practice in democratic government.

The term 'conflict of interest' apparently first appeared in a court decision in the United States in 1949 (Luebke 1987). Now the term is everywhere in probably hundreds of statutes governing behaviour of public officials and private citizens whose activities – such as insider trading – are subject to legal regulation. Most of us face conflicts of interest in our lives. Until little over a hundred years ago, almost no one thought that was a problem except in extreme cases, such as bribery. Today it is a central problem in public trust. Why? In part because big organizations, especially government institutions, control so much of our lives and are among our most powerful resources for getting things done.

We might wish to go further and say that public officials should avoid even the appearance of a conflict of interest. Should we require that? The answer largely should turn on how much difference we think it makes to their functioning in office and, more generally, to the functioning of public agencies overall. If an appearance of conflict of interest means that public bodies such as relevant legislative committees or ethics boards must invest great effort in investigating and establishing whether there is an actual conflict of interest, that is one reason for treating mere appearance as something that should be corrected. Or, and perhaps more important, if an appearance of conflict of interest casts public doubt on an official's trustworthiness, that is a strong reason for the public to want not even appearances of conflict of interest from their officials.

Moreover, when there are external effects of acting under the role morality of any professional, we might impose constraints on fulfilling the professional's function. In the case of elected officials, we might make some of those constraints legally binding, as when we block them from accepting large honoraria for speaking to private groups or when we put constraints on their campaign financing. Politicians could rightly argue that such constraints make it more difficult for them to fulfil their roles because they make it harder to gain election. Such constraints might be morally grounded, but they are independent of, and can even trump, the specific role morality of elected officials. This is, of course, no different from professional ethics more generally.

Alternatively, one might wish to say that we have a convention or practice of official lying according to official judgment. Unlike the supposed conventions of the unwritten English constitution, however, this is a convention that has not been debated or in any sense approved by popular assessment. Indeed, the only public debate about lying has largely been on very abstract general lines. Seemingly the most common position is that all lying is wrong, but very few people likely follow such a rigorist principle in practice, although many might assert the view (see quote from Orwell below; see also Bok 1978; but see Nyberg 1993). Rigorists hold that lying per se is wrong independently of the reasons for or consequences of lying or telling the truth. Public policy is inherently consequentialist in the sense that it is intended to cause particular things to happen in the world. To judge official lying independently of its consequences, therefore, is potentially disabling for public policy making in the sense that lying might actually enable us to accomplish some things that telling the truth would block. In sum, there is no clearly prevailing conventional morality to govern official mendacity in general.

In typical instances of official deceit, the goal is secrecy of certain actions. Therefore, we must analyze these two matters together. This is probably a defining characteristic of deceit in a democracy, where the purpose of deceit must be to override what would happen under democratic choice or to protect a presumptively democratic choice. There are two general classes of problem at issue: deceit in the adoption of policy and deceit in the implementation of policy. The former is primarily by legislators and by executives when acting in their legislative capacity, as when a US president proposes or signs legislation; the latter is primarily by administrative agencies and agents. I will focus on the former. Deceit by administrative agencies could be substantially at issue here only if it is on behalf of legislators.

In advanced democracies, we usually do not need to worry very much about lack of transparency in the adoption of official policies that have the form of laws or legal regulations or even of executive orders. The latter are commonly employed by American presidents but they must be openly promulgated. Their use is stimulated by the difficulty of acting through standard legislative channels, especially in times of crisis; but they are also very commonly stimulated by a desire to impose regulatory rules on administrative agencies that have not acted on relevant issues or have acted in ways that the president does not like, or to by-pass Congress when it might be thought to oppose presidential preferences on some issue. George W. Bush, lacking strong legislative support for much of his extremely conservative program, has made extensive use of executive orders. In all of these policy contexts, whether action is taken through legislative law making, regulatory rule setting, or executive order, the actions are relatively transparent. Yet, they can still be deceitful, as will be argued below for the demoralizing case of the recent congressional attack on the Internal Revenue Service (IRS).

There are two ranges of what we might perversely call ideal types of official deceit: when one could suppose that the public would prefer official lying as likely to help accomplish the relevant public goal; and when one cannot suppose that the public would approve of official subterfuge. The seemingly most interesting cases, however, are mixes of these two types.

Deceit in the Public Interest

There are some relatively clear examples of deceit that putatively serves the public interest. The public would presumably prefer that plans of action during war not be made public if that would tip off the enemy, and the public would prefer that the police not publicize some of their actions in searching for a reputed criminal or fugitive. In the war case, we want to shield relevant knowledge from non-citizens. For example, before D-Day, Allied military and political leaders wanted to mislead the Wehrmacht about plans for the invasion of Nazi controlled Europe. The way to keep plans secret from the Wehrmacht was to keep them secret from as many people as possible to reduce the possibilities of leaks. A similar argument applies to the criminal or fugitive case.

George Orwell rejected lying in all cases, even to deceive the enemy in wartime. Ian Slater (1985, 209-10) attributes to him the view that: "Lying becomes the norm, and one cannot, even by an act of will, confine it to just military matters." This suggests that any short-term gain from lying (winning World War II with fewer casualties) must be outweighed by long-term losses (the general corruption of government). There is a causal psychological claim here that cannot go without questioning. And there is an even more important structural claim implicit in this stark view, as attributed to Orwell. He seems to suppose that there will not be effective oversight of some kind to reduce the incentive to lie and to exact costs of those who do lie under certain circumstances. A remarkable feature of lying in wartime to deceive the enemy is that it might be approved after the fact, or, more likely, it would not be questioned even once it became known. After-the-fact tales of tricks by the English and the Americans to deceive the Germans during World War II seem to be well-received and even taken to be humorous by the populations whose interests were served by the trickery and deceit. Orwell's inference that lying therefore must have become the norm seems far off the mark. General Eisenhower probably did lie about actions in the European theatre, and President Eisenhower probably lied about many things. But it is far-fetched to say that lying was his norm or that his lying infected others to make it their norm.

Consider a more complex example: vaccination to eliminate polio in the 1950s in the United States and thereafter everywhere (see Hardin 2003, chap. 3). A complication of the US program was that the public might have mobilized to wreck the program if they had fully understood it. Superficially, the program seemed to serve the mutual advantage of everyone – and it did so relative to no vaccination program, although it was not an optimal program. The vaccine of choice was the attenuated but still live Sabin polio vaccine, which caused one case of polio per 560,000 first doses of the vaccine in the United States (Roberts 1988). But, as is typical of diseases that require human carriers as vectors, we might be able to reduce the total number of infections from vaccination by vaccinating only some large fraction of all children. The disease may not be capable of spreading even if only some fraction of the population is vaccinated. (This fact was used in the worldwide eradication of smallpox by the United Nations, because everyone in the vicinity of a smallpox victim could be quarantined and vaccinated to stop the spread of the disease, which was exclusively by inhalation of the airborne virus from an infected person or perhaps from the deposit of exhaled, virus-laden, aerosol on open sores or mucous membranes. A similar program is now underway for polio.)

Now we could say that, ex ante, it would be mutually advantageous to all children to vaccinate only, say, fifty percent of them. Those who are vaccinated will be put at greater risk than those who are not. The actual choosing of which children to vaccinate is then not a matter of mutual advantage even though selecting the percentage to vaccinate could be. (Of course, those children who do eventually contract polio do not ex post join in the mutual advantage of the vaccination program; they benefit only ex ante.) Vaccinating all children, as was virtually done in the United States, meant that twice as many deaths from the vaccine than if only fifty percent had been vaccinated.

Choosing which children to vaccinate has more the character of the choices made in a typical cost-benefit analysis, in which the costs to all are weighed against the benefits to all, although some may be net beneficiaries while others are net losers. In the United States, people have sued vaccine makers for their children's illnesses (see Sun 1985). The more sensible program would be to indemnify, from public funds, those who are harmed by publicly mandated programs. Then the ex ante burden would not be quite as far from the ex post burden as it traditionally has been. It is hard to imagine that many people would accept a promise of compensation in return for having their children become ill from vaccination gone awry, however, and one might therefore expect the officials running the vaccination program not to publicize the fact that, say, only half of all children in a town need to be vaccinated to protect all of them. It sounds perverse to suppose that keeping people ignorant might actually be mutually advantageous. But in this case, popular ignorance might enable government to act beneficially.

Deceit against the Public Interest

Committees in both houses of the US congress carried on a so-called investigation of the practices of the IRS in trying to collect taxes, which is the purpose of the IRS. They brought in tax payers who testified that the IRS had treated them abusively in trying to collect taxes they did not owe. On its face such a claim seems implausible.

Indeed, one can imagine that the IRS is among the most competent agencies of the Federal government, not least perhaps because its mandate is relatively clear and well defined and because much of its work is done by taxpayers and their private accountants. Moreover, its actions, when taxpayers disagree, are always subject to review by independent courts that are well known frequently to go against IRS interpretations of the law. In any justice system, there are bound to be cases that go wrong, but systematic abuse in the IRS seems very unlikely. (Part of the agency's problem was that it was forced to join the war on drugs and given police powers that IRS leaders did not want, police powers forced upon it by Congress [Johnston 1998]).

Yet Congress took the taxpayers' complaints seriously without bringing in IRS agents to find out why they thought those people owed money. Congressional behaviour was tantamount to holding a kangaroo court (an extra-legal, prejudicial proceeding that mocks principles of law and justice) to convict the IRS. The end result in Congress was legislation to restrict IRS behaviour, reduce its budget, and impose penalties on so-called rogue agents. Most of the testimony in the original hearings has been discredited, and some of it was disproved in subsequent court proceedings (Johnston 1999 and 2000). Now, however, the IRS has been reduced in its capacities in ways that are almost certain to enable many taxpayers to avoid payment of taxes they are legally obligated to pay. As a rule, that will typically mean high income taxpayers, who are the chief financial backers of the leaders of the congressional investigation into IRS practices. Hence there was a – perhaps small – public whose interest was served by the congressional sham action.

If one simply looked at this congressional exercise as an honest effort to find out whether there were abusive practices at the IRS, one would expect that the committee members, many of them lawyers, would insist on standard fact-finding, adversarial proceedings to collect information from both the accusing taxpayers and the IRS, perhaps bringing in independent auditors to check the claims of taxes due. If lawyers did not insist on proceeding in such a way, one would have difficulty believing that they genuinely sought to find out the truth. They wanted to convict the IRS and they proceeded in a way that was virtually guaranteed to convict. It was they who were abusive and their kangaroo-court proceedings were a disgrace as well as a public disservice (but see Nixon and Roth 1999).

As is typical of many big news stories, the original investigations into IRS practices and the outlandish accusations against the agency were front-page news. The later exoneration of the IRS and its agents was relegated to brief stories (Johnston 2000; the *New York Times* also ran an editorial, 'Phantom Rogues at the I.R.S.' 19 August 2000). Of the first 830 complaints by taxpayers filed against the IRS under the new rules, not one was upheld by the newly created independent watchdog, the Treasury Inspector General for Tax Administration. That agency found some of the complaints to be bogus efforts to avoid payment. The claim that there were many rogue agents has similarly proved to be unfounded. A spokeswoman for Senator William Roth (Republican of Delaware), sponsor of the bill to rein in the IRS, rejected the view that the bill had been misconceived with the asinine claim that IRS employees 'are adhering to the [new] law' because 'perhaps the restructuring act and its threat of termination has kept them from violating the law' (Johnston 2000).

The partial destruction of IRS capacities for enforcement and auditing of returns has been de facto permanent. As a result, the tax system of the United States has become more nearly redistributive upwards. The only gainers of the changes imposed by an abusive Congress are high-income taxpayers and many members of Congress, whose campaign chests have benefited. In 2002 tax revenues were inexplicably down $100 billion below expected levels over about half the year (*New York Times*, 1 September 2002, 4.2). Perhaps part of the shortfall is from reduced efforts to enforce compliance, as predicted by tax lawyers (Johnston 1999). The so-called tax gap – the difference between revenue actually collected and government estimates of what the revenue should be – was running about $195 billion (eleven percent of the total federal budget) in 1998 (Stevenson 1998). That number can only have risen after the legislation eviscerating the IRS.

In this case, as in many others, it would be difficult to prove that the actions of members of Congress were deliberately deceitful, but it is almost as difficult to believe that their purpose was not clearly to disrupt tax collections for, especially, small business operators. In any case, truth was not an issue for the committees because they – or at least the lawyers among them – knew professionally that their procedure would not elicit the truth. One might conclude that the members of Congress who ran this kangaroo court proceeding with extensive media coverage were stupid, not mendacious. That conclusion does not seem to be plausible for many of these people, who actively seem to have wanted to damage the IRS and also wanted to gain financial support from those who welcomed the weakening of IRS audit capacities.

Mixed cases

An important general category of secrecy is in constitutional deliberations, where secrecy might be seen as a device for making the final product more authoritative and definitive, as well as, of course, a device for keeping the public out of the debates in progress. The latter concern might be seen as a protection for the citizenry. Consider, for example, the differences in the US and French constitutional experiences two centuries ago (Manin 1997, 168; Elster 2000). These were the first two modern nations to adopt constitutions through popular procedures. It seems likely that the constitutions were substantially affected by the different degrees of openness of the deliberations. Indeed, even the stability of them was affected; the constitution written in secret in the United States is still in place whereas the French adopted one constitution after another in the few years after 1789. The French revolutionary constitutional assemblies were very large and carried on their deliberations openly, with massive coverage by many different presses and with an often loud audience of interested citizens.

The US constitutional convention (not called that at the time because its mandate was not to create a constitution but merely to propose amendments to the then governing Articles of Confederation) was very small with only several dozen people in attendance, and its deliberations were kept virtually secret. As Clinton Rossiter (1966, 332) remarks, it is 'one of the intriguing facts of American constitutional history that the people in whose name and by whose power the great charter of 1787 was proclaimed should have had to wait more than half a century to learn how it came to be written'. Indeed, records of its deliberations were not published for many years after the constitution was already long in place. The fullest of all the records, the notes of James Madison, were not published until 1840, so that by the time they were read by a wider public, that public included almost no one who had been adult at the time of the convention. The obvious response to Rossiter's remark is that the people voted on the constitution, thereby empowering it and the government it designed. Maybe it was better that they did not vote on it line by line but only as a complete document. Once that document was placed before the states, it seemed likely that for the lifetime of those then deciding, voting pro or con on the constitution was equivalent to voting for union or no union.

There is a meaningful sense in which the relevant groups – or at least leading figures in those groups – were apprised of the deliberations in Philadelphia. There were essentially three major interests and one very numerous but not very involved interest. A fifth group with a large stake in the outcome of the deliberations were slaves, who were completely excluded from the constitutional design and adoption proceedings. The three major interests were southern plantation owners, urban business interests (banking, shipping, and trade), and agrarian communities in the north that were not slave holding and that were governed locally by a somewhat aristocratic class of large land holders. The neglected group was the large bulk of the population: small holding farmers. Although they constituted more than eighty percent of the adult male population, this group was itself not actively involved in politics, largely failed even to vote on ratification of the constitution (Fink and Riker 1989), and may well not have appreciated any interest that they had in common with any of the other groups. Some of them were locally under the sway of one of the other two farming groups and might well have wanted out from under their political control, but we have very little direct testimony on their views.

The public debates were almost entirely among virtual aristocrats, including self-made aristocrats, such as Alexander Hamilton, among the business leaders. The great democratic revolution was democratic primarily for such aristocrats. The northern agricultural interests mostly boycotted the convention, some of them leaving only after it was clear that the agenda was to create a new constitution and that they were too few to block such a move. They eventually came to be known as the Anti-Federalists because they opposed the new national government with its legislative bodies that were clearly too small to represent the large number of small communities. The Anti-Federalists supposed that each community was distinctive and special in its interests and therefore each needed to be represented individually in the legislature. They boycotted the convention presumably because they thought they could stop any new constitution from being adopted, because the extant government under the Articles of Confederation would surely kill the constitution. The constitutionalists, however, proposed to have adoption be determined by the states, not by the extant Continental Congress, in which any state could veto any constitutional amendment and in which Rhode Island was certain to veto the new constitution (as well as any of the amendments of the Articles that the convention ostensibly was called to propose). In a sense, therefore, the deliberations of the Philadelphia convention were secret in their day to day detail but not in their larger political import. When two Anti-Federalist New York delegates left the convention, their complaints were public. Moreover, the constitution that was written there was put to the entire citizenry (male property holders) for ratification, so that there was a kind of retrospective voting on the procedure. That the constitution was adopted suggests that the secrecy that had helped to get it into shape was at least minimally acceptable.

One might argue that the US constitutional convention was deceitful in exceeding its mandate and writing a constitution that many Americans would not support. But it would probably still be reasonable to claim that the participants in that convention genuinely were concerned to create a generally good government and not merely concerned to further their own personal interests – although in their view, their interest and the public interest were closely related on the structure of government. Apart from the mostly absent Anti-Federalists, the delegates to that convention were sorely frustrated by the veto power of tiny Rhode Island in the Continental Congress and they wanted to create a government that would not be rendered so ineffective. In the Congress of the Articles, each of the thirteen states had one vote, and one negative was enough to block any constitutional amendment. Rhode Island and New York engaged in abusive trading practices. They would import goods from England and the Caribbean at low or no tariff and then re-export the goods to Massachusetts and New Jersey, which had high tariffs. They could undercut both domestic and import prices in those states while making a substantial profit. A main motive for calling the Philadelphia convention was to find a way to regularize trade between the thirteen states and between them and foreign nations and to eliminate such abusive practices. To do that, however, would require constitutional change to transfer power over tariffs and interstate trade from the individual states to the national government. James Madison and others at the convention understood very well that the way to accomplish that purpose was to end Rhode Island's veto power, and he supposed that the way to do that was to create a new nation and government without resorting to the hopeless Continental Congress.

Compare the very different French experience. The French constitutional assembly included more than a thousand delegates and was wide open in its day to day debates on details. It was also a dramatic failure from the perspective of virtually all the major interests. It was a forum for charismatic speakers. The best known charismatic speakers in the United States at the time of the Philadelphia convention – Richard Henry Lee and Tom Paine – were not at the convention. And the great force of the convention was Madison, who was a relatively poor speaker. Galvanizing speeches are not the media for constructing carefully thought out institutional structures, although they might play a role in getting a design accepted once it has been worked out. The incentive to make grand speeches was heightened in the French revolutionary assemblies by the presence of large numbers of spectators from the general public. The Estates-General of 1789 opted from the outset for the principle of openness. As Manin (1997, 168) says, "Pressure (not to mention threats) from the galleries notoriously influenced the debates… It is reasonable to think that the American public as a whole had a better opportunity of forming opinions about its Constitution (between the end of the Philadelphia Convention and the ratification debates) than the French public ever had with respect to the various revolutionary constitutions."

As is true of the vaccination program, many policy issues have an element of expertise that seems to justify acting without full public understanding. The supposition is that the public cannot understand. In the polio case, the public probably could have understood but might have faced conflict over which children had to take the risk of vaccination on behalf of all. There is a widespread push toward greater democracy on the side of decision making. If expertise is a difficult enough issue, however, increased citizen participation in decisions might actually make the policies less effective. Those who assert that we want democratic outcomes (what citizens would want to have happened) and not merely democratic procedures can argue that democratic procedures would sometimes conflict with democratic outcomes.

The rise of ongoing public participation in government has radically changed the way we understand both participation and political decision making. In its more extreme versions, especially in local politics, participation seems to be a way of life for many people. Participation by ordinary people often runs against expertise. For example, civil engineers might tell us how to design a road but citizens might prefer to do it differently and to ignore the experts. In Menlo Park, California, where popular participation seems to affect all significant actions by local government, citizens insisted on making a main street through the town less easily used by putting obstacles in the way of traffic. Ostensibly, their purpose was to reduce auto traffic by giving people incentive to take their cars elsewhere and to make bicycling and walking safer. Among the obstacles were high curbs built around spaces for plants at intersections and left turn lanes with curbing and centre islands that restricted the flow of passing cars. These actually blocked the bike paths, making it seemingly more dangerous to bicycle, and they impeded the movement of emergency vehicles such as fire trucks, which could not make some of the turns that curbs blocked. After most of this project was completed at fairly high cost, the townspeople objected to the problems the new curbs and obstacles caused. The city then tore out much of what had been done, at additional high cost. (Other road projects in Menlo Park have been equally or even more foolish.)

A problem with such participation is that the participants are self-selected and not very likely to be representative. One could say so much the worse for those who do not participate. But one might sooner say that life is too important to waste very much of it squabbling over minor political decisions. Participation can be too demanding for its value and, in the Menlo Park case, it can even be destructive because it is too ephemeral, erratic, and amateurish in its attempts to determine policy on even moderately complex issues.

Mixed cases in which legislators have a personal stake in secrecy or lies but in which the secrecy or lies might be seen to be in the interest of the public or at least part of the public are especially important for the problem of complex agency to be discussed below.

Citizens' Knowledge

Clearly, much of citizens' knowledge comes from sources other than their political representatives. It comes from the media, talking with associates, taking part in various political or quasi political activities, and dealings with government agencies. Hence if democracy depends on citizens' knowledge, as noted at the outset of this chapter, then duplicity by officials may not be the biggest obstacle to making democracy work. As a rule, we can suppose that most citizens know very little about politics and policies. Indeed, an informal survey suggests that most of my professional political science colleagues do not recall the congressional attack on the IRS, which was front-page news a few years ago. It is extremely unlikely that typical citizens know very much about policy issues except in the cases of extremely urgent and important issues. For example, most Americans likely knew a lot about the events of September 11 and the policy responses to them, at least in broad outline. But it was general ignorance about whether it was plausible that the IRS was as abusive as the congressional hearings suggested that gave such a suggestion what credence it had.

That the vast majority of citizens have had no complaint against the proceedings of the IRS (they do complain about taxes, but the IRS does not determine the tax laws) gives them no information on whether their experience is usual or unusual. Without such knowledge, they could not judge the kangaroo court proceedings of congress on any ground other than the abstract one of judging that the proceedings were conspicuously biased against discovering the truth of the accusers' claims. The media were derelict in not giving some factual background to enable the public to interpret the fiasco, although some of the media likely supported the sham proceedings.

The problem of citizens' knowledge is far deeper than this problem of media failure. Joseph Schumpeter argued that voters have no interest in coming to know much about the issues that their votes will affect. This follows from the fact that individually they cannot affect elections anyway. If my vote makes no difference to the outcome of an election, I have no great interest in coming to know enough to vote well – either in my interest or in support of some general policy position. As Schumpeter (1942/1950, 262) wrote, 'without the initiative that comes from immediate responsibility, ignorance will persist in the face of masses of information however complete and correct.' I may have reason to acquire knowledge because it gives me pleasure or because my associates constantly talk politics, but not because it will be useful in my causing good public effects through my role as citizen and voter (Hardin 2002).

The ideal of political participation from the Progressive era in the United States was informed citizenship. Michael Schudson argues that this is too demanding for current conditions, which involve political participation in many more parts of life than would have been included in the politics of the Progressive era. Indeed, one may note, informed citizenship was too demanding even a hundred years ago when it arose as the ideal. He commends 'monitorial citizens,' who engage in surveillance more than information gathering (Schudson 2001, 311). That is, they are activated by need when an acute issue arises and, presumably, they vote more nearly retrospectively than prospectively.

Strangely, experience may run against Schudson's hope here. In great crises, such as war, citizens seem to acquiesce all the more readily in government decisions without being activated to try to affect those decisions. The immediate response to September 11 in the United States was to rely more heavily on the government than before and even to express greater 'trust' in government – the very government that had failed to take any of the prior clues of the impending disaster seriously (*Economist* 2002). We might suppose, therefore, that citizens will be activated to question and to influence government when provoked by lesser crises but virtually not at all by major threats. Monitorial citizens might rise to protest corruption or crime, but not get involved in ordinary issues or in grievous crises. Indeed, we might expect citizens in this supposedly participatory era to be activated by local issues far more than by larger national issues. This makes sense on the causal account of how much effect their actions can have at the two levels.

Moreover, we might suspect that citizens will be subject to manipulation by public leaders such as the congressional committees that investigated the IRS and its supposed abuses.

Perhaps the cleanest class of issues on which citizens regularly make decisions are referendums, which typically focus on a single issue. The experience with many referendums on fundamentally important public issues in California suggests that either voters are not very competent to make such choices in their own interest or they are manipulated into making choices they would not make if they were adequately well informed (Gerber et al. 2001). While supposedly attempting to accomplish very different things, they have voted de facto to end California participation in national party nominating conventions and to sentence to a minimum of twenty years in prison certain of those who commit trivial crimes (petty felonies, such as stealing a carton of cigarettes or a single slice of pizza).

Problems with referendums are that they are sometimes deceptively worded and their backers are sometimes kept secret (Elias 2002). A particularly egregious example of deceptive wording was the group that called itself 'Californians for Statewide Smoking Restrictions.' Its initiative would have banned local laws restricting smoking. Keeping the donors secret violates the spirit of California laws requiring disclosure of names of contributors of more than $100 to any political campaign, including campaigns for initiatives. This requirement is easily subverted.

Ward Connerly proposed the Racial Privacy Initiative for the 2002 ballot. Rather than have contributors donate directly to his campaign, he collected funds through a private non-profit organization, the American Civil Rights Coalition, which then spends money in support of the initiative, which would prohibit state and local governments from classifying people by race or ethnic background. Connerly's campaign need only report massive donations from this organization, which has no legal obligation to disclose names of its donors. Presumably, the reason for keeping names of the actual donors secret is to keep the electorate from knowing that these donors are large corporate entities that would benefit from racial discrimination (see further, Broder 2000).

Apart from such overt subversions, the most grievous failing of the referendum process is voter failings. Consider the referendum (Proposition 198 of 1996) requiring open primaries (Gerber et al., 71-4). Voters apparently displayed substantial misunderstanding of the issues in this referendum, which was put on the ballot and passed despite opposition to it from both major parties and most state political leaders. Adhering to this referendum would likely have disallowed California representation at the national party nominating conventions in the year 2000 because the two major parties require closed primaries to protect against manipulation by voters of the other party. Republicans understandably do not want to have Democrats select their candidate for president. Unfortunately, once a referendum has created a law, the legislature cannot revise it; it can only be revised by referendum. A second referendum (Proposition 3 of 1998), repealing Proposition 198, failed by a substantial margin, although it seems inconceivable that Californians genuinely wanted to block their own participation in the national party conventions. After the electorate failed on this issue, the California secretary of state, Bill Jones, introduced administrative devices to enable the state to distinguish Democratic and Republican voters in primary elections in presumable violation of the referendum (*New York Times* 1998). In this failure, democracy was a charade and, when it failed from ignorance, we let a knowledgeable bureaucratic agency act against the democratic result. The referendum legislation was eventually voided by the US Supreme Court as violating the right of assembly of the political parties, but the primary election of 2000 was still governed by it, although only through Jones's subterfuge.

As their title, 'Stealing the Initiative,' suggests, Gerber et al. show that the striking fact of many of the most important referendums in California is that they are not implemented in ways their sponsors would have expected from the wording of the initiatives. State and other political agents affect what the popularly adopted laws can accomplish. Gerber et al. (2001, 109) characterize the post-election fates of referendums as "wildly varying." In their history, elected and appointed officials often assert control over the policies that have been popularly adopted. As in the case of Jones's salvation of the state's primaries in 2000, these officials often very likely believe they are acting in the public interest even while rejecting the public's expressed preferences.

Agency and Representative Government

There are two ways representative government could work for complex cases such as the polio vaccination program. Decisions might be seen as simply turned over to the representatives to decide as they see fit, presumably by taking citizens' interests into account. Or they might be seen as still subject to public inspection and input so that, although the representatives formally make decisions, still they do so in transparent proceedings with public participation. In the vaccination case, complete transparency would undercut the program, so that some degree of secrecy or avoidance of public understanding of how it worked was arguably necessary to make it a success. Transparency after the fact would allow retrospective voting on an issue, although few single issues would be taken as sufficient to decide for or against an elected official. Anti-abortion and pro-gun groups reputedly can mobilize voters to vote against those who hold the 'wrong' views on their single issues, but most groups cannot do this because most voters are not so rabidly focused on a single issue.

The possibilities for individually distinct choices by members of parties in parliamentary systems, in which voting is often organized by a whip to conform with party positions rather than with individual discretion, are relatively limited. Moreover, legislators in such systems are commonly elected much more nearly as members of their parties than as individuals. Certain issues, such as abortion and the death penalty, might be left to the conscience of individual legislators even if the party takes a position. The way government works in the United States is a compromise between these two possibilities. Representatives have enormous discretion simply to act on many issues but they are also sometimes held to account for their actions.

In both kinds of system, vocal opposition can prevent secretive actions by the majority. Indeed, in the US system, opposition by a single vocal legislator can block such action. Still, the complexity of issues can make it very difficult to communicate to citizens what is at stake, so that legislatures can still have great discretion on the whole. Administrative agencies that have the power to act can, of course, be very secretive, even abusively so. For a complex issue, such as the polio vaccination campaign, secrecy can be achieved simply by not going to the trouble of explaining the issue fully.

Consider the most striking difference between traditional professional ethics and any plausible ethics for elected officials. Both professionals and public officials are agents on our behalf. They are trustees and we want them to act as trustees. The politician's position is, however, substantially more complex than the professional's in that all doctors, for example, should be the agent of every patient they deal with. An elected politician – Senator A – might be seen as your agent but not mine because I voted against A and A's policies commonly go against my interests. I cannot claim that A is bound to serve my interests in the way I can claim that a doctor should because A may do what a majority of the electorate wants.

This collective complication might not seem to be a grievous problem, but in fact it can undercut the claim that a conflict of interest harms the constituency of an elected official. Suppose you value having Meese as the Attorney General so much that you willingly ignore his self-interested behaviour in order to use his public power to reward people who benefited him personally. You now might rightly be able to claim that Meese with his conflict of interest represents your interests better than any much cleaner politician who is likely to replace Meese. One might wish to say that Meese's actions violate the public interest, but the public interest is not well defined in this context. You and I are both part of the public and we have conflicting interests. But even you, with your preference for keeping Meese in office, might readily see that his behaviour should be subject to rebuke and constraint short of removing him from office, so that, ex ante, you would support regulation of such behaviour as Meese's. Ex ante, the political valence of the regulation would be neutral.

Legal Regulation of Politicians' Ethics

It is important not to confuse public officials' ethics and its enforcement, if it is to be publicly and not merely 'internally' enforced, with criminal enforcement. We have many protections of accused criminals that have strong justifications and that are commonly turned into legal rights. Principally, those rights protect not only those who may be guilty of crimes but also those who are not. When public officials are accused of crimes or civil offences, as President Richard Nixon, Vice President Spiro Agnew, President Bill Clinton, and many others have been, the *criminal* investigation of them is subject to their normal rights against excessive measures by anyone in the criminal justice system. For example, mere refusal on their part to testify about their activities cannot be used as prima facie evidence of their criminal guilt.

When public officials are questioned about the ethics of their behaviour in office, however, we need not suppose they are protected by such rights. To say that they are is to say that they somehow have the right to hold their offices just as we and they have the right to lead our private lives without certain public intrusions. Citizens' private actions are not required to be transparent, but politicians' official actions are. Citizens have civil liberties that protect them against the government and its potentially overly zealous conduct. It would be odd to suppose that office holders in the government should be protected against the government, and the US and British constitutions offer no such protection. Both these constitutions permit overtly political removal from office in their provisions for impeachment and removal. Nixon and some of his defenders objected that he was being treated worse than a common criminal would be, with violation of his civil liberties. He and they got it badly wrong. He was being treated as only a president or other high official could be treated. Moreover, if he, Agnew, and many others had been treated like common criminals, they would have gone to jail and would have disappeared from public life.

When a legislative ethics committee or an ethics board even calls a public official's apparent conflict of interest into question, it *can* take refusal to answer questions about it as prima facie evidence of actual conflict of interest. If there is ground for criminal action, that generally goes beyond the legislative committee's or the ethics board's power and can be referred to proper legal authorities.

There is a side benefit of making ethics a matter of regulation and law and not merely of political discretion. Making clear in advance what the rules and expectations are is likely to induce people to be less careless about their actions. The most common experience of the early days of the Board of Ethics of the City of Chicago was such learning. Many, perhaps most, of the cases that arise at that board are requests for advice in advance or soon after various actions to clarify whether they are prohibited under the ethics ordinance. Many office holders have seemed to be at first mildly irritated or even offended when the Board has initiated inquiries. In the longer run, one may expect them to be more attentive to natural concerns about the appearance of conflict of interest in their actions. One contractor for the city complained that the law got in the way of how he did business by blocking him from giving meaningful gifts to City Council members from whom he sought business. Precisely.

Concluding Remarks

Ethics in public office is first and foremost a political problem in this sense: the rules for behaviour will generally be what the political process has established them to be. In a democracy it is the public who decide what the definition of agency is for their representatives. No moral philosopher, no lawyer, no religious leader can tell us what those rules have to be. They might help us understand the problems and resolve our minds on what to expect and what to do. They cannot tell us what the "right" rules ought to be. There are very few, if any, "right" rules. A hundred years ago, there was evidently no real sense of a conflict of interest in politics. In the United States, reform of the federal civil service – to base government employment on merit and not political affiliation – was a response to the assassination in 1881 of newly elected President James A. Garfield, whose new administration had not rewarded his assassin with a civil service post.

For the fifty years between Andrew Jackson's presidency and Garfield's assassination, the use of federal jobs to reward party stalwarts was the standard expectation. It is still acceptable practice in certain high ranking positions, in which loyalty to the president might seem to count for a lot. But it is not acceptable practice in staffing the lower rungs of the government bureaucracy. One might wish to say that the earlier practice was morally wrong. Such a judgment would largely be irrelevant. What is true is that it has been democratically ruled out. In debates over President George W. Bush's desire to have the discretion to hire and fire employees in the new national security agency to protect against terrorism, critics framed their objection in terms of job protections. The unspoken word was 'patronage.'

At the same time, the enforcement of morals is not purely political. We do not let the mood of the public at the relevant moment decide every case as it arises any more than we let the mood of the public decide on the guilt or innocence of an accused in the criminal law. There are rules and standard procedures including, for more than fifty years, rules against certain kinds of conflict of interest. We democratically want politics today to establish rules and even laws for tomorrow. As much as possible I think we want to take actual cases out of politics, although of course in some cases – such as the forced resignation of Spiro Agnew, and the impeachment of Richard Nixon and Bill Clinton – the issue and the resolution may be inherently political to a large extent.

Depoliticizing everyday cases can yield substantial benefits. It should lead politicians and public officials to give more attention to public policies, less to personalities. It is interesting that the US Congress has been at its best in reprimanding and even punishing its own members and at its abysmal worst in attacking presidents, beginning with Andrew Johnson, who succeeded to the presidency upon Abraham Lincoln's assassination. All of the impeachment moves have been highly politicized, whereas the handling of members of congress has been relatively apolitical. In the latter, the focus could be on the de facto professional ethics or role morality of legislators.

More generally, any laws or rules it would make sense to adopt would fit some functional account of the role of elected officials. If we had a clear account of agency that could handle the oddly complex relations of representatives to their constituencies, we could devise good policies from that account. For certain classes of issues, such as financial conflict of interest, we can readily imagine that the agency relation at stake is essentially agent to the whole public, because the whole public shares an interest in reducing the costs of graft and so forth, which can be seen as a deadweight loss to the whole society.

References

Bok, S. (1978), *Lying: Moral Choice in Public and Private Life.* (New York: Pantheon).

Broder, D. (2000), *Democracy Derailed: Initiative Campaigns and the Power of Money.* (New York: Harcourt).

Campbell, J. (2001), *The Liar's Tale: A History of Falsehood.* (New York: W. W. Norton).

Economist (2002), 'What September 11th Really Wrought', (12 January), 23-5.

Elias, T. (2002), 'Connerly Tries to Keep Names of Donors Secret', *Palo Alto Daily News* (9 August), 6.

Elster, J. (2000), 'Arguing and Bargaining in Two Constituent Assemblies', *University of Pennsylvania Journal of Constitutional Law* 2, 345-421.

Fink, E. and Riker, W. (1989), 'The Strategy of Ratification' in Grofman, B. and Wittman, D. (eds.), 220-55.

Gerber, E., Lupia, A. McCubbins, M. and Kiewiet, D. (2001), *Stealing the Initiative: How State Government Responds to Direct Democracy.* (Upper Saddle River, NJ: Prentice-Hall).

Grofman, B. and Wittman, D. (eds.) (1989), *The Federalist Papers and the New Institutionalism.* (New York: Agathon).

Hardin, R. (2002), 'The Street-Level Epistemology of Democratic Participation', *Journal of Political Philosophy* 10:2, 212-29; Reprinted in Fishkin, J. and Laslett, P. (eds.), *Philosophy, Politics and Society.* Vol. 7. (London: Blackwell), 163-81.

_____ (2003), *Indeterminacy and Society.* (Princeton, NJ: Princeton University Press).

Johnston, D. (1998), 'Senate Committee Is Told of a Vast Range of Abuses by I.R.S.', *New York Times* (29 April), A.16.

_____ (1999), 'Tax Professionals See Pitfalls in the New I.R.S.', *New York Times*, 1.21.

_____ (2000), 'Investigations Uncover Little Harassment by I.R.S.', *New York Times*.

Luebke, N. (1987), 'Conflict of Interest As a Moral Category', *Business and Professional Ethics Journal* 6:1, 66-81.

New York Times (1998), 'California Scrambles after Measure Fails', 1.20.

Nixon, W. and Roth, W. (1999), *The Power to Destroy.* (Boston: Atlantic Monthly Press).

Nyberg, D. (1993), *The Varnished Truth: Truth Telling and Deceiving in Ordinary Life.* (Chicago: University of Chicago Press).

Roberts, L. (1988), 'Change in Polio Strategy?', *Science* 240 (27 May), 1145.

Rossiter, C. (1966), *1787: The Grand Convention.* (New York: Macmillan).

Schumpeter, J. (1942/1950), *Capitalism, Socialism and Democracy*, 3rd Edition. (New York: Harper).

Slater, I. (1985), *Orwell: The Road to Airstrip One.* (New York: W. W. Norton).

Stevenson, R. (1998), 'The Morning After: Waking Up to Reality of a Toothless I.R.S.', *New York Times* (28 June), 4.6.

Sun, M. (1985), 'The Vexing Problems of Vaccine Compensation', *Science* 227 (1 March): 1012-14.

Chapter 3

Transparency and Efficiency

Albert Breton

Introduction

A general theory of rational obfuscation and transparency in politics (or in other domains of inquiry) is not available. Indeed, it seems that propositions about transparency (and obfuscation) are intimately related to the theory or model one adopts to analyse a particularity reality.[1] To see this, consider bureaucracy. In the early theory – that of Max Weber (1925) and his followers, a theory which is no longer accepted either by economists, political scientists, or sociologists, though it still has wide currency in the legal profession – superiors give orders or instructions to their subordinates. These orders are announced and therefore have a public character: they are implicitly assumed to be transparent.

This approach to bureaucracy can be contrasted to that suggested by William Niskanen (1971) – a view of bureaucracy that is still widely accepted in Public Choice circles and even outside that discipline. In that model, subordinates are assumed capable, on the basis of their presumed superior knowledge, to trick their superiors into accepting a budget larger than is necessary for the production of public output.

In the niskanenian model it is subordinates that in effect 'give orders' to superiors. But the orders are neither announced nor public because they are based on deceit and falsehoods. In that model, the relationships of superiors and subordinates are not transparent. As Barbara Spencer (1980) has shown, transparency, even of the most limited variety, would simply void the niskanenian model.

There is another problem. Both the weberian and the niskanenian models suffer from a tacit assumption that rules out competition. In both models, bureaucracies are presumed to be monolithic. To put it differently, neither conceives of bureaucracies as bodies made up of bureaus that compete with each other. It is as if the smallest production unit on the supply-side of microeconomics was the industry – not the firm or the plant. Industries appear to compete among themselves but in reality, unless they are monopolies, it is the firms that make decisions and compete for larger shares of household budgets. But bureaucracies, in Weber's and Niskanen's

1 Though I was unaware of this when writing *Competitive Governments* (1996), the discussion I provide of 'budget secrecy' (99-108) and the contrast I make to alternative approaches could easily be translated into a comparative analysis of transparency.

views of the world, do not compete. Given that, by assumption, bureaus do not exist – only bureaucracies do – competition is of necessity ruled out. In the presence of competition, there would be less transparency than would exist in the clear-cut chain of command structure presumed to exist in the weberian bureaucracy, but there would be more than would exist in the deceitful niskanenian bureaucracy.

In what follows, I will use the model of bureaucracy developed by Breton and Ronald Wintrobe (1982). In that model, unlike in the approaches of Weber and Niskanen, transparency is not a trivial problem.

Recent history has brought to our attention the fact that in many societies the professions – the accounting, legal, medical, and social work professions, the police and national defence forces, to name only a few – are privately policed or, more precisely, are self-policed. That fact poses a number of interesting questions: Why are (all?)[2] professions self-policed while many occupations are publicly policed? Does self-policing lead to obfuscation or, to put it differently, does self-policing of professional activities lead to the generation of relationships that are, in some sense, less than optimally transparent? If transparency in professional self-policing is less than optimal, will that lack beget the sort of corporate corruption that seems to be turning up almost everywhere these days?

A theory of public sector decentralization is emerging. There are still many problems to be resolved but a model articulated on horizontal and vertical competition among public sector units based on benchmark or yardstick competition exists. Both types of competitions do, however, require that citizens be in a position to make trans-frontier comparisons of government policies. This in turn requires that information be forthcoming, and information will be available only if there exists some degree of transparency. I look at each of these realities in more detail in the remainder of the chapter.

Bureaucracy

As is now generally recognized in the literature on organizations (see, among many, Mintzberg 1979, 1983), bureaus and bureaucracies are constituted of both formal and informal structures – not exclusively of a formal structure as in Weber, or of an informal structure alone as in Niskanen. It would seem that one could make the assumption that the formal structure is transparent as it is constituted of the chain of command and channels of communication often embodied in organizational charts; the official rules governing promotions, advancements, and dismissals; the codified rules governing behaviour and the procedures to be followed if the rules are broken; the operating manuals describing the tasks associated with particular jobs; and so on. It is no doubt because of this feature that courts and tribunals – judges and lawyers – focus so much of their attention on the formal structure when trying to establish

2 To decide on whether all professions are self-policing, one needs a precise definition of profession.

guilt or innocence. Still, because of one role that it must play in the management of bureaucratic conduct, the formal structure, as we will see shortly, cannot be fully transparent.

There is no ambiguity in regards to the informal structure. In 1982, Breton and Wintrobe (see also Breton 1998) argued that this structure is based on *exchanges* between superiors and subordinates. The exchanges are of informal services for informal payments. Informal implies that neither the services nor the payments are codified. They are, indeed, private and *sub rosa* to a degree.

Specifically, informal structures are the networks of unofficial relations which play a continuous role in the transmission of commands, in the collection and communication of information, in the coordination of tasks inside and, at times, beyond the confines of organizations. Informal services can sometimes be beneficial to superiors and sometimes harmful. To put it differently, commands can be forwarded swiftly and clearly or they can be deferred, distorted, or shelved; information can be transmitted whole and intact or it can be garbled and falsified; and coordination can be expeditious and effective or it can be haphazard and unproductive. I return to this point below.

Each of these informal services has a unit price. To understand the nature of these prices, it is important to recognize that the exchanges consummated in the internal markets that constitute the informal structure of bureaus and bureaucracies are based on trust – a reality that substitutes for legally enforceable property rights.[3] More precisely, the pattern of trades and prices will depend on the distribution of trust between superiors and subordinates on the one hand and among subordinates on the other.

Much is known about how trust is born, grows, and is endangered or mutilated (see Breton and Wintrobe 1982; Salmon 1988, 2001; Brennan 1998; Hardin 2000, 2002). However, much remains to be learnt. For the purpose of the present exercise, it is sufficient to understand that trust is a capital asset in which persons (and collectives) invest. To put it differently, the accumulation of trust – as a result of the satisfactory conclusion of a transaction under incomplete information about one's trading partner – absorbs resources, but once trust has been amassed it yields a flow of benefits over time to those who own it. However, trust is context-specific, that is, it yields a benefit only when engaging in further transactions with the same trading partner. For this reason, the trust that accumulates within an organization is clustered in separate 'networks'.

In complex social systems, of which bureaucracies are an example, what matters in addition to the amount of trust is the distribution of these amounts over groups of persons. A useful assumption about the distribution of trust treats informal vertical structures (operationally defined as structures in which superiors are members) as vertical trust networks and horizontal structures (those from which superiors are absent) as horizontal trust networks and takes the ratio of the amount of trust in

3 Though in many instances the substitution will be nearly complete, this need not always be the case.

each type of network as the relevant distributional variable. If it is further assumed that vertical networks produce *efficient*, and horizontal networks, *inefficient* results from the point of view of superiors, the stage is set for the incorporation of informal structures in a general theory of bureaucracy.

It is sometimes objected that horizontal cooperation – 'team' production – enhances the productivity of subordinates and, through that channel, the utility of superiors and that, as a consequence, the second part of the foregoing assumption is of dubious value. A necessary (though not sufficient) condition for horizontal cooperation to raise productivity is that the number of subordinates be small (see Davis 1982). In an assembly line, for example, cooperation among *some* subordinates can only be used to slow the line down, not to speed it up. To do the latter, cooperation among *everyone* working on the line is required, often a difficult goal to achieve (Wintrobe and Breton 1986).

Because the authority of superiors is incomplete and because, as a consequence, subordinates have the power to subvert, to a degree, the ability of their superiors to achieve their goals, there necessarily exist potential gains from trade that superiors and subordinates can exploit to their mutual benefit. It is the existence of these gains that set the stage for how superiors and subordinates relate to each other. To see this, assume that in the absence of such trades, the present value of the flow of benefits accruing to the organization is V_f. Now consider what happens to V_f when the existence of an informal structure made up of vertical and horizontal trust networks – which can be labelled v and h – is recognized. If it is assumed that $v/h < 1$, which is to say that the amount of trust among subordinates is greater than that between superiors and subordinates, the latter will make use of that greater trust among themselves to exploit the power they possess to appropriate resources that would otherwise go to their superiors, as happens in Crozier (1963), Niskanen (1971), Breton and Wintrobe (1982), Tirole (1986), and Laffont (1990). That $v/h < 1$ is sufficient for this outcome follows from the fact that trust is costly to accumulate and, as a consequence, will only be accumulated if it is expected to yield a return. Superiors cannot be assumed to reward subordinates who form collusive trust networks to distort information, manipulate agendas, sabotage organizational strategies, entrap fellow workers, or engage in slowdowns (work to rule). The return on accumulated trust can only be arrogated or captured by the subordinates themselves and for that reason can be called 'takings'.

In general, takings cannot be effected by a subordinate acting alone. An agreement among a coalition of subordinates is required – an agreement that trust among these subordinates can serve to enforce. In addition, if takings are to be successfully effected, it is necessary that the strategies used by the subordinates to achieve that end be concealed from superiors or at least that there be no single subordinate whom the superiors can isolate as responsible. For this reason, when horizontal trust networks are being profitably used in the conduct of particular activities, vertical trust networks must be in abeyance in respect of the same activities. Therefore when $v/h < 1$, subordinates make use of their power and rely on trust to avoid punishment and benefit from takings. This inefficiency (from the superiors' point of view) is reflected in the fact that the present value of the flow of benefits going to the organization is now less than V_f.

Now suppose that superiors recognize that subordinates can be made to pursue the goals of the organization – in effect, be induced to show initiative and enterprise, to the benefit of superiors, by 'zealously' obeying the necessarily incomplete commands emanating from these same superiors – only if they are rewarded for doing so. The initiative and zeal of subordinates will manifest itself in many ways such as offering more effort, providing more accurate information, cutting through red tape (turning a blind eye to pointless rules), being more inventive, and so on. In exchange superiors can offer amenities such as use of company cars, expense accounts, accelerated promotions, free long-distance telephone calls, well-decorated offices, and better working conditions. It should be noted that these amenities cannot be components of the formal structure because they have to be discretionary – and hence elements of the informal structure – otherwise, should they accrue to everyone, they could not serve as incentives in transactional relationships. Because these informal exchanges are mostly inter-temporal, the ability of superiors to trade with their subordinates and to pay for initiative and enterprise – at the same time as putting an end to takings by subordinates – will require the accumulation of more trust between themselves and their subordinates, the control and possibly even the destruction of trust relationships among subordinates, or both. Superiors, in a word, must act to make $v/h > 1$.

The foregoing should make clear that superiors have a preference for transparency regarding the behaviour of their subordinates, but that they cannot satisfy this preference at zero cost. In other words, they do not want their subordinates to hide and conceal what they are doing, or to deceive and double-cross them. But unless they invest in *v*-trust that is what they will get. Transparency is not a free good. The amount 'purchased' will depend on the unit cost of *v*-trust relative to that of *h*-trust.

Superiors also want their subordinates to know that, whenever $v/h > 1$, informal services beget their rewards. That may not always be an easy matter to manage. Indeed, though superiors want the fact that they honour their obligations to be known in the organization, they do not, in general, want the precise terms of trade for informal services to be known, given that these can vary from individual to individual for what is essentially the same service. In other words, markets for informal services are imperfect. One way of achieving this result is to allow the prices paid to become public knowledge within the organization, while suppressing information about the informal services supplied.

Let me consider anew the two types of networks I have been examining: the one made up exclusively of subordinates and the one constituted of superiors and subordinates. In the first, the interaction is not only face-to-face, it is often among individuals with essentially the same educational and social backgrounds and having similar status. In the second, the interaction is most of the time not face-to-face – superiors may not even be in the same physical location as their subordinates – but is mediated and orchestrated by managing, modulating, and fine tuning the formal structure. If subordinates are not aware that the formal structure is managed in such a way as to ensure that the informal services provided are paid for, the management of that structure will be in vain. The formal structure and its modulation must therefore be transparent. The problem, however, is the same as with the informal structure: it must be known that prices are paid, but the exact informal services that beget those prices in each individual transaction must remain unknown to the organization's personnel.

The theory of single bureaus tells us that bureaus will be efficient – and ultimately survive – if superiors actively accumulate vertical trust and control horizontal trust. It is not obvious that superiors would be actively engaged in these tasks in the absence of competition. As already noted, whenever bureaus and bureaucracies have been treated as identical and the possibility of competition thus eliminated, the literature has (tacitly) assumed that superiors were passive. If for no other reason than to recognize that superiors are actively involved in the pursuit of their own interest, the theory of bureaucracy has to be a theory of competition among bureaus for resources (budgets).

Self-Policing and Regulatory Capture

In many societies, the professions police themselves. In effect, a governance structure is set up, rules are devised and promulgated, a monitoring and enforcement mechanism put in place, and a tribunal with the power to adjudicate, acquit, convict, and punish created – all within the profession. It is not obvious why elected and even non-elected governments should bestow all that power onto private bodies who, as a consequence, become accountable to no one but themselves, except possibly at times of great 'scandal'.

It could be, and has been, argued that the knowledge required to regulate the professions is so specialized that only those who possess that kind of knowledge can be effective regulators. Society is better-off as a consequence of professional self-policing both because the cost of monitoring and enforcing rules are less than they would be if non-specialists were carrying out these activities and because the benefits that derive from more apposite rules and regulations are greater. Or, in a contrary manner, one could argue with Karl Marx and Frederick Engels (1848) and George Stigler (1971) that there is a general tendency, whatever the form of government, for special private interests (in Marxist theory, the bourgeoisie) to capture the apparatus of state or its power and use it in the pursuit of their own interests.[4] Richard Posner (1974) has pointed to some important differences between Marx and Engels' and Stigler's models of capture, but it remains the case that the end result is the same with the two hypotheses: private groups override the interests of citizens. The rent-seeking literature, though generally less specific than Marx and Engels and Stigler on the *dramatis personae* involved in the game, nevertheless also

4 Marx and Engels (1848) put their view succinctly as follows: 'The executive of the modern State is but a committee for managing the common affairs of the whole bourgeoisie.'

offers a view of collective action in which the citizenry's interests are shanghaied by special interests.

However that may be, we must recognize that professional self-policing is necessarily less transparent than genuine (non-capture) public policing would be. It is furthermore difficult not to assume that what goes on behind what we may call the 'veil of obfuscation' is not in the interests of the self-policing professionals themselves. To examine some of the implications of these propositions, assume that the social cost of producing transparency in professional accounting (law, medicine, social work, internal security, etc.) is the volume of resources used up in the collection and processing of information (including its orderly diffusion), and in dealing with information overload. If we let T stand for transparency, C for production costs, and Z_1 for a portmanteau of variables that are held constant, then $C = C(T, Z_1)$ with $\partial C/\partial T > 0$, assuming that at the margin production costs increase, with $\partial^2 C/\partial T^2 > 0$. The benefits generated by transparency derive from the increased quality or improved performance standards of the services produced. With B denoting benefits and Z_2 the variables we hold constant, we have $B = B(T, Z_2)$ with $\partial B/\partial T > 0$, on the conventional assumption of an increasing marginal rate of substitution between it and a pre-selected numeraire, with $\partial^2 B/\partial T^2 < 0$. If we now equate the marginal costs and the marginal benefits of transparency, we obtain a social equilibrium volume of transparency equal to T^*.

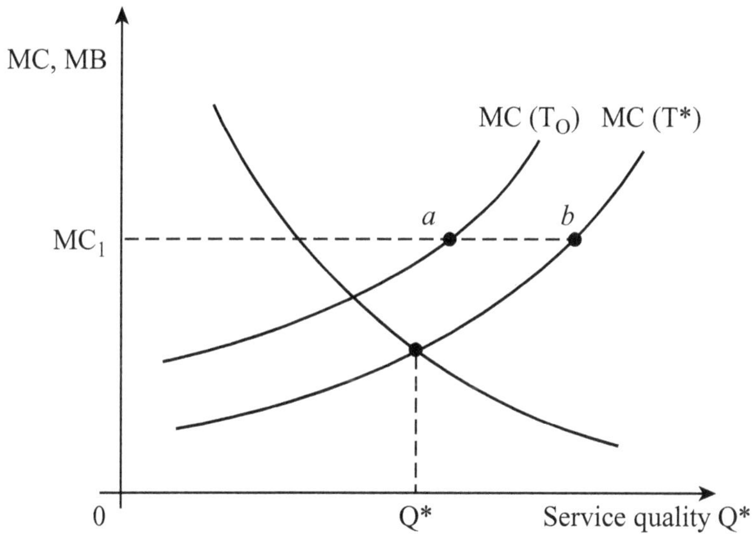

Figure 3.1 Measuring the Spoils of Obfuscation

If we now consider the quality or performance standard (Q) associated with a given service X (kilowatt-hours, legal and medical services, etc.), we can picture, as in Figure 3.1, the marginal benefit to consumers and the marginal cost to service providers for a level of transparency T^*. The social equilibrium is at Q^*. Now suppose that the volume of transparency is exogenously reduced to T_0 ($< T^*$). The marginal cost of Q moves from MC (T^*) to MC (T_0). For any MC – say MC_1 – the reduction in service quality or the lower standards of performance by the agency producing X is equal to *ab*. That line interval also measures the size of the 'amenities' or the 'spoils' generated by way of rents – associated with the monopoly-like character of the 'veil of obfuscation' – and with the lower costs of monitoring and enforcement.

If, as was the case in the Enron-Arthur Andersen saga, the commodity X and the quality of the professional accounting service Q were produced by two different agencies (Enron and Andersen), a further question begs for attention – that of the division of the spoils between them. That division, standard economic theory tells us, will be determined by the elasticities of the demand and supply functions for the professional service at the relevant price. Institutionally, the elasticities are embodied in the 'other' services – the so-called 'conflict-of-interest' services (the most important being consultancy) – which the professionals sold to the providers of X. A conclusion of the foregoing is that conflict-of interest activities govern the *division* of the spoils, not their *size*. The latter derives from self-policing.

The question therefore arises of whether the spoils can be made smaller. The answer to this question is that they can. That will occur if self-policing is more strictly regulated and thus becomes more transparent. It is important to bear in mind, however, that public regulation need not be socially efficient – generate T^* of transparency. For that to happen, the public regulatory process must itself be transparent. Otherwise, the spoils would be divided between the agencies – say, Enron, Arthur Andersen, and the Washington regulators. Who can say that this is not often the case!

Decentralization

The case for the decentralization of the public sector is not different from that for the decentralization of the private sector. In both instances, the purpose is to garner the advantages of competition. In the two sectors, problems of externalities (spillovers), economies of scale, collusion, and the like have to be resolved, but in such a way as to preserve as much of the benefits of competition as possible.

When considering the public sector, it is essential to distinguish between horizontal and vertical competition – between the competition that rules among governments located at the same jurisdictional level, and that among governments inhabiting different tiers. In most of the work on decentralization, attention is restricted to the first of these two. It is furthermore assumed that the motor behind this intergovernmental competition is the interjurisdictional mobility of persons and capital searching for the best and lowest cost bundles of goods and services.

The assumption has its roots in the early work of Charles Tiebout (1956). It is not known however, if interjurisdictional mobility is strong enough a force to motivate intergovernmental competition. If, as is generally believed by American scholars, it is powerful enough in the United States, I share Dieter Bös's view (1983) that it does not have that power in the other decentralized governmental systems to be found in the rest of the world. However, even if the mobility mechanism was powerful enough to motivate horizontal competition, it would still be lacking, because it would have nothing to say about vertical competition. Indeed, even if individuals are able to move from jurisdiction to jurisdiction they cannot move from one jurisdictional tier to another. In decentralized systems, one is a citizen of *all* the tiers that are constitutive of the governmental system. If mobility can tell us something about the allocation of resources at a particular jurisdictional level, it has nothing to say about the assignment of powers to different jurisdictional tiers.[5] To deal with this problem we need to refer to vertical competition.

A decade and a half ago, Pierre Salmon (1987) applied the theory of labour tournaments initially proposed by Edward Lazear and Sherwin Rosen (1981) to horizontal intergovernmental competition arguing, in effect, that if the citizens of a jurisdiction evaluate the performance of their government by comparing it to the performance of governments elsewhere but at the same jurisdictional tier, they would induce their own government to do as well or better than these governments and in the process would prompt their opposition politicians to compete with their governing politicians. One virtue of what may be called the Salmon mechanism, in addition to the fact that it is a complement to the Tiebout mechanism whenever that last mechanism is operative, is that it will also motivate vertical competition whenever citizens use the performance of governments located at other jurisdictional tiers as benchmarks to evaluate what their own government is doing.

The initial formulation of the Salmon mechanism and, to my knowledge, all subsequent formulations, assumed that citizens compared the performance of their own government to that of a benchmark government in terms of the 'levels and qualities of services, of levels of taxes or of more general economic and social indicators' (Salmon 1987, 32). However, as argued by Breton (1996), competition in governmental systems compels all centres of power to forge wicksellian connections (defined in the next two paragraphs) that are as tight as possible so as to be granted the consent (vote) of citizens.[6] In the light of this result, Breton and Angela Fraschini (2003) suggested that citizens evaluate the relative performance of governments in terms of the tightness of wicksellian connections – both for horizontal and vertical

5 In the Tiebout model and in the models that derive from that seminal contribution, the division of powers is a consequence of the 'span' of public goods – local public goods are assigned to local governments and the other public goods to a central government which, however, plays no role in the models. This last point is powerfully made in Keen (1998).

6 For a defense of that assumption see Breton (1996, 48-57).

competition.[7] In other words if there are n centres of power indexed i and if we let w_i ($i = 1, \dots, n$) be a measure of the tightness of the wicksellian connection generated by centre of power i, with w_i normalized so that $0 \leq w_i \leq 1$, citizens will rank the centres of power that make up compound governments in terms of w_i.

What are wicksellian connections and why is it an improvement to articulate the Salmon mechanism on them rather than on the vector of goods, services, taxes, and other indicators on which the mechanism has hitherto been articulated? A wicksellian connection is a link between the quantity of a particular good or service supplied by centres of power and the taxprice that citizens pay for that good or service. Knut Wicksell (1896)[8] showed that if decisions regarding public expenditures and their financing were taken simultaneously and under a rule of (quasi) unanimity, a perfectly tight nexus between the two variables would emerge. Breton (1996) argued that competition between centres of power, if it was perfect and not distorted by informational and transparency problems, would also generate completely tight wicksellian connections. In the real world, competition is, of course, never perfect and, as we shall shortly discover, informational and obfuscation problems abound and, as a consequence, wicksellian connections are less than perfectly tight. Still, as long as some competition exists, there will be wicksellian connections.

The virtue of a Salmon mechanism expressed in terms of wicksellian connections is that a given citizen can carry out comparisons of performance in terms of a common standardized variable, whatever jurisdictional level benchmark governments inhabit. A variable that serves that purpose well is the size of the utility losses inflicted on citizens whenever the volume of goods and services provided by centres of power differs from the volume desired at given taxprices. Put differently, citizens experience the same kind of utility losses from decisions made by governments whatever the jurisdictional tier the governments inhabit. The goods and services supplied can differ, but the efforts to achieve tightness in wicksellian connections will not.[9] Indeed, the ability to compare performance horizontally is likely to reinforce the ability to execute vertical comparisons and *vice versa.*

How does vertical competition manifest itself? When powers are assigned to different levels of government, the assignment is never precise or explicit enough to cover all possible contingencies. Adapting the theory of contracts, which says that a contract is incomplete whenever possible future contingencies are not included in the contract and remedies to potential conflict among the signatories are not specified, we could say that assignments are always incomplete in the sense that even if their meaning appeared to be fully transparent to those who drafted and endorsed the initial constitutional document, that meaning can no longer be clear to

7 The Breton-Fraschini (2003) paper was presented at the 2000 Villa Colombella Seminar, but not included in the published volume of proceedings of that Seminar.

8 See also Lindahl (1919) and Johansen (1965).

9 As in the tournament model suggested by Nalebuff and Stiglitz (1983), the comparison of performance will be more precise if the random disturbances affecting performance are common to all centers of power instead of being idiosyncratic to each.

successor generations because innumerable contingencies were not addressed at the time of drafting and remedies not specified. Constitutions or other documents that spell out the assignment of powers are therefore, of necessity, also incomplete and therefore imprecise. As a consequence, it is always possible for governments at one jurisdictional tier to invade – to make inroads, incursions, or forays into – the policy domain of governments located at a different tier. The invasions need not actually take place – it is sufficient that they be possible. It is easy to provide evidence that confirms that governments, more or less continuously, invade the policy domains of governments inhabiting other tiers.

If it is assumed that the outcomes of vertical competition are stable, by which I mean no more than that the equilibrium outcomes of that type of competition, once achieved, will persist when the system is subject to ordinary shocks, then vertical competition will generate outcomes that are also efficient. The reason for this is the same as that which underlies every argument put forward to demonstrate that competition generates efficient outcomes.

I assume that governing politicians maximize expected consent. This implies that, given taxprices, these politicians will endeavour to supply goods and services (including regulation and redistribution) to their citizens in quantities and qualities that match as closely as possible what these citizens desire. As a consequence, governing politicians will only invade the policy domain of governments located at other tiers when they expect the invasion to increase the consent their citizens will grant them. Sometimes the invasion will not be successful; it will then be transitory. At other times however it will be successful and become permanent. In this second case the invasion will, in time, become entrenched in a constitutional document or in a convention to which all parties acquiesce. When that happens, vertical competition will have led to a new permanent division of powers between jurisdictional tiers.

This mechanism is important. It generates re-assignments of powers that reflect the relative efficiency or comparative advantage of governments at different tiers to generate tight wicksellian connections in respect of particular bundles of goods and/or services. Vertical competition, driven by the modified Salmon mechanism, therefore leads to assignment of powers according to which the provision of goods and services by governments at all tiers is as efficient as possible as efficiency is defined by Wicksell. Vertical competition then generates an assignment of powers that allows governments to supply goods and services at the lowest taxprice possible. It exists and is activated by the desire of all centres of powers at all the jurisdictional tiers that constitute a governmental system to maximize expected consent.[10]

The foregoing should have made clear that the modified Salmon mechanism requires transparency if it is to operate efficiently.[11] However, transparency is easier to achieve with the modified mechanism than it is with the original. Indeed, when

10 One can add that vertical competition may also lead to the creation of new permanent or transitory tiers if that will increase supply efficiency – temporary or permanent associations of a limited number of provinces or states for the provision of a particular good or service.

11 This point is also made by Brosio in his contribution to this volume.

comparison is over goods, services, taxes, and the like, those engaged in making the comparisons must know, not only about those variables, but also about the preferences of the citizens in the benchmark jurisdiction. No such transparency is needed for the modified version of the Salmon mechanism to work effectively. All that is needed in that case is transparency with respect to the efforts of the benchmark government to forge wicksellian connections whatever the preferences of citizens. It goes without saying that the greater this transparency, the more efficient the mechanism.

However, the re-assignment of powers from one jurisdictional tier to another or, in different words, the invasion mechanism will work better if constitutional documents and conventions are not fully transparent. Indeed, full transparency in this matter implies that the constitutional arrangements are not subject to interpretation and the political system denied constitutional flexibility. This line of reasoning allows us to distinguish between those whose doctrine of constitutional interpretation and evolution is based on so-called 'original intent' and those who are more 'activists' supporting constitutional changes adjusted to the problems of the time.

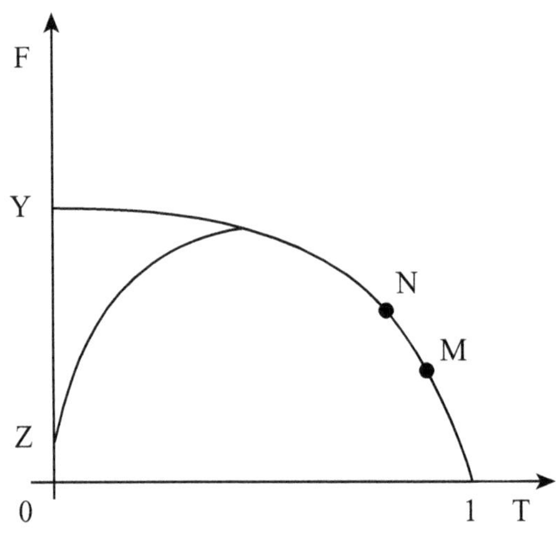

Figure 3.2 "Original Intent" and "Activist" Courts

In Figure 3.2, transparency (T) is measured along the abscissa and the degree of constitutional flexibility (F) along the ordinate. If T is normalized to vary between zero and one, then at T = 1, flexibility is, let us say, zero (or some very small number). As T is reduced, flexibility increases. Whether the curve looks like the Y1 or Z1 contours in Figure 3.2 – that is, whether flexibility increases, in all likelihood at a decreasing rate, or starts to fall – is a 'technical' problem. I incline to the view that the real world trade-off looks more like Z1 as courts and other adjudicating bodies rely on jurisprudence to formulate judgements. Jurisprudence to be useful must be somewhat transparent.

Whether point M or point N is selected by society depends on the distribution of political power in the society as well as on the ruling *zeitgeist*. A point like M, or one in its neighbourhood, will rule if the dominant powers and the *zeitgeist* favour original intent. Otherwise, a point like N will be chosen.

Conclusion

Though only in very broad and general terms, the above discussion has come to three conclusions. I have argued that in bureaucracies the actions of superiors in managing the formal structure must be as transparent as possible if the informal markets that make up the informal structure of bureaucracies are to work efficiently. I have further argued that efficiency also demands that the nature and size of the informal services provided by subordinates not be known to the organization's personnel, whereas the prices paid for these services be transparent public knowledge. In the matter of regulatory capture, I have made the point that transparency always reduces the spoils that accrue to self-policing professionals and the incidence of corporate corruption. Finally, I have argued that in decentralized governmental systems, the competition based on a modified Salmon mechanism is more efficient the greater the transparency in the doings of benchmark governments. However, the efficient re-assignment of powers from one jurisdictional tier to another through an invasion mechanism requires less than full constitutional transparency.

References

Aubert, F. and Sylvestre, J.-P. (eds.) (2001), *Confiance et rationalité*. (Paris and Versailles: INRA-Editions).

Bös, D. (1983), 'Commentary' on Roger Gordon's "An Optimal Taxation Approach to Fiscal Federalism", in McLure Jr. (ed.), 43-45.

Braithwaite, V. and Levi, M. (eds.) (1998), *Trust and Governance*. (New York: Russell Sage Foundation).

Brennan, G. (1998), 'Democratic Trust: A Rational-Choice Theory View', in Braithwaite and Levi, (eds.), 197-217.

Breton, A. (1996), *Competitive Governments. An Economic Theory of Politics and Public Finance*. (New York: Cambridge University Press).

_______ (1998), 'Bureaucracy', in Newman (ed.), 185-192.

_______ and Wintrobe, R. (1982), *The Logic of Bureaucratic Conduct. An Analysis of Competition, Exchange, and Efficiency in Private and Public Organizations*. (New York: Cambridge University Press).

_______ and Fraschini, A. (2003), 'Vertical Competition in Unitary States: The Case of Italy', *Public Choice*, 114(1-2), 57-77.

_______ Galeotti, G., Salmon, P., and Wintrobe R. (eds.) (1988), *Villa Colombella Papers on Bureaucracy, European Journal of Political Economy*, 4(Extra Issue).

Crozier, M. (1963), *Le phénomène bureaucratique*. (Paris: Seuil). Translated by Crozier as *The Bureaucratic Phenomenon*. (Chicago: University of Chicago Press).

Davis, L. E. (1982), 'Organization Design', in Salvendy (ed.).

Galeotti, G., Salmon, P. and Wintrobe, R. (eds.) (2000), *Competition and Structure. The Political Economy of Collective Decisions: Essays in Honor of Albert Breton*. (New York: Cambridge University Press).

Gerth, H. H. and Mills, C. W. (eds.) (1946), *From Max Weber: Essays in Sociology* (New York: Oxford University Press).

Hardin, R. (2000), 'Trust and Society', in Galeotti et al. (eds.), 17-46.

_______ (2002), *Trust and Trustworthiness*. (New York: Russell Sage Foundation).

Johansen, L. (1965), *Public Economics*. (Amsterdam: North Holland).

Keen, M. (1998), 'Vertical Tax Externalities in the Theory of Fiscal Federalism', *IMF Staff Papers*, 45(3), 454-85.

Laffont, J.-J. (1990), 'Analysis of Hidden Gaming in a Three-Level Hierarchy', *Journal of Law, Economics, and Organization*, 6(2), 301-324.

Lazear, E. P. and Rosen, S. (1981), 'Rank-Order Tournaments as Optimum Labor Contracts', *Journal of Political Economy*, 89(5), 841-64.

Lindahl, E. (1919), 'Just Taxation – A Positive Solution', in Musgrave and Peacock (eds.), 168-176.

Marx, K. and Engels, F. (1848), *Manifesto of the Communist Party*, in Marx and Engels, Vol. 6, 476-519.

_______(1975-) *The Collected Works of Karl Marx and Friedrick Engels*. (New York: International Publishers).

McLure Jr., C. E. (ed.) (1983), *Tax Assignment in Federal Countries* (Canberra: Australian National University).

Mintzberg, H. (1979), *The Structuring of Organizations. A Synthesis of the Research* (Englewood Cliffs: Prentice-Hall).

_______ (1983), *Power in and Around Organizations*. (Englewood Cliffs: Prentice Hall).

Musgrave, R. A. and Peacock, A. T. (eds.) (1964), *Classics in the Theory of Public Finance*. (London: Macmillan).

Nalebuff, B. J. and Stiglitz, J. E. 'Prizes and Incentives: Towards a General Theory of Compensation and Competition', *Bell Journal of Economics*, 14(1), 21-43.

Newman, P. (ed.) (1998), *The New Palgrave Dictionary of Economics and the Law*, Volume 1 (London: Macmillan).

Niskanen, W. A. Jr. (1971), *Bureaucracy and Representative Government* (Chicago: Aldine-Atherton).

Posner, R. A. (1974), 'Theories of Economic Regulation', *Bell Journal of Economics* 5(2), 335-358.

Salmon, P. (1987), 'Decentralization as an Incentive Scheme', *Oxford Review of Economic Policy*, 3(2), 24-43.

_______ (1988), 'Trust and Trans-Bureau Networks in Organizations', in Breton, Galeotti, Salmon, and Wintrobe (eds.), 229-52.

_______ (2001), 'Accumulation et destruction de la confiance: un schéma d'inspiration poppérienne', in Aubert and Sylvestre (eds.), 31-44.

Salvendy, G. (ed.) (1982), *Handbook of Industrial Engineering*. (New York: Wiley & Sons).

Spencer, B. J. (1980), 'Outside Information and the Degree of Monopoly Power of a Public Bureau', *Southern Economic Journal*, 47(1), 228-33.

Stigler, G. J. (1971), 'The Theory of Economic Regulation', *Bell Journal of Economics and Management Science*, 2(1), 3-21. Reprinted in Stigler (1975), *The Citizen and the State. Essays on Regulation*. (Chicago: University of Chicago Press), 114-41.

Tiebout, C. M. (1956), 'A Pure Theory of Local Expenditure', *Journal of Political Economy*, 64(5), 416-24.

Tirole, J. (1986), 'Hierarchies and Bureaucracies: On the Role of Collusion in Organizations', *Journal of Law, Economics, and Organizations*, 2(2), 181-214.

Weber, M. (1925), 'Bureaucracy', in Gerth and Mills (eds.).

Wicksell, K. (1896), 'A New Principle of Just Taxation', in Musgrave and Peacock (eds.).

Wintrobe, R. and Breton, A. (1986), 'Organizational Structure and Productivity', *American Economic Review*, 76(3), 530-38.

PART 2
In International Settings

Chapter 4

The Artist as a Secret Agent: Liberalism Against Populism

Manfred J. Holler[1]

Introduction

Art is the laboratory of great emotions, deep thoughts, intense beliefs, and new ideas. If this is so, it would seem appropriate to look for the effects and impacts of rational obfuscation and transparency in art when it meets politics. The Cold War period provides ample material on this issue. In order to illustrate the interplay of rational obfuscation and transparency in politics, I have proposed that during the Cold War the CIA (Central Intelligence Agency) supported art, more specifically, Abstract Expressionist painting in becoming the dominating Western aesthetic culture. 'In the world of art, Abstract Expressionism constituted the ideal style for these propaganda activities. I was the perfect contrast to "the regimented, traditional, and narrow" nature of "socialist realism"' (Cockroft 1974, 40).

This example seems appropriate to discuss the issue of obfuscation in politics because it is not at all obvious that the CIA's secret cultural policy was a 'bad thing' while its more or less transparent counterpart at the government level was the better alternative. For example, "America's pre-eminent liberal historian," Arthur Schlesinger, maintained that the CIA's influence was not "always, or often, reactionary and sinister."[2] Schlesinger saw its leadership as politically enlightened and sophisticated. In her study of *The Cultural Cold War*, Frances Saunders (2000, 3) concludes that 'this view of the CIA as a haven of liberalism acted as a powerful inducement to collaborate with it, or, if not this, at least to acquiesce to the myth that it was well motivated'.

As we shall see, the CIA gave, directly and indirectly, financial and logistic support to modern art. Abstract Expressionism became the vehicle for America's imperial burden and this vehicle needed fuel. However, why did support of modern art and, more generally, cultural policy depend on covert fuel? President Harry Truman did not think much of modern art and even less of the artists who produced it. This evaluation was shared by many politicians, at least, when they talked in

1 The three sections that follow the Introduction are taken from Holler (2000).

2 See Saunders (2000, 3).

public. George Dondero, a Republican Congressman from Michigan,[3] attacked modern art as an instrument of Communist subversion and declared that 'modernism to be quite simply part of a worldwide conspiracy to weaken American resolve' (Saunders 2000, 253). Modern art became emblematic of 'un-Americanism' – 'in short, cultural heresy' (de Hart Matthews 1976, 763).

George Dondero succeeded to force the withdrawal of a State Department exhibition called 'Advancing American Art'. It was shown with great success at Paris and Prague. In the Congress, however, it was denounced as subversive and 'un-American'. The State Department issued a directive ordering that in the future no American artist with Communist or fellow-travelling associations be exhibited at government expense. In the period of McCarthy witch-hunts this meant that politicians who, in principle, looked benevolently at modern art hesitated to become officially involved.[4] It was the rich, well-educated, venturous, liberal East-Cost elite who had (a) the insight that Abstract Expressionism could be excellent weapon in the Cold War, (b) the financial means and the social connections to do this on their own account, and (c) strong personal connections to the CIA – as did Nelson Rockefeller – partly as a result of earlier wartime intelligence work. In addition this group had the conviction that they had to fight oppressive Russian communism in order to defend freedom – and that Abstract Expressionism is a most exiting art project, adequate to their liberal taste.

This sets the stage. On the one hand, we had the politicians, constrained by their desire for majority support and popular assistance; and on the other, we had the East-Coast elite, determined to use modern art to defend American liberalism against the Russian communist threat, and, to some degree, also against the corruption of the political establishment and 'red-neck' art theories advocated by Republicans from Michigan.

The scene very much looked like a contest of 'liberalism against populism.'[5] However, what looked like a fundamental conflict was solved through recourse to obfuscation and secrecy – private political action under public umbrella and state interventions in the costume of private organizations. Major players of this game were the CIA, the Museum of Modern Art, and the Congress of Cultural Freedom. In the next section, we will give a more detailed account of these institutions to clarify this relationship. After that I look at the pawns of cultural warfare, the artists. The section contains a brief introduction into Abstract Expressionism and its message of individualism and universalism which simultaneously enthused liberal Cold War strategists, alienated the American public, and discriminated against artists which were not part of the canon, i.e., non-white, female, homosexual and

---

3 Eva Cockroft (1974, 41) and Jane de Hart Mathews (1976) relate George Dondero with Michigan while Frances Saunders relates him with Missouri.

4 See Hauptman (1973) for details on cultural policy during the McCarthy Decade.

5 This reflects the title of Riker (1982). Although Riker's book has been motivated by theoretical results of social choice theory, it refers to the same basic dilemma which was already discussed in Tocqueville's *Democracy in America* (1835 and 1940/1956).

non-American artists. Then I try to evaluate the result of the 'undercover cultural policy'. The question here is not whether it was good or bad, but how it affected politics and cultural life. Following this discussion, I suggest an evolutionary model which discusses the effects of obfuscation policy to the implementation of social standards and dominating aesthetic culture. The model applies the model of *optimal obfuscation*, proposed in Magee et al. (1989) to clarify political implications in terms of votes gained from campaign contributions and votes lost from distortion effects is then applied. This expanded to incorporate the experience of covert policymaking and privatization of the public domain. Optimal obfuscation turns into a radical obfuscation as cultural politics is no longer identified with politicians and democratic control. An afterward concludes the chapter.

Major Players

Figure 4.1 illustrates the relationship of the intermediate agents in the 'American battle against Russian communism': the CIA, the Museum of Modern Art, and the Congress of Cultural Freedom. The relationship was the result of historical ties, personal links, and ongoing collaboration.[6]

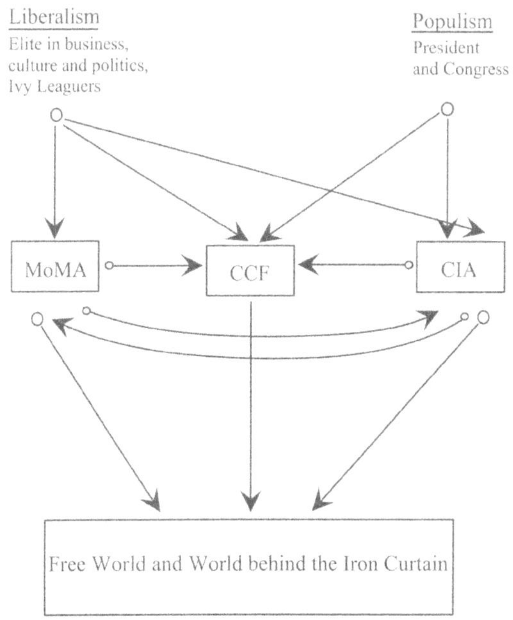

Figure 4.1 The Major Players

6 The following 'portrait' of the three organizations summarizes the corresponding material in Saunders (2000). In parts, the description is very close to Saunders's text and quotation marks could be adequate.

The CIA was created by the National Security Act of 26 July 1947 in order to coordinate military and diplomatic intelligence. Although the Agency was not explicitly authorized to collect intelligence or intervene secretly in the affairs of other nations, the Act mentioned "services of common concern" which was used to move it into espionage, covert action, paramilitary operations, and technical intelligence collection. Frances Saunders (2000, 32ff) points out that 'the terms under which the Agency was established institutionalized the concepts of "the necessary lie" and "plausible deniability" as legitimate peacetime strategies'. The CIA's officers were dedicated to the mission to save 'western freedom from Communist darkness.' This was the result of a training in solid Christian morality, the principles of a robust intellect which most of them enjoyed at some Ivy League school, and a spirit of the Declaration of Independence which they had inhaled in their social environment. Some of them had already experienced intelligence work for the Office of Strategic Service (OSS) during wartime. OSS collected family members of the Vanderbilt, DuPont, Archbold, Weil and Whitney in its ranks. A son of Ernest Hemingway and the two sons of J.P. Morgan worked for the OSS. To some OSS members, the Service was an exiting adventure. In any case, it offered a possibility to enhance reputation and another network to combine with the old school tie. Some of OSS and most of its spirit carried over to the newly created CIA. Young Ivy Leaguers flocked in the Agency to fight the threat of communism and to enjoy the privileges of power and secret brotherhood.

The CIA had substantial finances at its disposal to be spent with minimum of bureaucratic control; and it used various institutions to make it difficult to trace its transactions and the financial support it gave to other organizations and cooperating individuals through private donations. In 1967, for instance, Whitney's charity trust was exposed as a CIA conduit (see Cockroft 1974) In 1949, the US Congress passed an Act which allowed the Director of the CIA to spend funds without having to account for disbursement. Some of this money was spent to support the Congress of Cultural Freedom.

At end June 1950, more than 4000 intellectuals of the 'free world' gathered in Berlin. They all were invited to stand up and be counted. The invitation committee included Berlin's Mayer Ernst Reuter and several prominent German academics. Reuter delivered an opening speech in which the word 'freedom' appeared with high frequency. During four days, participants moved from one panel session to the next and discussed issues such as 'good' and 'bad' atom bombs. The actor Robert Montgomery declared that 'there is no neutral corner in the Freedom's room!'

Not everyone subscribed to this rhetorical crusade against neutrality or at the option of a middle way between Russia and America. Some wondered about the independence of the meeting and about the substantial financial resources that made the event and their participation possible. Others received covert benefaction via the Information Research Department of the Foreign Office. In an interview in 1994,

Tom Braden, OSS officer in his youth and former head of the IOD,[7] the greatest single concentration of covert political and propaganda activities of the CIA, reflected on the financing of the event at Berlin: 'We've got to remember that when we're speaking of those years that Europe was broke ... There wasn't any money. So they naturally looked to the United States for money.'[8] Simple common sense was enough to find out who was behind the Berlin Congress. Delegates who speculated about who was footing the bill concluded that this was not quite the spontaneous event its organizers claimed.

Despite some irritations, the Berlin Congress was celebrated by US government officials and the CIA as a success. The Congress of Cultural Freedom (CCF) became institutionalized. It became a precious instrument of the CIA tool box. Its principle task was: the winning over the waivers. 'It was not to be a centre of agitation, but a beachhead in western Europe from which the advance of Communist ideas could be halted. It was to engage in a widespread and cohesive campaign of peer pressure to persuade intellectuals to dissociate themselves from Communist fronts or fellow travelling organizations. It was to encourage the intelligentsia to develop theories and arguments which were directed not at a mass audience, but at the small elite of pressure groups and statesmen who in turn determined government policy. It was not an intelligence-gathering source, and agents in the other CIA divisions were warned not to attempt to use it as such' (Saunders 2000, 98ff).

The CCF managers were answerable to Tom Braden, then head of the CIA's International Organizations Divisions (IOD). Its activities were either directly financed by CIA's Farfield Foundation or, indirectly, by one of the many foundations that were more than willing to transfer CIA money to CCF officials or to be contributors to CCF projects, e.g., museum directors, gallery owners, art critics, journalists or artists.[9]

Some contributors were supported by their own foundation, and thus did not depend on CIA money. This did not hinder them in closely cooperating with the CCF. Most of the 1940s and 1950s, Nelson Rockefeller was the president of the Museum of Modern Art (MoMA). His mother was one of the museum's five founders in 1929. MoMA represented the 'enlightened rich,' the future of American culture.

During World War II, Nelson Rockefeller was in charge of all intelligence in Latin America. His organization sponsored touring exhibitions of 'contemporary American painting' of which nineteen were contracted to MoMA. Rockefeller was not involved in OSS but his close friendship with Allen Dulles, who was in charge of OSS wartimes operations in Europe, younger brother to secretary of state

---

7 The IOD, the International Organizations Division of the CIA, aimed at uniting the intellectuals of the 'free world' against what was being offered in the Soviet Union.

8 Quoted after Saunders (2000, 82).

9 The CIA undercover activities were generously subsidized by Marshall Plan money. Recipient countries were ask to deposit an amount equal to the US contribution in its central bank. 95 percent of the currency funds remained the legal property of the recipient country's government, while 5 per cent became the property of the US government – and were made available as a war chest for the CIA (Saunders, 2000, 1005ff).

John Foster Dulles and CIA's director in the period 1953-61, compensated for this shortcoming. Allen Dulles and Tom Braden delivered briefings on covert activities of the CIA on a regular basis and, in 1954, Nelson Rockefeller was appointed as Eisenhower's special advisor on Cold War strategy. He was also chairman of the Planning Coordination Group which controlled the National Security Council and CIA's covert operations.

The various engagements of William Burden,[10] a great-great-grandson of Commodore Vanderbilt, illustrates the connection between CIA, CCF and MoMA. During the war, he worked for Nelson Rockefeller's intelligence service. After the war, he became director of CIA's Farfield Foundation and thus decided on the financial support to CCF, sat as chairman of an advisory committee of the MoMA, and became MoMA's president in 1956. Frances Saunders introduces several other high ranking officials to us who held similar links to at least two of these institutions. There are however also actions in which these institutions repeatedly collaborated. However, in the case of MoMA's activities, 'unlike those of CIA, it was not necessary to use subterfuge. Similar aims as those of CIA's cultural operations could be pursued openly with the support of Nelson Rockefeller's millions' (Cockroft 1974, 41).

By 1956, the International Program of MoMA hat organized 33 exhibitions, including the US participation in the Venice Biennale. 'The State Department refused to take the responsibility for U.S. representation at the Venice Biennale, perhaps the most important international-cultural-political art event, where all European countries including the Soviet Union competed for cultural honours. MoMA bought the U.S. pavilion in Venice and took the sole responsibility for the exhibitions from 1954 to 1962. This was the only case of privately owned (instead of government-owned) pavilion at the Venice Biennale.' (Cockroft 1974, 40). The Government's difficulties in handling the delicate issues of free speech and free artistic expression, generated by the McCarthy hysteria of the early 1950s, made it necessary and convenient for MoMA to assume this role of international representation of the United States. This was consistent with the neo-liberal principle that there is nothing to prevent an individual from exerting as much influence through his work in a private foundation as he could through work in the government (Saunders 2000, 139). Moreover, it is a hallmark of the 'artistic free enterprise' strategy identified with Abstract Expressionism.

When MoMA contracted to supply the art material for CCF's 1952 Masterpieces festival in Paris, 'it did so under the auspices of trustees who were fully cognizant of the CIA's role in that organization' (Saunders 2000, 268) and of its propaganda value. On the other hand, the collaboration with the CCF brought MoMA and its favoured Abstract Expressionism access to many of the most prestigious art institutions in Europe whose directors were sitting on the Arts Committee of the CCF.

During 1953-54, MoMA organized a tour of Europe, dedicated exclusively to Abstract Expressionism. The show, entitled 'Twelve Contemporary American

---

10 See Saunders (2000, 137) for this short portrait and further details illustrating William Burden's political and cultural role.

Painters and Sculptures', had its opening at the *Musée National d'Art Moderne* in Paris. This was achieved with the help of the American Embassy at Paris (which acted as a quiet liaison between MoMA and its French hosts) and with the financial support of the Nelson Rockefeller Fund which was partly conducted through the *Association Française d'Action Artistique*. This association was a donor to the CCF and its director, Philippe Erlanger, was a designated CIA contact at the French Foreign Office (Saunders 2000, 270).

In a 1974 piece, Eva Cockroft discussed the relationship of CIA's cultural apparatus and MoMA's international program. The functions of both institutions were similar and 'mutually supportive'. Frances Saunders (2000, p.264) concludes that 'there is no *prima facie* evidence for any formal agreement between the CIA and the Museum of Modern Art. The fact is, it simply wasn't necessary.' The motivations of both institutions, being at least functionally divergent, converged in the support for the Abstract Expressionism and its advance throughout the 'free world' and to some dissident circles behind the Iron Curtain. Why Abstract Expressionism? Was it not that precisely the form of expression that had been rejected by America's silent majority and by some of its very out-spoken politicians?

Individualism and Universalism

If the CIA, the Museum of Modern Art, and the Congress of Cultural Freedom were major players in the cultural warfare game, then the Abstract Expressionist artists were the pawns. In fact, the major players did not really care about the individual artists but focused on their work and the ideology behind their work. This was, in a sense, paradoxical because individualism was one of the cornerstones of Abstract Expressionism and a major reason why this art was supported as an alternative to the 'collectivistic art of socialism'. The art works showed substantial variety, but the variation among the artists seemed even larger and 'most of them were people who had very little respect for the government in particular and certainly not for the CIA', said Donald Jameson in an interview in Washington in June 1994.[11] Jackson Pollock was a drunk and was killed in a car crash. Mark Rothko and Adolph Gottlieb were committed anti-Communists. Barnett Newman was painting for America[12] while Robert Motherwell and Willem de Kooning, born Dutch, did not think highly of a national context for their work. Ad Reinhardt participated in the March on Washington for black rights in August 1963. It seems that nothing remarkable has been said about Clyfford Still's life and political orientation. There were times when he refused to be co-opted by the museums and the critical establishment, directed by

11 Reproduced in Saunders (2000, 260).

12 However, he '...clung throughout his life to the independent anarchistic views he had formulated in youth' and even '...wrote a foreword to a new edition of Kropotkin's memoirs' (Golding, 2003, 32).

a Clement Greenberg,[13] but he still wished to be perceived as a spiritual leader of the Abstract Expressionist movement. To some extent, he was the mentor of colour-field painters such as Barnett Newman and Mark Rothko and, different from Pollock, Motherwell and de Kooning, rejected Freud and Surrealism and 'all cultural opiates, past and present' (Cox 1083, 51).

These artists formed the 'essential eight' of Abstract Expressionism. Others who were added to this group are William Baziotes, Arshil Gorky (who hanged himself), Philip Guston, Hans Hofmann, Fritz Kline, Richard Pousette-Dart, Mark Tobey, and Bradley Walker Tomlin (see Gibson 1997, *xx*). However, instead of going deeper into the individual history and political beliefs of these people, I will follow the strategy of the three major players and focus on the ideology of art which made Abstract Expressionism.

Danto (1999, 75) summarizes the essence of Abstract Expressionism, 'with its celebration of the self, of the inner states that painting allegedly made objective, and of paint itself as the medium par excellence through which this inner states were externally transcribed. In a certain sense, abstract expressionist painting was a kind of private pictorial language, a turning away from the public and the political in the interest of producing an art that was, in the words of Robert Motherwell, "plastic, mysterious, and sublime".' The focus on colour instead of form or narrative expressions represented the abstract dimension. The discovery of the Unconscious with the help of colour contained the expressionist dimension. The two dimensions met in automatic drawing and painting, doodling, gesture and action painting, and Jackson Pollock's dripping method. The 'fluid space, lack of closed shapes, a deliberately unfinished quality, and an "overall" composition that diffused any notion of focus' of Abstract Expressionist work – complex, cosmopolitan, and ever-changing – 'was intrinsically at odds with the need for certitude and control' (de Hart Mathews 1976, 785) strongly looked for by many Americans in the times of Cold War.

'Marxism gave way to psychiatry' (Guilbaut 1983, 165). Several Abstract Expressionist artists had political roots in the Marxism of the 1930s, and their analysis of the new political situation and their own position in it bore the imprint of the Marxist tradition. However, in the 1940s, there was an important shift away from critical studies of the social and political environment, alienation in the capitalist society, etc. Gottlieb and Rothko were dedicated readers of Freud and Jung. This concurred with the focus on creativity (or originality) as one of the core principles of Abstract Expressionism. 'Originality, like abstraction, was an important way predicated on the denial of politics' (Gibson 1997, *xxviii*). Alienation became a purely individualistic (psychological) phenomenon which, according to Clement Greenberg, self-appointed prophet and spokesman of Abstract Expressionism, made the American artist the 'most modern' of all artists and enabled him to express

13 March 1948, art critic Clement Greenberg was the first to declare that New York had achieved international status as a cultural centre and even replaced Paris as the cultural symbol of the Western world: American art was the foremost in the world.

the modern age. However, Abstract Expressionists rejected machine imagery and industrial and urban landscape, they 'entered into a pastoral world that was primitive and elemental' (Cox 1983, 48). On the other hand, abstraction made it possible to lead into an active dialogue with the age and private material could be treated as a public declaration. However, to art historian Serge Gilbaut (1983, 197), 'the freedom of expression and existential violence that leap to the eye in the work of abstract expressionists were in fact products of fear and the impossibility of representation, of the need to avoid the literary expression…'.

'The American problem,' Robert Motherwell emphasized, 'was to find a creative principle that was not a style, not stylistic, not an imposed aesthetic.'[14] Many Abstract Expressionist artists were followers of Carl Jung. As Jungians they believed that the collective unconscious was universal and 'self-identical' in all human beings (Gibson, 1997, 48). The function of art was considered as the invention of codes to transpose universal, rather than local, meaning into visual form. 'Turning … to private visions, insights, and most especially the subconscious, the abstract expressionists plumbed the depths of their own experience for metaphors and symbols that would somehow possess universal meaning' (de Hart Mathews 1976, 783). This was the spiritual-intellectual basis for the claim on universalism and the discharge of the isolationist spirit of pre-war America – a pre-condition for applying art to cultural warfare.

Paradoxically, to some extent Abstract Expressionism contained a turning away from the market. Before it was discovered as an instrument of Cold War its main representatives were not very much of a success on the art market. By the simple fact that this art often used immense formats – different from its European predecessors – it necessitated museums and other public spaces which were only made available in the course of Cold War cultural policy. In principle, this conflicted with the private pictorial language of Abstract Expressionism, its 'artistic free enterprise' strategy and non-political attitude, and made its dissemination dependent on semi-public (political) entrepreneurship as developed by the CIA, MoMA, and CCF.

There are many paradoxes embedded in Abstract Expressionism; some are embedded in the inconsistency of its claim of individualism and freedom, on the one hand, and its policy effects which focus on dominance of ideas, ideology, and power on the other. Eva Cockroft (1974, 41) concludes that 'attempts to claim that styles of art are politically neutral when there is no overt political subject matter are as simplistic as Dondero-ish attacks on all abstract art as "subversive".'

Paradoxically, the discriminatory edge of Abstract Expressionism was its claim for universalism. And it was this claim, together with its individualistic ideology that made this style and the artists a canon of interest to Cold War strategists. Does not Communism also make a universalist claim?

To Eva Cockroft (1974, 41), it is evident that 'rich and powerful patrons of the art, men like Rockefeller and Whitney, who control the museums and help oversee foreign policy, also recognize the value of culture in the political arena. The artist creates freely. But his work is promoted and used by others for their own purposes.

14 Quotation taken from Danto (1999, 23).

Rockefeller, through Barr and others at the Museum his mother founded and the family controlled, consciously used Abstract Expressionism, "the symbol of political freedom," for political ends.'

Basic Questions

Frances Saunders (2000, 5) raised a number of questions which could serve as a starting point for evaluating the CIA's engagement in the cultural warfare. The first question addresses the issue of freedom. 'Clearly, by camouflaging its investment, the CIA acted on the supposition that its blandishments would be refused if offered openly. What kind of freedom can be advanced by such deception?' Of course, this question was relevant for the Free World and its frontier states towards the Soviet Empire. However, it was also of interest to the political, economic and social life within the borders of the USA. A preliminary answer to this question is: a liberal freedom controlled by an elite and the elite's principle. For instance, with respect to the contribution of MoMA and the various private foundations which supported the cultural warfare, liberalism implies that there is nothing to prevent an individual from exerting as much influence through his work in a private foundation as he could through work in the government.

The Founding Fathers, and more specifically James Madison, wanted to refine the voice of people in government, not replicate it. They proposed various restraints to majority voting which were thought to shelter the governing elite from direct popular impact. Voting was considered a method of controlling officials by subjecting their tenure to periodic electoral tests, but not a method for citizens to participate directly in making law, supposedly the 'Will of the People.' To create and to use a policy frame which is independent of parliamentary support is a natural consequence of this principle of American liberalism as soon as the elite finds the elected representatives too narrow-minded, and too close to popular values, to collaborate in the pursuit of the grand scheme.

More specifically, Frances Saunders (2000, 5) asks: 'Did financial aid distort the process by which intellectuals and artists were advanced? – Were reputations secured or enhanced by membership of the CIA's cultural consortium?' Ex-post one can conclude that most of the writers, film makers and artists selected by the CIA sponsorship were of extremely high quality. The Abstract Expressionists such as Jackson Pollock, Willem de Kooning, and Mark Rothko have defined the world art of their period and are still prominent contributors to museums of modern art around the globe. (See Marc Rothko's room at Tate Modern.) But it seems impossible to answer whether they could have done this without the support which they derived, directly or indirectly, from the resources which the CIA invested in the secret cultural warfare.[15] We have to see that Abstract Expressionism entails a high degree of exclusiveness and of cartelization so that its support had a substantial

15 However, 'there is ....incontrovertible evidence that the CIA was an active component in the machinery which promoted Abstract Expressionism' (Saunders 2000, 273).

discriminating effect on American art – with precarious consequences for those who were not members of the cartel. Abstract Expressionism 'was sealed inside a belljar and protected from infection by any unwanted Germs, from intrusion by any outsider who might disturb the cherished harmony' (Guilbaut 1983, 10). There was no (gallery) space left for Byron Browne, Carl Holty, Karl Knath, and Charles Seliger, painters who were successful before the Abstract Expressionists conquered the stage: their works were too European, too close to Paris, and too un-American – to become enlisted by governmental agencies and private organizations in the fight against the expansion of Communism[16].

Ann Eden Gibson (1997, *xxxi*) summarizes: 'To the extent that the work of an artist who is not in the canon looks like that of one who is, the non canonical artist's work is derivative. To the extent that the non canonical work does not resemble that in the canon, the contending work is not Abstract Expressionist'. Paradoxically, the discriminating effect resulted from the focus on universality. This excluded artists whose identity did not generalize 'in a postwar society whose standards were racist, misogynist, and homophobic' (Gibson, 1997 *xxii*). The mechanism of this society functioned to reinforce the power of European, male and heterosexual identity and discriminated against artists who did not fit in this pattern. The CIA was grateful for this pre-selection of artists and their work; it made it less cumbersome to transfer Western values to the rest of the world. The standards of the post war society were racist, misogynist, and homophobic not only in America.

However, 'was there any real justification for assuming that the principles of western democracy couldn't be revived in post-war Europe according to some internal mechanism? Or for not assuming that democracy could be more complex than was implied by the lauding of American liberalism?' (Saunders 2000, 5) Indeed, democracy is a complex concept. Left to the internal mechanism it is not obvious that a democratic equilibrium evolves. From a theoretical point of view, coordination on a democratic equilibrium seems to be easily solvable by the implementation of American liberalism – and the American way of life as the focal point. However, when it comes to modern art as a vehicle to disseminate American liberalism, it faced, as we have seen, popular resistance from inside. Undercover operations was a way to circumvent this problem. This violates the majority principle of democracy but not necessarily the liberal perspective of it. As Gordon Wood, author of *The American Revolution: A History* writes 'What really counts in maintaining democracy are the liberties protected by the Bill of Rights and the underlying conditions of the country – its culture, its social arrangements, its economic well-being, and the political experience of its citizens and their leaders' (Wood 2002, 21).

If the financing were done openly, the liberal elite would see itself in conflict with the political sector which (a) relies on majorities and thus depends on popularity, and (b) whose members are, in general, not as well equipped to enjoy modern art as the members of the elite. Moreover, it seems that some participants of the Berlin

16 On February 25, 1948, Czechoslovakia went over to the Soviet bloc after the Czech Communist succeeded in out-manoeuvring the divided Social Democratic Party.

Congress and affiliates to the CCF did not know that they were, directly or indirectly, financed by the CIA. Had they known they would have left the projects it supported or publicly distanced themselves from their donor. In both cases the effect would have probably been negative.

Other participants claimed that they did not know that they were financed by the CIA. They needed this umbrella to (a) keep up social respect, (b) be acceptable for the cultural or political community, and (c) avoid political or social resistance and concomitant backlashes about their work. Secrecy was helpful and, to some extent, necessary for the conquest of the Western art community through sponsored exhibitions and gallery work. Were the shows which finally installed Abstract Expressionism in Western Europe during the post-war period openly financed by the US government, their impact is likely to have been much reduced: the success of America's Cold War program depended on its ability to appear independent from government, to seem to represent the spontaneous convictions of freedom loving individuals. This was the credo of Allen Dulles, younger brother to secretary of state John Foster Dulles, close friend of Nelson Rockefeller and director of CIA in the period 1953-61, who was already in charge of covert operations in Europe during World War II (Saunders 2000, 130).

The Model Analysis

Georges Duby claims that 'the most startling discoveries that remain to be made ...will come from the attempt to find out what was left out of the discourse, whether voluntarily or involuntarily, to determine what was hidden, consciously or unconsciously.'[17] Naturally, a lot is left out when politics makes use of obfuscation and secrecy. Duby concludes 'What we need are new scholarly tools, tools better adapted than those we now have to bringing out the negative in what we are shown, to laying bare the things that men deliberately cover up. At times these suddenly reveal themselves quite by accident, but most of the time they must be carefully deciphered between the lines of what is actually said.'[18]

Game theory is often applied to model and analyze counter-factual or, in more popular terms, the paradoxical events and thus seems an adequate instrument to lay bare the things that 'men' cover up. Of course, game theoretic models are highly stylized, but this is unavoidable if we want to analyze complex phenomena. The stylizations and simplifications help us in uncovering general principles, defining relevant problems, and find new questions.

17 Quotation taken from Guilbaut (1983, 6).

18 Quotation taken from Guilbaut (1983, 6).

The Wickström Model

The model that will be applied here has been used by Holler and Wickström (1999) to analyze the use of scandals in the progress of society. Here, we will analyze the impact of secrecy on social dynamics. In the model we assume that there are many players in society who randomly encounter one another. At each encounter one has to behave according to one of two conventions, I and II (the strategies I and II). Such a convention could be on which side of the street to travel or which language to speak, or whether we like avant-garde art or whether we prefer a more traditional alternative. If two players, i and j, encounter one another and adopt the same convention, the payoffs are positive for both: (v_i, v_j) for convention I and (w_i, w_j) for convention II. If they adopt different conventions the payoff is zero for both players.

i, j	I	II
I	v_i, v_j	0,0
II	0,0	w_i, w_j

Figure 4.2 Game of Convention

Now, let us assume that the status quo is characterized by convention I. That means everyone adopts this convention if they encounter another player. If player i chooses convention I, then the expected payoff for player i from an encounter with j:

$$u_i(\mathrm{I}) = 1 \cdot v_i + 0 \cdot 0 = v_i$$

because i adheres to convention I with probability one. Applying the same logic to convention II, if individual i chooses convention II, his expected payoff is:

$$u_i(\mathrm{II}) = 1 \cdot 0 + 0 \cdot w_i = 0$$

It is clear that the player will adhere to convention I. In fact, everyone will adhere to convention I because everyone else adheres to it. A single player in a large population cannot make a difference; the society is locked into convention I. Only the concerted effort of a large number of individuals could change this. In adopting convention II, a single player can only cause his own misery and that of others who adhere to convention I.

This situation could change through a concerted effort of several individuals. In fact, there exists for each individual i a smallest fraction of the population that would have to use convention II for it to be rational for individual i to also adopt convention II. This fraction of the population is known as the *critical mass* for player i.

Note that this measure of critical mass is related to an individual player while the concept of critical mass as applied in network theory (see, e.g., Peters 1997) is defined respect to the population or subgroups of the population. However, we will see that the two concepts coincide for the critical mass equilibrium.

It is straightforward to find the critical mass for an individual i. Denoting the proportion of the population adhering to convention II by δ, we can again find the expected payoffs of individual i which are given by:

$$u'_A(c_A) = u'_B(c_B) = H'_A(g_A) = H'_B(g_B)$$

$$c_A^{FB} = c_B^{FB} = g_A^{FB} = g_B^{FB} = \frac{(k+1)w}{4}$$

Obviously, individual i will prefer convention II to convention I if u_i (II) > u_i(I)

$$U_A^{FB} = U_B^{FB} = \log\left[\frac{(k+1)^2 w^2}{16}\right]$$

This is the case if

where we have defined m_i as player i's *revolutionary propensity*, i.e., the player's valuation of a society adhering to convention II in comparison to one adhering to convention I. The parameter δ_i is player i's critical mass.

The revolutionary propensity is greater than 1 for players who would prefer convention II to be the norm; and it is smaller than 1 for people who prefer convention I. Similarly, the critical mass for a player who prefers status quo is greater than 0.5. For those who prefer a new norm the critical mass is less than 0.5.

We can now order the individuals according to their critical mass, *i.e.* in reverse according to their revolutionary propensities. We further denote by $\theta(\delta_i)$ the fraction of the total population with a critical mass $\delta_i = \delta$ or smaller. That is, $\theta(\delta_i)$ is the fraction of the population that would adopt convention II if at least a fraction δ has already done so. Figure 4.3 illustrates a possible function $\theta(\delta_i)$.

The critical mass of the most revolutionary member of society is denoted by δ_m, and that of the most reactionary by δ^M. If we assume, as in Figure 4.3, that the function U_i is increasing at a rate larger than 1, then it has only one point intersecting a 45° line, that is, a point where $\theta(\delta_i) = \delta$. This point is denoted by $\delta = \delta^*$ in the figure and is known as a *fixed point*. The important property of this fixed point is that it is the 'true' critical mass of the society as a whole: δ^* represents a *critical mass equilibrium*.

If a fraction slightly larger than δ^* adopts convention II, then there is even a greater fraction U_i that finds it advantageous to adopt convention II. After they have done so, even more would like to do so, and the bandwagon starts rolling and does not stop until all individuals have adopted convention II. In other words, the fixed point of our evolutionary process does not represent a stable equilibrium for the critical mass function $\theta(\delta_i)$ in Figure 4.3. Hence, in order to arrive at a change in convention, it is necessary to coordinate at least a fraction d^* consisting of the most revolutionary individuals in the society to take the first step. Needless to say that coordinating on convention II is no problem, irrespective of the *revolutionary propensity* of *j*, if the meeting game is sequential and *i* is a first mover to propose convention II.

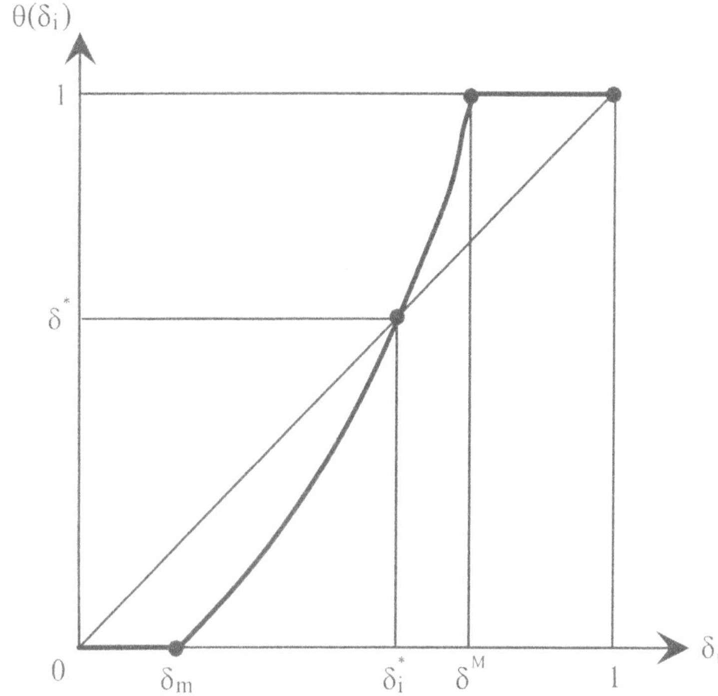

Figure 4.3 The Distribution of Expectations

If, however, players choose their convention strategies simultaneously, i.e., without knowing the choice of the other, then the decision situation is more complex: (a) The individual members do in general not know the distribution of individual critical mass measures, i.e., the function $\theta(\delta_i)$. (b) Even if player *i* knows $\theta(\delta_i)$ and also knows that a sufficient number of players know $\theta(\delta_i)$, then there is still no guarantee for *i*, choosing convention II, to encounter a second player who chooses convention II. However, if $\delta > \delta^*$, then an player *i* with $\delta_i < \delta^*$ has a large enough *revolutionary propensity* μ_i to propose convention II in a meeting with *j*. But how will the players come to know the function $\theta(\delta_i)$? If encounters occur repeatedly then a player can obtain an estimate of $\theta(\delta_i)$ from experience, e.g., applying the Bayesian rule for updating his a priori assumption on relevant values of $\theta(\delta_i)$. If you think that a sufficient share of members of a society, $\delta > \delta i$, shake hands, and you want to follow this convention, but in every encounter you offer your hand is ignored, you will revise your estimate of δ and choose another convention as soon as $\delta < \delta_i$.

In general, there is also exogenous information – created by events or delivered by external players – from which players can derive updates of their beliefs on $\theta(\delta_i)$. Holler and Wickström (1999) suggested that the mobilization and coordination can be achieved through a scandal. In this chapter we will argue that the prominence of the evolutionary elements has been organized and enhanced by the CIA and private players, such as MoMA, who shared the value and methods of its Cold War cultural policy.

Interpretation

There were two alternatives which specified the status quo characterizing American art in the early 1940s. First, the already mentioned Byron Browne, Carl Holty, Karl Knath, and Charles Seliger painted in European style, i.e., by and large, they followed the art program which was popular in Paris. In fact, in his early paintings, Arshil Gorky also borrowed from Paris, however, he succeeded in becoming accepted as member of the second layer of Abstract Expressionists.[19] The work of a second group of painters such as Edward Hopper, Georgia O'Keefe, Mark Tobey and Stuart Davis was identified as truly American but the art industry considered their example 'too parochial in coloration, and thus too "unmodern" to provide models for mainstream work' (Kozloff 1973, 43). Their work was not abstract and as such it was representative of what middle-class Americans called modern art.

The two alternatives operated on segmented markets which were clearly identified. There was no coordination problem and it did not happen very often that the participant of one market – buyer, gallery, artist, art critic – was trapped into the other. The balance was washed away when Abstract Expressionism entered the scene. From one day to the other, the influential Kootz Gallery at New York no longer exhibited works of Browne, Holty (see Guilbaut 1983, p.178f.) and Hopper.[20] What has happened?

Alfred Barr's support of Abstract Expressionist artists played an influential role in their success. In addition to his role at MoMA, Barr was an artistic advisor to Peggy Guggenheim, whose Surrealist-oriented *Art of This Century* gallery gave some of these artists their first shows in the mid-1940s. For example, in her East River gallery, Peggy Guggenheim offered one-man shows to Jackson Pollock in

---

19 One could also argue that there is a very strong link from Picasso's *Demoiselles d'Avignon* of 1906, which is part of the permanent collection of MoMA, to Adolph Gottlieb's adaptations of primitive concepts. However, Gottlieb was a member of the 'essential eight' of Abstract Expressionism.

20 Later, in 1952, 'some fifty American artists, including Edward Hopper, Charles Burchfield, Yasuo Kuniyoshi and Jack Levine, attacked MoMA, in what came to be known as the "Reality Manifest", for "coming to be more and more identified in the public eye with abstract and non-objective art", a "dogma" which they felt stemmed "very largely from the Modern Museum and its unquestionable influence throughout the country"'(Saunders, 1999, 265).

1943, 1945, 1947, Hans Hofmann in 1944, Robert Motherwell in 1944, and Mark Rothko in 1945. On the occasion of his solo show in May and June 1943, Pollock sold nothing but Peggy Guggenheim offered him another show, together with the painter Matta in November 1943 and an annual contract of US$1,800 a year for his entire output (Russell, 2002).

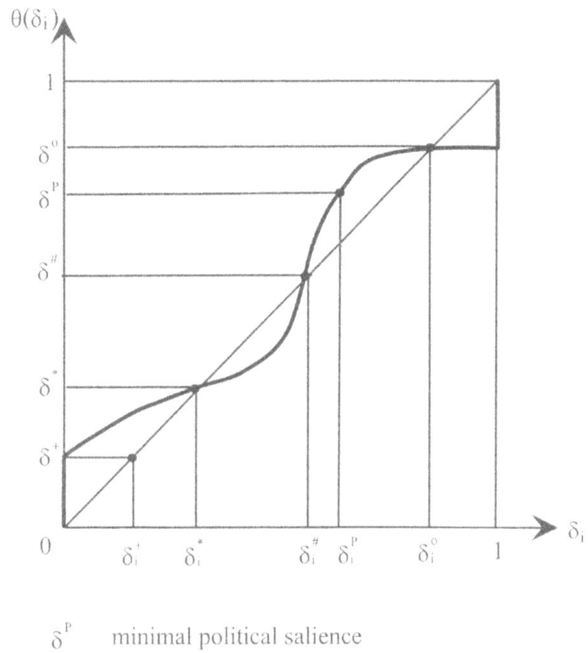

Figure 4.4 Bi-polar Expectations and Political Science

Figure 4.4 shows two prominent types of players. The first one is characterized by δ^+, a group of players who will choose the convention II even if nobody else is choosing this convention. Such an autonomous change δ^+ can be attributed to the MoMA and its friends and supporters, represented by Nelson Rockefeller. The other group of prominent players is described by $\delta^\circ < 1$, the upper level of δ for $\delta < 1$. The Donderos will only accept Abstract Expressionism if all players accept this style of art, *including themselves*. However, since the Donderos are not prepared to accept this style at any costs, δ° expresses the upper level of δ. If δ^P represents the "amount of players" necessary to make Abstract Expressionism politically salient so that it defines the style of the Free World, then δ^P has to satisfy the inequality $\delta^P < \delta^\circ$. Otherwise δ^P cannot be achieved.

Obviously, the 'amount of players' is not well defined in this context where the social relevance of the various players and peer group behaviour matter; not all players are of equal weight in a liberal society.[21] Different weights can be expressed through nonmarginal steps in the $\theta(\delta_i)$ function. However, $\theta(\delta_i)$ assumes that players form identical expectations with respect to the contributions of the various players to satisfy the critical masses δ_i: the expectations on $\theta(\delta_i)$ are identical for all players, only the δ_i values differ. Needless to say that the assumption of identical expectations is rather heroic, but convenient for the lucidity of the analysis.

In Andreozzi (2002, 201), player *i* will switch to convention II 'if at least a fraction δ^+ of the entire population has already switched.' However, as it is assumed that the entire population initially plays convention I, all players will stick to this convention in the situation described in Figure 4.4. That is, players do not form expectations but simply imitate observed behaviour. Perhaps it seems more realistic to assume players having identical observations than having identical expectations, but even in the case of observations different players may assign different social weights to players. If so, then the assumption of a unique function $\theta(\delta_i)$ is inconsistent. That is: the simplifying assumption a unique function $\theta(\delta_i)$ implies that every *i* has the same expectation with respect to the distribution of critical mass values.[22]

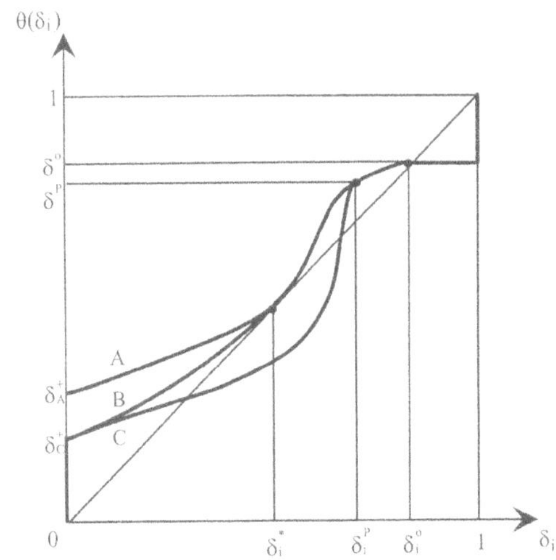

Figure 4.5 Shaping Expectations

---

21 Binmore (1998) discusses the evolutionary determination of social weights in the context of a norm of fairness. In principle, these weights could be applied here as a measure of the social relevance of agents. However, the Binmore's evolutionary model is not conclusive (see Holler and Napel, 2001).

22 Andreozzi (2002) endogenizes the differentiation in critical masses by assuming that players get a higher payoff out of a specific strategy the more experienced they get in playing this strategy. It does not seem obvious that this principle can be applied to the distribution of δ_i , i.e., to Abstract Expressionism. Political history teaches us that the simple left-right dimension, possibly structured with age, does not always apply to the appreciation of modern art as the latter is generally detested by both the extreme right and the extreme left.

If players react to observed changes from convention I to convention II, then the fraction δ^+ changes in the situation of Figure 4.4. Under the assumption that players form expectations, an additional fraction $\delta^*-\delta^+$ will be motivated by the autonomous change and a fraction $\delta = \delta^+$ will follow convention II. However, if $\delta^* < \delta^P$, as illustrated in Figure 4, then political salience has not been achieved. If decisions are based on expectations, player who are interested in political salience have the option to augment expectations, by, for instance choosing a larger autonomous change, increasing the social weight of players with a high revolutionary propensity and thus a low δ_i – a likely implication of liberal policy – or influencing the learning process by manipulating the a priori beliefs. If the a priori δ is large then many players are willing to choose convention II; and then it is more likely that a player will meet another who has chosen convention II.

The interaction of MoMA, CIA, and CCF offered a tool box of instruments to manipulate $\theta(\delta_i)$ so that, in the end, $\delta^* > \delta^P$ was satisfied. In Figure 4.5, alternative $\theta(\delta_i)$ functions are represented. Curve A illustrates the choice of larger autonomous change while B illustrates successful manipulation of $\theta(\delta_i)$. Both curves leave the expectations of the Donderos 'intact.' Curve C represents the 'without manipulation' curve of Figure 4.4. Curves A and B are drawn such that the critical value δ^* is identical for both distributions. Of course, this is not necessarily the case. As long as $\delta > \delta_i$ and agents behave in accordance with their expectations d will grow. If $\delta = \delta^* = \delta_i$, MoMA has to organize an extra exhibition to overcome this (instable) rest point.

Of course, there are many alternatives as to how the manipulated expectations of curve B can be explained. What we know so far of the interaction of MoMA, CIA and CCF offers rich material for speculation. For example, the success which Abstract Expressionism had in Europe due to Cold War policy seems to be an important factor to explain the recognition it gained by the U.S. middle class in the 1950s. Another important fact was the overnight change in *Life* magazine's policy towards Jackson Pollok and the Abstract Expressionism, "transforming the alienated avant-garde artist into a cultural hero" (Guilbaut 1983, 193). It was Alfred Barr of MoMA who 'persuaded Henry Luce of *Time-Life* to change his editorial policy toward the new art, telling him in a letter that it should be especially protected, not criticized as in the Soviet Union, because this, after all, was "artistic free enterprise". Thus it was Luce – who held the phrase "American's intellectual health" permanently on the end of his tongue who won over to Barr's and MoMA's interests. In August 1949, *Life* magazine gave its centre-page spread to Jackson Pollock, landing the artist and his work on every coffee table in America' (Saunders 2000, 267).

Radical Obfuscation

The cooperation of CIA, MoMA and CCF added an additional dimension to the model of *optimal obfuscation* suggested by Magee et al. (1989) and applied, for example, in Magee (1997) and Hojman (2002). The public component of this cooperation, the CIA and its share in CCF activities, was secret, at least before it was gradually unveiled in later years, while the rather active private component, represented by MoMA, was outside the range for which voters will sanction government for its policy. If we map this additional dimension into the two-dimensional diagram proposed in Magee et al. (1989, 261) to illustrate their theory we get Figure 4.6.

The G-curve illustrates the 'votes gained from campaign contributions' while the L-curve represents 'votes lost from distribution effects'. The standard hypothesis is that interest groups are less inclined to support the governing party the more difficult it is to see who benefits from its policy. By definition, an increase of obfuscation decreases 'visibility'. This explains the decreasing shape of the G-curve. The shape of the L-curve derives from the fact that increasing social waste related to greater obfuscation becomes less recognizable to voters. Magee et al. (1989) illustrate the curves in Figure 4.6 with the example of an economically inefficient tariff policy. If the government wants to gain the votes of labour and thus support labour-intensive industry, then a labour subsidy would be, economically, the most efficient policy. Labour unions are likely to honour this policy through campaign contributions; non-labour voters will, however, tend not to vote for the government party because of its obvious partisanship which is not in their favour. Social choice theory says that whenever policy boils down to the redistribution of a constant sum, and voters are aware of it, the government runs into the problem of cyclical majority and the opposition, being second move to issue its election platform, can always propose a distribution scheme which guarantees a majority of votes. This is just another way to say that the core of the voting game is empty or, alternatively, a Condorcet winner does not exist for this game. If, however, the government avoids the distribution issue, it is unlikely to gain substantial campaign contributions. Moreover, most policy problems have redistributive implications. Obfuscation seems to be a natural way out of this dilemma. The redistributive effects of tariffs on imports of labour-intensive goods seems to be less obvious than the redistributive effects of labour subsidies. As a consequence, labour union are less inclined to honour this policy in the form of campaign contributions while more non-labour voters are likely to support the government. The redistributive effects of quotas on imports of labour-intensive goods seems even less obvious, and the redistributive effects of so-called voluntary export restraint agreements (VER) by foreign suppliers of labour-intensive goods seem to be the least obvious in the chain of alternative trade barriers so far developed to favour the vote clientele of a party.

Needless to say that corresponding instruments are available to gain support of capital-intensive industry and its major stakeholders. Starting with direct subsidies and ending with VER, the obfuscation will increase and economic policy will be more an more distorted with the result of increasing social waste. The L-curve reflects, in addition to the redistribution effect, the evaluation of the distortion as experienced by the voters. However, as better informed voters are expected to punish government for economic inefficiency, parties tend to increase obfuscation. Magee et al. (1989, p. 263) observe a *voter information paradox*: If voters tend to be better informed, parties increase obfuscation, and more economic inefficiency results. The change from tariffs to VERs illustrates this argument.

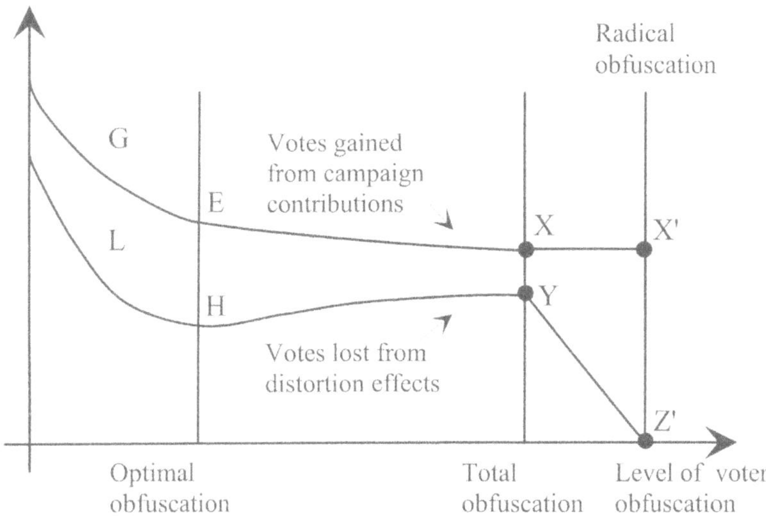

Figure 4.6 Optimal and Radical Obfuscation

Obviously, in Figure 4.6, an obfuscation optimum (i.e. *optimal obfuscation*) exists for the range between *no obfuscation* and *total obfuscation*. It is determined by the degree of obfuscation for which the distance of the two curves is maximal, i.e. where the "marginal votes gained from campaign contributions" equal "marginal votes lost from distortion effects". In this example, *total obfuscation* is not optimal as a comparison of the distances XY and EH shows. Of course, this marginalistic interpretation assumes a cardinality for the obfuscation scale which is difficult to justify.

In the case of CIA's Cold War cultural policy, obfuscation was not only total but *radical*: voters did not relate the emergence of Abstract Expressionism to the government. On the contrary, the government's preferences were reflected in President Truman's verdict and Congressman Dondero's preventive actions. When Eisenhower became President, the official cultural climate became, perhaps, less hostile towards Abstract Expressionism but active public support was still not visible. The public abstention on this issue marks a point which is outside the range defined by the interval between *no obfuscation* and *total obfuscation*. If it is somewhere on the scale of obfuscation then it has to be to the right of *total obfuscation* (see Figure 4.6). Of course, both the G-curve and the L-curve have to be redefined for the cooperation of CIA, MoMA, and CCF on Cold War cultural policy. The G-curve reflects the votes gained from the supporting the Dondero-ish position which decrease if support becomes more and more obfuscated. The L-curve illustrates votes lost by those who were alienated by the statements on art and culture by the political establishment. Here we have to observe that an obvious difference between government officials and the opposition party on this issue did not exist.

There are redistributive effects of cultural policy, however, in general, they do not define majority interests. Non-singlepeakedness of preferences seem to be a more serious problem which politicians face who try to win an election. Often politicians are very hesitant to be explicit in this arena. In the case of Abstract Expressionism, however, preferences seemed to be single-peaked with a median at the Dondero-ish position. Correspondingly, the optimal obfuscation equilibrium is close to its left extreme. But the fast popularity gains of Abstract Expressionism in the second half of the 1940s and in the early 1950s show that these preferences were not stable; or at any rate where easy to destabilize by policies which relied on the evolutionary changes.

If the distance X'Z' is larger than EH, then Figure 4.6 indicates a corner optimum for the government related to *radical obfuscation* and the difference between the two measures expresses the benefits of secrecy as compared to *optimal obfuscation*. The G-curve shows vote gains which are identical to the vote gains of total obfuscation. In fact, we could even think that the vote gains for radical obfuscation are identical to the vote gains for the case of no obfuscation as the position of the government is not obfuscated. However, if government policy is only verbal, and hardly active, as in the case of Cold War cultural policy, many voters will decide on the basis of a different issue on allocating their votes. If so, then the government's vote gains out of cultural policy should be close to what it gains in case of total obfuscation. What really makes the difference between total obfuscation and radical obfuscation, is that government is not held responsible for developing the culture sector. Thus the L-curve should have a minimum with radical obfuscation. Of course, to accept the abstention of the government in active cultural policy presupposes that culture is foremost a private issue. This position is widely shared in the American society when culture is reduced to art.

Afterward

In 1966, a series of articles was published in the New York Times on the CIA's covert operations. Amidst reports on political assassinations and ruthless political intervention came details about the support which the CIA gave to the cultural sector. The upshot was that the moral authority which the intellectuals enjoyed during the height of the Cold War was "seriously undermined and frequently mocked" (Saunders 2000, 6). Was this intended? Or, was it just the consequence of a change in art style: from Jackson Pollock's *drippings* to Andy Warhols *Brillo Box* and his *Campbell's Soup Cans*, the latter perhaps more appropriate to reflect the consumerism of capitalism than the worship of colour and celebration of the lonely hero of the former.

References

Andreozzi, L. (2002), 'Society Saved by Children: The Role of Youngsters in the Generation of Scandals', in Holler, M.J. *Scandal and Its Theory II, Homo Oeconomicus* 19, 199-205, (Munich: Accedo-Verlag).

Binmore. K. (1998), 'The Evolution of Fairness Norms', *Rationality and Society* 10, 275-301.

Cockroft, E. (1974), 'Abstract Expressionism. Weapon of the Cold War', *Artforum* 12, 39-41.

Cox, A. (1983), *Art-as-Politics: The Abstract Expressionist Avant-Garde and Society* (Ann Arbor: University of Michigan Research Press).

Danto, A. (1992), *Beyond the Brillo Box: The visual Arts in Post-historical Perspective* (New York: Farrar Straus Giroux).

_______ (1999), *Philosophizing Art: Selected Essays* (Los Angeles and London: University of California Press).

de Hart Mathews, J. (1976), 'Art and Politics in Cold War America', *American Historical Review* 81, 762-87.

Gibson, A. (1997), *Abstract Expressionism. Other Politics* (New Haven and London: Yale University Press).

Golding, J. (2003), 'Divide and Conquer', *New York Review of Books* 50, 32-5.

Guilbaut, S. (1983), *How New York Stole the Idea of Modern Art* (Chicago: University of Chicago Press).

Hauptman, W. (1973), 'The Suppression of Art in the McCarthy Decade', *Artforum* 12, 48-52.

Hojman, D. (2002), 'Obfuscation, Inequality and Votes: A Model of Policy Choice Under Rent Seeking', *Liverpool Research Papers in Economics, Finance and Accounting, No: 0204*.

Holler, M. (2002), 'Artists, Secrets, and CIA's cultural policy,' in: Priddat, B. and Hegmann, H. (eds.), *Finanzpolitik in der Informationsgesellschaft. Festschrift für Gunther Engelhardt* (Marburg: Metropolis-Verlag).

_______ and Napel, S. (2001), 'On interpersonal comparison of value,' in Nevalainen, K. (ed.), *Justice, Charity, and the Welfare State: Moral and Social Dimensions* (*Acta Philosophica Fennica* 68), (Helsinki: Hakapaino).

_______ and Wickström, B.-A. (1999), 'The Use of Scandals in the Progress of Society' in Holler, M.J. *Scandal and Its Theory* (*Homo Oeconomicus* 16, 97-110, Munich: Accedo-Verlag).

Kozloff, M. (1973), 'American painting during the Cold War', *Artforum* 11, 43-54.

Magee, S. (1997), 'Endogenous Protection: The Empirical Evidence', in Mueller, D.C. (ed.), *Perspectives on Public Choice: A Handbook* (Cambridge: Cambridge University Press).

_______ Brock, W.A., Young, L. (1989), *Black Hole Tariffs and Endogenous Policy Theory* (Cambridge: Cambridge University Press).

Peters, R. (1997), 'The Stability of Networks: An Evolutionary Approach to Standardization", in Holler, M. and Niskanen, E. (eds.), *EURAS Yearbook of Standardization,* Vol 1, (Munich: Accedo-Verlag).

Riker, W. (1982), *Liberalism Against Populism* (San Francisco: Freeman).

Russell, J. (2002), 'Modern Art Groupie', Review of 'Art Lover: A Biography of Peggy Guggenheim, by Anton Gill', *New York Review of Books* 49, 23-25.

Saunders, F. (2000), *The Cultural Cold War. The CIA and the World of Arts and Letters* (New York: Free Press).

Tocqueville, A. (1835 and 1840/1956), *Democracy in America* (New York: Mentor Books).

Woods, G. (2002), 'Rambunctious American Democracy', *New York Review of Books* 49, 20-23.

Chapter 5

Jihad vs. McWorld: A Rational Choice Approach

Ronald Wintrobe[1]

Introduction

According to many, the fall in the costs of acquiring and transmitting information and of transacting across borders generally dictates, via the logic of economic efficiency, a global world order in which countries specialize according to comparative advantage and the international division of labour is as complete as possible. Part of this new order is that economic relations become as transparent as possible, since greater transparency implies lower transactions costs. Democracy, too, thrives on transparency, and dictatorship on obfuscation. Consequently, on this point of view, it is obvious that the new global world order must be governed by the most transparent systems possible, both to promote democracy and economic efficiency.[2]

To some extent, transparency and globalization go together in that both are the result of the information revolution. However, transparency is not the same thing as globalization – transparency, in part, is what many in the *anti* globalization movement want from organizations such as the IMF, the World Bank and the WTO with respect to their own deliberations. All of these organizations which 'manage' the international order have been accused of lack of transparency, perhaps most notably by Stiglitz (2002) in his powerful indictment of their operation. But with this qualification, transparency and globalization obviously belong together: both are the result of new technologies which reduce the costs of transmitting information via fax, email, internet, etc.

However, transparency is not always desirable, and it is surprisingly easy to think of examples of this undesirability. Here are a few:

1. In simple theoretical models, an increase in transparency is just as likely to

1 Previous versions of this chapter were presented at the Villa Colombella Seminar in September 2002, and at the meetings of the European Public Choice Society, April 2003. I am grateful to Geoffrey Brennan, David Hojman, Michael Parkin and participants in those seminars for helpful comments and suggestions. Any errors remain my own.

2 I conjecture that many, perhaps a majority of economists would subscribe to these views. Among the more well known advocates are Barro (1998), Bhagwati (2000), and Sachs (2000).

increase the volatility of prices as to decrease it (Furman and Stiglitz 1993).
2. Politicians are typically not transparent, even in democracies. In many models of democratic political competition, the strategy of ambiguity is preferable.[3]
3. Redistribution may sometimes be possible only with lack of transparency. Thus one reason for universal Medicare that is often mentioned is that only in this way can the poor be effectively insured. More generally, the desire to obfuscate the true level of redistribution is one reason why redistribution often takes place in kind and not in money.[4]

Another possibility, to which I shall return, is that while real transparency would indeed be nice, transparency as we know it is often an illusion. To illustrate, the surrealist painters knew that transparency was illusory, as shown by the painting *The Key to the Fields* (1936) by Rene Magritte of a window which is shattered but in which the shattered pieces of glass turn out to have been painted to look exactly like the landscape behind the window. Thus, before the window was broken, the glass appeared transparent but was actually opaque and therefore, in one sense, it revealed nothing. In another sense, the glass 'reflected' the landscape perfectly, since the painted glass and the landscape behind it were identical. So there is no mystery ... or is there?

Less poetically, the sometimes illusory quality of transparency is shown by the recent corporate scandals in the US in which billions of dollars in expenses somehow did not show up on the balance sheet as costs to the companies, and so the profits of the companies were considerably overstated. And could there be anything more surreal than the sight of powerful American CEOs in handcuffs being led off to jail? In turn, was this treatment a transparent warning to American executives to clean up their act? Or, as Paul Krugman has suggested[5] was it a trick to fool the voters into thinking something is being done when in fact very little is being done to solve this problem?

These scandals apart, many have suggested that the American system of political and corporate governance is the most transparent and, partly for that reason, the system of the future and to which the world is going to converge (e.g., De Souza 2002; Friedman 1999).Other systems of production, such as the Italian solidarity system, the German social democratic model, and East Asian systems like that in Japan and South Korea and that in China appear less transparent than the American way, but they have also been successful in terms of generating economic growth. These are often lumped together (apart from the Chinese system which is really a special case[6]) as 'stakeholder' systems in contrast to the American 'shareholder' system and I will follow this practice. The stakeholder system appears to combine

3 See for example, Glazer (1990); or Alesina and Cukierman (1990).

4 On the other hand, it is often asserted that paying merit differentials is easier with non-transparency: i.e., that only by rewarding merit *in secret* can merit pay be used at all.

5 *New York Times*, August 11, 2002.

6 The Chinese system is discussed below.

economic progress with a greater capacity to spread the wealth and to cushion the risks inherent in the market. Put simply, there seems to be greater solidarity in this type of system. Perhaps it is worth discarding a little transparency in exchange for more solidarity? On the other hand, economic growth in many European countries, especially Germany,[7] has stalled in recent years. And while some Asian countries with stakeholder – type systems have had spectacular growth, this sometimes seems to be either accompanied by corruption (South Korea) or authoritarianism (Singapore), or both (China). Indeed, in the most spectacular case of growth (China) it appears that growth is being pursued in part by 'liquidating' solidarity, as discussed below.

The outline of the chapter is as follows. In the next section I discuss several different meanings and contexts of the word 'transparency'. I then focus on one context: transparency in the system of political economy or political and corporate governance. I look at this issue through the lens of Benjamin Barber's analysis of globalization in his prophetic 1995 book, *Jihad vs McWorld.* In this context, transparency, now identified as the forces of McWorld, is pitted against another powerful force, jihad. I then outline this conflict in a more prosaic manner by identifying two broad systems, the shareholder and stakeholder systems, and suggests that the shareholder system is superior in terms of transparency. After that, I explain why the stakeholder system is better at generating and promoting solidarity. I then use this analysis to present a simple rational choice explanation of Barber's most obscure proposition – how McWorld actually stimulates jihad. In the last substantive section of the chapter, I turn to the solidarity system, and look at economic growth and corruption, particularly with respect to the Korean and Chinese systems, where there appears to have been both spectacular growth and a great deal of corruption. This raises a number of questions: if growth is what is desired, is corruption necessary for that growth, especially in the stakeholder system? Is this price worth paying? And is the American system, on the surface so transparent, free from this flaw?

The Meaning of Transparency and Its Role in Economic Systems

Dictionary definitions of transparency stress clarity and visibility: thus Webster's defines it as 'easily seen through, recognized, or detected'. Typical synonyms include 'clear, open', or 'visible'. In economics, transparency has recently become a 'buzz' word, especially since the 1997-8 East Asian crisis. It usually refers to the quality of information. Thus, Vishwanath and Kaufman (2001) suggest that transparency has a number of dimensions, such as the level of access to information, its comprehensiveness, relevance, quality and reliability. In political economy, it often refers to 'the absence of perceived corruption', which is what is measured by the Transparency International index (see for example: Lambsdorff 2002). Clearly, it is possible to have a lack of transparency in the first sense – obscurity – without necessarily implying the second – corruption. One oft-used illustration (e.g.

7 See Sinn (2002) for a discussion of the German case.

Furman and Stiglitz 1993) is the difficulty of reading the balance sheet of a Korean *Chaebol*.[8]

Yet another meaning of transparency arises from the fact that in many quarters the promotion of transparency is really a code word or Trojan horse for what I shall call, following Benjamin Barber, 'McWorld'. McWorld is shorthand for global, US style capitalism, its signature products like MTV, Coca Cola and Hollywood cinema ('McWorld's storyteller'), and most of all its way of life. Barber's book *Jihad* vs. *McWorld*, which appeared in 1995, seems to have foreseen the future as we are now experiencing it better than more famous prognosticators like Samuel Huntington and Frances Fukuyama. Barber saw a world increasingly pit between two alternatives:

> The first scenario ... holds out the grim prospect of a retribalization of large swaths of humankind by war and bloodshed: a threatened balkanization of nation-states in which culture is pitted against culture, people against people, tribe against tribe, a Jihad in the name of a hundred narrowly conceived faiths against every kind of interdependence, every kind of artificial social cooperation and mutuality. The second paints that future in *shimmering* pastels, a busy portrait of onrushing economic, technological, and ecological forces that demand *integration* and *uniformity* and that mesmerizes peoples everywhere with *fast* music, *fast* computers, and *fast* food – MTV, Macintosh, and McDonald's – pressing nations into one *homogenous* global theme park, one McWorld tied together by communications, information, entertainment, and commerce. Caught between Babel and Disneyland, the planet is falling precipitously apart and coming reluctantly together at the very same moment. (Barber, 1995, 4; italics added)

It is safe to say that the conflict between the two poles was not seen by the originators of the 'Washington consensus' – the recipe for what countries should do in order to prosper formalized in a set of conditions by the economist John Williamson (1990). Indeed, it is not obvious at all what the implications of jihad are for economic theory. The word jihad of course means struggle, usually with others in a common cause such as religion.[9]

With respect to McWorld, note that I have italicized all the phrases in the quote from Barber above which refer to its transparency. Some aspects of it include: 1) transparency requires *standardization* of inputs and outputs; this is what allows everything to be *fast* in the quote above; 2) transparency was not part of the original Washington consensus, but it is safe to assume it is part of the current one:[10] many have blamed lack of transparency for the depths of the 1997-8 East Asian crisis; 3) its illusory quality: thus McDonald's food is not really good; the cast of 'Friends' are not really representative of everyday American life nor will emulating them

8 But see below on the role of solidarity.

9 Wintrobe, 2006.

10 See Williamson (2000). The other major change in the ideas which make up the consensus is probably the idea, supported by people as diverse as Krugman, Bhagwati and Sachs that there is a fundamental difference between goods markets and capital markets and that the latter always need careful regulation (including the possibility of controls on international capital movements) whereas the former may not.

necessarily make you happy; if you buy a Lexus, beautiful women will not actually jump into the front seat beside you when you stop at a red light, and so on.

The more general point is that the forces of McWorld *promote* transparency, i.e., the more transparent the relationship the closer it gets to the kind of relationship characteristic of McWorld. Thomas Friedman (1999) sees economic transparency and political democratization being promoted through the globalization of capital markets – a process he calls 'globalution'. He suggests that the 'Electronic Herd' of international investors insist on transparency before they will invest in a country (Friedman 1999, 147ff) – especially since the East Asian crisis of 1997-8. The conventional interpretation of the role of transparency in that crisis is perhaps that while it is difficult to understand how lack of transparency could have *initiated* the crisis (Furman and Stiglitz 1993), there is evidence that the crisis lasted longer and was deeper in less transparent countries (Vishwanath and Kaufman 2001).

Jihad and McWorld are opposites in many respects, but in others they are similar. Both aspects are illustrated by the story Barber cites from a *New Republic* report by Slavenka Drakulic of Admira and Bosko, two young star-crossed lovers from Sarajevo:

> They were born in the 1960s. They watched Spielberg movies; they listened to Iggy Pop; they read John Le Carré; they went to a disco every Saturday night and fantasized about traveling to Paris or London. Longing for safety, it seems they finally negotiated with all sides for safe passage, and readied their departure from Sarajevo. Before they could cross the magical border that separates their impoverished land from the seeming sanctuary of McWorld, Jihad caught up to them. Their bodies lay along the river bank, riddled with bullets from anonymous snipers for whom safe passage signaled an invitation for target practice. The murdered young lovers, as befits émigrés to McWorld, were clothed in jeans and sneakers. So, too, one imagines, were their murderers. (Barber, 19)

Jihad and McWorld have other things in common besides blue jeans and sneakers: For one thing, *both forces are anti democratic*. We know from public choice theory that the "consumers" of McWorld don't make good citizens. Jihad is political but demands the subservience of individual values to a common, often authoritarian, cause. And to some extent, it is McWorld that makes jihad possible, which for some was the true meaning of September 11th.[11] It is not just that McWorld facilitates jihad by providing the means for messages to be broadcast and for terrorists to fly around the world, etc. (what Barber refers to as jihad *via* McWorld), though that is not unimportant. McWorld stimulates jihad. It is difficult to understand exactly why this might be so from Barber's dialectical arguments and poetic metaphors, but the essence of his argument seems to be that McWorld empties the body of its soul,

---

11 For others, (for example Adjami 2003), 9/11 was just a fight *within* Islam, which had really nothing to do with the United States except insofar as it insulted the religion and interfered with the expansion of Islamic religious rule, for example by stationing troops in the holy cities of Mecca and Medina.

which then craves jihad in order to restore it. I will return to this point below in the less poetic language of rational choice.

Social cohesion in the extreme form of jihad comes from struggle, but in less virulent forms it also comes from relationships to particular people, places or things. McWorld tends to destroy local relationships and particularity along with many sources of social cohesion like common pensions, welfare programs, etc, as we shall see later. This leaves the population, especially its less mobile elements, vulnerable to more extreme and less organized sources of social cohesion.[12] In production, it involves the substitution of general for specific human capital, thus obviating the need for implicit contracts or trust relationships within the firm. In consumption, Gertrude Stein's famous aphorism is perhaps never more true than of a (any) McDonalds's restaurant: there is (indeed, by design!) no 'there' there.

In addition, there is something Barber, a sociologist, doesn't mention, which is that markets are not free but require police and courts to enforce contracts. Those who protest against recent US foreign policies may not be against the US way of life as expressed in free markets and free expression but against the way America uses its enforcer role. That is, it is America's iron fist that they do not like. So, once account is taken of the idea that markets and property rights are not free, the correct analysis might be jihad *vs* jihad.

Is there a third way? Perhaps other systems can supply enough solidarity, along with reasonable economic growth, even though they are not perfectly transparent, so that the forces of jihad are not aroused? In that case, maybe it is one of these (European or Asian) systems, rather than the American shareholder system to which the world should look in the future? We begin our exploration of this possibility in the next section.

Shareholder vs. Stakeholder Systems

A contrast is often drawn between two types of systems – the American or shareholder system and a 'stakeholder' system characteristic of much of Europe and especially Japan and South Korea. In the shareholder system, the objective of the firm is said to be to the maximization of the value of the firm. However, such firms are often widely held, with no shareholder maintaining a controlling ownership and so there is considerable room for managerial objectives to enter the system (as discussed further below). In the stakeholder systems, by contrast, capital is typically raised through an affiliated bank, and the objectives of the firm are more complex, involving the interests of various stakeholders such as the bank and the firm's employees.

The two systems can be compared on three dimensions:(1) industrial relations; (2) corporate governance; and (3) the role of the government. To consider industrial relations first, the simplest way to derive the existence of the two types of system is via efficiency wage theory (Shapiro and Stiglitz 1984; Bulow and Summers 1986).

12 McWorld also makes many other kinds of relationships possible, such as email relationships or those within transatlantic groups such as the noted Villa Colombella Group.

In this line of thought, the productivity of employees is assumed to be difficult to measure. Firms are therefore faced with a potential shirking problem. A firm can deter employees from shirking basically in one of two ways: by monitoring them more closely or by paying them higher wages. Thus firms face a choice between: (1) relatively low pay combined with high monitoring, or (2) high pay and low monitoring. Gordon (1996) suggests that the industrial relations characteristic of different countries fall into these two types. For example he contrasts the low-wage, high monitoring system used especially in the shareholder systems of the US and Canada with the high-wage, low monitoring "stakeholder" system in Europe[13] and Asia. (Gordon, 1996, 85). To give some illustrations of magnitude, in 1980 the supervisory ratio in the US was about 11.5%, while real wages were virtually flat over the period 1973-89; in Germany the supervisory ration was about 3 percent and real wages increased over the period in question by about 3 percent *per annum*. Looking at a cross- section of 12 countries, they do seem to cluster into the two types and, as predicted, the average annual real wage change for production workers in manufacturing over the period 1973 to 1989 is negatively related to a measure of supervision – what Gordon calls the 'bureaucratic burden' – the percentage of total non-farm employment working in administrative and managerial occupations in 1980.

Like Americans, many Europeans are proud of their system and many European politicians especially in France and Germany are adamant that they do not wish to adopt the American system of industrial relations. The main problem that is often alluded to with respect to the European system is that growth has been stagnating there recently. However, many countries in Europe seem to be extremely reluctant to part with the solidarity features of the system. The history of recent labour market reforms in Germany illustrate this point,[14] as does continued opposition to a more 'flexible' system in France[15] and the recent struggle over the modification of Article 18 in Italy (which provides that an employee who is found to have been fired unjustly is entitled, not merely to compensation, but to have his job back).

The second difference between the two systems is the system of corporate governance. Under the stakeholder system, managers bear some responsibility towards their employees and to the affiliated bank which provides the firm with the capital. Both of these stakeholders often have a say in how the corporation is run. Under the US system, the manager or CEO is charged with the task of maximizing the value of the firm (as expressed by the share price) and is responsible only to its board of directors. However, the CEO is typically not the owner of the firm and so, as has been recognized ever since the work of Berle and Means in the 1930's, the manager may pursue his own, so-called 'managerial' objectives such as hiring excess staff or

---

13 Is it possible that European welfare state has grown up along with the 'stakeholder' production systems? Or that proportional representation and 'stakeholder' production relations go together?

14 See the *New York Herald Tribune* (August 17, 2002).

15 See Hoffman (2002).

building luxurious headquarters at the expense of those of the shareholders. This is perhaps the weakest point of the system as members of the board are often alleged to be "in the pocket" of the manager (that is the manager and the board constitute a solidarity group), or at least not sufficiently independent, well informed and active enough to credibly police his activity. One indication of this is that managers in the United States are hardly ever fired (Murphy 1999, 2543).

There are corrective mechanisms in the shareholder system, including incentives like stock ownership or options that are supposed to align the interests of the manager with the owners of the firm, and the possibility of hostile takeovers (the so-called 'market for corporate control'). One consequence of the first is that the pay of American executives, which is partly set by the executives themselves, is larger by an order of magnitude than compensation in Europe or Asia (Murphy 1999). The takeover mechanism is also deeply flawed on both theoretical and empirical grounds, as a substantial literature has now demonstrated.[16]

Finally, the third difference between the two systems is the role of the government. In Europe and most especially in some Asian countries like Japan and South Korea, the government takes a very active role in deciding matters of corporate policy, such as where investments are to be made, while in the shareholder system, intervention by the government is, by comparison highly limited.[17] In addition, democracy is more typically associated with the shareholder system than with at least some variants of the stakeholder system.

What does this have to do with transparency? It seems that in all three aspects, the American or shareholder system is more transparent. To take the industrial relations aspect first, the US system pays employees relatively low wages and monitors them intensively. Gordon's 'bureaucratic burden' is highest in the United States. Now, monitoring obviously requires transparency while higher wages do not.[18] The shareholder system therefore promotes transparency within the company partly

16 The basic theoretical problem with the market for corporate control, first pointed out by Grossman and Hart (1980), is that, for a hostile takeover bid to be successful, the firm's current shareholders would have to be induced to sell their shares to a group which is bidding for the firm with the aim of raising the value of those shares once the takeover is complete. So why would the current shareholders sell, unless the bidder offers them the entire value of the prospective improvement? But, if that is what has to be offered, what motive is there left for the bidder to take over the firm? Empirical evidence does bear out the prediction of these models that a substantial premium must be offered to the firm's existing shareholders. Other predictions of the models are more controversial. For a range of views, see, for example, the papers in *The Journal of Perspectives* symposium on this subject (Varian 1988).

17 Of course, there is a huge literature as to whether the increased role of the government has helped or hurt economic performance in the Asian countries. The classic references are Johnson (1982) and Wade (1990).

18 One might try to rationalize the combination of low pay for employees with enormous executive compensation packages if the actions of the CEO were harder to monitor by an order of magnitude than other employees. However, if it is the CEO who is to be held responsible for the performance of the firm as measured by its stock price, then this is obviously untrue as

in order to more easily monitor the activities of employees. In terms of corporate governance, the actions of corporate executives are said to be transparently reflected in the share price of the corporation, an easily observable number. By contrast, the competence of the CEO and the value of enterprises under the stakeholder system is much more difficult to ascertain. Finally, the greater role of the government in stakeholder systems muddies their transparency still further, as it becomes less obvious whether a policy or strategy was the business idea or was mandated by the government. The next section turns to the role of solidarity in the two systems.

The Role of Solidarity

No organization runs on formal relations alone, and all rely to a considerable extent on informal organization that enables them to function relatively smoothly.[19] One can express this point in various ways. One is that, in addition to monitoring and compensation, employees within both the shareholder and the stakeholder systems are members of *networks*, or will have accumulated *social capital* within the firm. Alternatively, as I suggest here, an element of *solidarity* – a particular type of network or form of social capital – is retained in both the shareholder and stakeholder systems. These bring a capacity to operate without constant formal instruction and approval, without which any organization will drown in red tape.

Solidarity denotes 'unity' or 'oneness of purpose'. The more solidarity there is among the members of a group, the more they are capable of cooperating as a group towards some common goal.[20] The desire for group identification seems to be a fundamental characteristic of human beings.[21] It has been demonstrated in very simple experiments, such as the one where pupils were sorted by their teacher into groups with brown eyes and those with blue eyes, and the individuals within each group immediately began distinguishing between 'insiders' and 'outsiders' based on eye colour.[22] The nature of the group identified with appears to be subject to wide variation. A hierarchy of groups with which individuals identify can be listed, including the family, workplace, religion, political party, sporting clubs, ethnicity and the nation state.

However, working against solidarity within any group is the well-known 'free rider' problem: even though individuals within the group are better off when the group prospers as a whole, any individual can always gain through the pursuit of individual advantage even when that conflicts with the interests of the group. In

---

this variable is easily observable. On the other hand, if the CEO is not the determining factor of the firm's value, why pay such high compensation?

19 Breton and Wintrobe (1982) developed the role of social capital networks in production, emphasizing that some networks or kinds of trust increase productivity while others reduce it. Here I am taking a simpler point of view.

20 A formal proof of this proposition can be found in Wintrobe (1998, Chapter 11).

21 Brown (1991).

22 Rubin (2002) reviews some of these experiments.

biology, this destroys the possibility of group selection (Williams 1966). In society, the pursuit of individual advantage can have the same effect on solidarity within groups. To put it simply, *markets do not create, but tend to destroy solidarity.*

Broadly speaking, I can think of three different mechanisms which generate group solidarity:

1. The first type are *mechanisms that ensure equality among the group* such as common pensions, universal Medicare, etc. The more everyone within a group receives exactly the same treatment, the less energy an individual in the group will put into trying to increase his or her own advantage at the expense of the group and the more will be put into seeking benefits for the group. Of course there is a free rider problem: each individual's attempt to maintain group solidarity benefits everyone in the group. If the group is large, free riding will limit the extent to which individuals will work for the group's advantage. However, as a substantial literature now demonstrates, there are various ways to overcome the free rider problem, including not only the classic Olsonian selective incentives but mobilization through networks and social ties (Opp and Hartmann 1989), and group leadership and the promise of rewards from successful action (Uhlaner 1989; Morton 1991; and Chong 1991). Given a constant level of these incentives, more equality of treatment within the group means more effort directed at group goals.
2. Group solidarity will also be larger, the larger the *barriers to entry and exit* from the group. The reasoning is similar: the harder it is to leave the group, the more members will be motivated to take measures that take care of it. The more membership is restricted, the less it will be felt that any improvement in the group's fortunes will be dissipated through opportunistic entry. Thus, the peculiar solidarity of ethnic groups comes from the fact that entry to and exit from the group are essentially blocked. And there are other ways to limit entry: among these must be included obfuscating the way the group works to outsiders, including in- group rituals and practices and in-group signals and symbolism. Groups also use stigma to raise the marginal rate of substitution of within-group consumption (as argued by Iannaccone (1992) for sects). Such practices make it more difficult for members of the group to interact pleasurably with outsiders and raise the value of in-group interaction.
3. Finally, and most obviously, group solidarity is most famously built through jihad against an external enemy, whether another nation, ethnic group, civilization, etc. The larger the perceived threat to individuals in the group from outside, the greater the solidarity of the group.[23]

23 I leave it to another occasion to consider the individual rationality of this response. After September 11th, it is particularly hard for North Americans to maintain that it does not exist.

To summarize, barriers to entry and exit, mechanisms to ensure equality and the struggle against an external enemy are alternative methods to raise solidarity. It follows that if one of the mechanisms becomes more costly to use, one or both of the others will be substituted for it. One implication is that it would be particularly important for the European Union, for example, in which historic enmities among the member countries have been foregone, to continue to subsidize the welfare state and labour market regulation if solidarity is to be maintained there. The next section discusses another implication of this argument.

How McWorld Stimulates Jihad

Now let us apply the reasoning of the last section to the industrial relations systems discussed earlier. What happens to the shareholder and stakeholder systems as the result of increased globalization (McWorld)? One important aspect of globalization is decreased transportation and information costs which also make it more feasible for companies to diversify production internationally. The result is an increase in the elasticity of demand for labour as firms can increasingly substitute foreign for domestic labour (Bhagwhati 2000; Rodrik 1997). This substitution is obviously easier in the shareholder system, in which workers do not have 'rights' to jobs and need not be compensated for their losses if terminated. Globalization insists on transparency, and this favours the expansion of the shareholder system as well. So globalization tends to favour the shareholder system over the stakeholder system.[24]

Globalization also changes the nature of both systems in that it reduces their demand for solidarity. Globalization detaches the CEO from relations within the firm and gives the firm a greater incentive to substitute non-specific for specific human capital (Cerny 1995).

Globalization also tends to inflate executive salaries in the shareholder system[25] and makes it more difficult for social capital to be created or maintained as it is more difficult to have exchanges between parties when they are very unequal (Zingales 2000). Finally the increased transparency demanded by McWorld reduces the forces making for social cohesion to the extent that social cohesion rests on equality and therefore requires that obvious inequalities be obfuscated.

For these reasons, then, globalization reduces the capacity of either system to generate solidarity via the mechanisms of equality of treatment within the firm, or raising barriers to entry and exit. It follows that the demand for solidarity via struggle

---

24 Some (for example Gilpin 2001) assert that the flashlight of transparency in Germany, along with increasingly high labour costs is pushing it towards the shareholder system. West Germany currently has the highest real wages in manufacturing world wide (Sinn 2002, 8).

25 Over the last 30 years the average annual salary in America expressed in 1998 dollars rose about 10% (from $32,522 to $35, 864). Over the same period the average real compensation of the top 100 CEO's in America went from $1.3 million (39 times the pay of an ordinary worker) to $37.5 million, more than 1000 times the pay of ordinary workers (Krugman 2002, 64).

against some external enemy is increased.[26] *Here, then, in rational choice terms, is how McWorld stimulates jihad.*

The same process presumably takes place at the national level. Thus the European welfare states build solidarity by providing pensions, Medicare, unemployment insurance and so forth. The American style system has fewer of these and considerably more inequality and real poverty (Alesina, Glaeser and Sacerdote 2001). The process of globalization, which to some extent spreads American style values (Friedman, 1999) of small government and flexible labour markets makes it more difficult for other countries to sustain different systems. If they do lose them, they may find that if their citizens have a real demand for solidarity, as I am suggesting in this chapter, jihad might have to take its place, as perhaps it has in America. Indeed, on this line of reasoning, it may be no accident that the previous peak of globalization occurred just before World War I.

If firms find it more difficult or are less interested in creating solidarity, other institutions will take their place if people have a real demand for solidarity as I assume they do. Moreover, the rent seeking activities of firms implies they need the support of politicians. So the partial withdrawal[27] of the firms from this task just increases the demand for other institutions to supply the needed solidarity. It follows that this task will increasingly fall to political and religious institutions.

It may be no accident, then, that the current United States administration makes war abroad at the same time as domestically it creates further opportunities and tax breaks for the rich.[28] In the absence of jihad against an external enemy, opposition to inequality – enhancing policies might spell their defeat. At the same time, the idea that competition against an external adversary can substitute for other solidarity-producing mechanisms explains how it can be that American conformism, noted since Tocqueville (who thought that America was the most conformist society he

---

26 It may be objected that there are probably other ways to create solidarity besides the three mentioned, so that if the first two become more difficult to do, others besides the third can be substituted. However, while this is surely true, the ones mentioned are not institutions but mechanisms, and they cover many of the institutions which can play this role. The easiest way to think about the proposition in the text is by analogy to the proposition in standard theory that an increase in the price of capital will raise the demand for labour. No doubt it will raise the prices of other factors of production as well, including some which are not usually mentioned in standard theory (Entrpreneurship? Organization?), and others which have yet to be discovered. But the basic proposition in the text still holds.

27 Firms as well as governments can use the principle of competition against an external enemy to substitute for equality mechanisms and barriers to entry and exit in creating solidarity within the firm.

28 Many analysts have noted that standard economic theories of the factors generating income inequality (skill- biased technical change, and increased international trade) cannot explain the recent increase in inequality in the U.S. (Krugman 2002) is one of these; he goes so far as to suggest that 'norms have unravelled' to explain it. So even if the present analysis is wrong, there is still a big problem which requires explanation.

had ever seen) can go hand in hand with the equally oft-noted competitiveness of American society.

Globalization not only acts as a tax on the mechanisms of equality and internal barriers to entry and exit, it may also act as a subsidy to the mechanism of jihad. Globalization helps in this task for both firms and governments by breeding contact with unfamiliar and little understood foreign entities which are easier to demonize as enemies than domestic competitors may be.[29]

Finally, the same process occurs again at the international level. The mechanisms of equality, barriers to entry and exit and jihad operate in all countries, and politicians, firms and religious leaders everywhere are eager to satisfy their citizens demands for solidarity. Dictatorships no less than democracies are interested in building support through this mechanism.[30] It follows that politicians everywhere are more eager to embrace the principle of jihad in a more globalized world. In turn, the interests of firms and politicians in potentially opposing sets of countries intertwine. As Posen (1993) was the first to note, the 'security dilemma' operates equally well with social cohesion (solidarity) instead of armaments. The social cohesion (solidarity) of armies is a prime element in their effectiveness. Increased social cohesion in one country therefore can be threatening to other countries if they are potential victims of aggression. So the increased cohesion in the threatening country stimulates increased solidarity in the threatened country in turn, which then causes solidarity to increase further in the threatening country and so on in an upward spiral.[31]

On this way of thinking, the 'Clash of Civilizations' discussed in Huntington's celebrated 1996 book of that title is not an inevitable outcome of differences among peoples but of political processes which have at their root a desire on the part of their citizens for solidarity. This desire is frustrated by the destruction to equality-enhancing processes and barriers to entry and exit caused by increased globalization, leaving only jihad to satisfy it. Similarly, people's needs for solidarity and what the exploitation of these can lead to may be what is left out of the optimistic predictions of an 'End of History' and the triumph of liberal democracy, or, more generally for a world increasingly characterized by democracy, human rights, free markets and

---

29 Many studies have been undertaken to investigate whether trade between countries stimulates friendship (the so-called "contact" hypothesis) or hostility, with the results approximately evenly divided between these two results (the studies are reviewed in detail in Forbes (1997). So if trade does not necessarily bring friendship even when there are mutual gains, it seems reasonable to suppose that the balance can easily be tipped towards hostility when this factor is absent, and there is a political intent to demonize. This is the justification for the conjecture in the text.

30 Whether dictatorships do this more or less than democracies is an interesting question. Dictatorships are more capable of imposing barriers to entry and exit from their societies. On this ground, their leaders should be less interested in jihad. But inequality tends to be greater under dictatorship, leading to the opposite prediction.

31 Elsewhere (Wintrobe 2002) I applied this way of thinking to the interaction between Serbs and Croatians which led to the spread, like 'wildfire' as it is often put, of nationalism in Serbia under Milosevic.

the peaceful resolution of conflicts by international institutions such as the Security Council.

Asian Growth Through Corruption: A Fourth Way?

Corrupt Tigers

The previous section suggested that two of the dynamic features of the American system – its openness, and its relative absence of a social safety net, come at a cost: a reduction in solidarity. The social welfare states of 'Old Europe' do not face this problem to the same degree. However, this analysis has been developed without reference to corruption, as is standard in the literature. But it is time to introduce it. In the stakeholder system, exchanges are made and enforced along network lines, in contrast to law-backed exchanges characteristic of the shareholder system. Network exchanges are often made in secret and enforced by informal mechanisms, and these kinds of exchanges lend themselves most easily to corruption.

Tanzi (1995, 167) defines corruption as 'the intentional non-compliance with the arms- length principle aimed at deriving some advantage for oneself or for related individuals from this behaviour'. He points out that the word 'corruption' comes from the Latin verb to break, *rumpere.* It thus implies that something – a rule, moral code, a promise, is broken in a corrupt act. Corruption also often means doing a favour for someone. In societies with high levels of social capital (solidarity), networks or connections among family and friends tend to be more extensive. Consequently such societies are especially prone to corruption.

To illustrate, among countries with extensive high growth experience the Italian economy has, somewhat surprisingly, been a standout in Europe and per capital growth there is now suggested to have been the largest in Europe since World War II. But Italy has also had many problems with corruption, as illustrated by the extensive scandals opened up by the *Mani Pulite* investigations (see Della Porta and Vanucci 1997).

The countries with the best growth performance over the last two decades or so are the Asian 'tigers'. At one time it was said that these countries grew quickly because there was less rent seeking there, thanks in some cases at least to the presence of authoritarian but efficiency minded dictatorships (Haggard 1990; Bardhan 1997). Bureaucrats in these countries were lauded for their neutrality, and it was said – and still is being said, for example, by Barro (1998) – that authoritarianism eliminated or at least reduced the rent seeking to be found in the corrupt democracies in the West. However, this myth seems to have come under a cloud recently. For example, while Singapore may indeed be the closest approximation to the myth, here is Lee Kwan Yew himself, responding to a 1996 report that his son, Deputy Minister Lee Hsien Loong accepted discounts of more than $700,000 in a soft sale of condominiums conducted before bids were opened to the public: 'I am me. It's not a level playing field' (quoted in Hutchcroft 1997, 223).

With respect to South Korea in particular, David Kang's detailed investigations (2002a and 2002b) have exploded the idea that Korea grew because its bureaucrats were neutral. His study shows that, as he puts it, 'Corruption was rampant, and the Korean state intervened in the way it did because doing so was in the interests of a small group of business and political elites' (Kang 2002, 178). The high-growth era is thought to have started with the Park regime. Kang's account of the process is straightforward: 'The basic process was simple: Business and political elites exchanged bribes for political favours. Businessmen used the rents from cheap capital to expand as rapidly as possible, thus ensuring their continued political and economic importance. Development and money politics proceeded hand in hand.' (Kang 2002, 185).

The extent of the corruption of the political process appears remarkable. According to Kang, leading members of the Democratic Republican Party took massive donations from the *chaebol* in return for loans and sweetheart deals. If businessmen did not provide sufficient funds when asked, the Bank of Korea called in their loans, or they suffered a tax audit, or their subsidy application was denied (Kang 2002, 186-7). But politicians did not dominate the process. Rather, business and the state were partners. The result was massive, probably excessive expansion of industrial capacity.

How could such rent seeking account for what is certainly one of the biggest success stories among the tigers? If one thinks about it, it is not hard to understand why economic growth could have been high at the same time as the state was handing out contracts in exchange for bribes. Growth benefits capital owners (producers) more than labour because the increased value of assets in the future implied by economic growth can be immediately capitalized into the price of capital assets today, whereas the increased value of labour or other assets such as a cleaner or safer environment can be realized only over time. Thus, if investment decisions by the government are based on bribes, it is to be expected that business groups will offer the most compared to labour or environmental groups and it is no accident that such a system, while corrupt, can result in a high rate of investment and growth.

Economists have been somewhat blind to this possibility since they have focused on the costs of 'rent seeking'. But in South Korea this process was well controlled under the authoritarian regimes and centralized in the highest offices of the party. Thus there was no unseemly rent seeking in the classic sense of a wasteful expenditure on lawyers and lobbyists to get the ear of the political party: the bribes were coming from the six or seven top *chaebols* and no other group need have bothered to bid. Secondly, since it was all cash, there was technically no waste in the economic sense – just a transfer from one party to another. And thirdly, since the firms providing the bribes were doing so in order to obtain investment funds, the process may have stimulated growth.

Campos and Root (1996) explain the performance of the 'tigers' in general by the idea that growth in these countries is shared, and in general I suspect that there is a great deal of truth to this view. There is no doubt, for example that real wages in South Korea have increased enormously over the last 40 years or so (see the figures in Sachs and Radelet 1998). This sharing is what makes the solidarity system so attractive. But the exposure of the corruption casts a shadow both on the idea that sharing was chiefly responsible for the spectacular growth performance and, in general, on the desirability of at least the East Asian version of stakeholder capitalism. And it is not comforting that the amount of corruption seems to have multiplied with the turn to democracy (Kang 2002, 196ff).

Corrupt Communist Chinese Capitalists

Perhaps the most remarkable story of growth over the last 20 years or so has been that of mainland China. Here there is no mystery about corruption to be exposed: China has been consistently ranked one of the most corrupt countries in the world since the indexes were begun. Yet its growth rate over the last 20 years or so has been spectacular. How is this to be explained? China's policies certainly do not conform to the prescriptions of the Washington consensus. And one cannot assert that the Communist Chinese bureaucrats, who still seem to control the political system even though central planning is dead and the state enterprises are in steep decline, are immune to offers of bribes or favours in exchange for rents. The system is *based* on the exchange of bribes and favours for rents.[32]

Some explanations have been offered: Fan and Grossman (2001, 8) argue that corruption provides an efficient inducement to local officials to promote economic reform that satisfies the objectives of the Communist Party. Their central claim is that 'those local officials who make the largest economic contribution are likely to be able to extract the largest bribes or nepotistic favours or to have the most valuable public property to appropriate'. However, the theoretical basis for this argument seems to be a little thin. Would the authors recommend, say, giving US customs officials the right to receive bribes as well? Why not, if it stimulates economic growth? And what they refer to as the 'evidence' for the efficiency claim – that the Chinese authorities have promoted fiscal decentralization, that there is no alternative incentive scheme, and that the authorities do not enforce anti corruption measures (12) – is entirely consistent with another hypothesis: corruption is widespread within the system, and no one has both the power and the desire to do anything about it.

Perhaps a more satisfactory line of thought is related to the idea that, possibly even more than South Korea, China has a powerful and authoritarian government that controls the corruption process. In bribery monopoly is better than competition. Under competition, so many bribes may be required that no investment project goes through. Perhaps the typical outcome of competitive bribery is illustrated by Peru, where competition in corruption has produced 'dead' capital, as discussed by De Soto (2000). So part of the explanation of how corruption works to promote growth in China is that the corruption is still tightly controlled by the Party.

Another piece of the puzzle is the increased prevalence of illegal asset-stripping, in which managers 'appropriate' the assets of SOE's (state enterprises) for their

32 A comprehensive picture of the process is presented in Lin (2001).

private use. In this way state assets are privatized. But the process destroys trust and solidarity. One description of this process is by Chen (1999). He notes that labour protests have increased in the 1990's by 'quantum leaps', involving over 3.6 million workers in 1998 alone, and explains these protests as follows. In pre-reform China, the crucial dimension of state-labour relations was an 'all-encompassing dependency of labour on the state enterprise' (Chen 1999, 43), in which workers receive medical care, housing, pensions and so on from the firm (what Andrew Walder calls 'neo-traditionalism'). The 1987 'Optimal Combination' reform, designed to reduce the excess workforce in state enterprises, gave managers the power to dismiss workers, but also insisted that a minimal living allowance be given to the laid off (Chen 1999, 46). However, in the 1990's many firms reneged on this obligation, and indeed many began not to pay the workers still employed by the firm or workers' pensions at all, claiming they had to reduce costs in order to be competitive in the market. At the same time, in many of these factories, managerial asset-stripping has become extensive. This takes various forms:

> In some cases, managers transfer the most profitable activities of the SOE's to their own businesses, leaving the debts with the parent enterprise, which eventually has to close down. In others, managers spend enterprise funds without restraint on luxury housing, extravagant entertaining, free overseas travel, and so on. Many managers become wealthy while their employees are close to liquidation. They are, in a phrase used by workers, 'rich Buddhist abbots in poor temples' (Chen 1999, 51).

Chen's study found that the circumstances which were particularly likely to give rise to protests were the combination of managers reneging on obligations to the workers along with evidence of managerial asset-stripping. In many cases, the Party has to intervene to prevent the demonstrations from getting out of control. A worker from Jianxi province told an interviewer:

> How pitiful we workers are! But how about the cadres? They are gambling, womanizing, living in luxury houses, and driving fancy cars. Where does that money come from? They cannot possibly earn that amount of money even in ten thousand years. What do we workers hope for? We hope that there will be another cultural revolution and all those corrupt cadres will be killed! (quoted in Chen 1999, 51).

Analyses and stories of asset -stripping abound in recent issues of Chinese economic journals (e.g. Wang 2002; Ding 2002; and especially He Qinglian's monumental 'China's Descent Into a Quagmire' serialized in three parts in *The Chinese Economy* (2000-2001)). He traces the rise of asset stripping to the introduction of 'shareholding' into state enterprises. The story, with its accompanying naiveté about the workings of corporate governance in shareholder systems, will be familiar to those who followed the privatization process in Russia:[33]

33 The case of Russia is discussed in Wintrobe (1998b).

> This system was seen by its creators as the "ruby slippers" (*fabao)* that would bring about a magical transformation in state-owned enterprises. The traditional role of 'shareholding' for raising capital was, in the eyes of both officials and economists in China, of only secondary consideration ... government officials and economists optimistically forecast that once shareholders gained the relevant property rights as owners, the management, development, and distribution of wealth generated by the entire enterprise would be under strict supervision by the newly created shareholders, thereby making management responsible to both its superiors (the board of directors) and its subordinates (employees). The latter in particular would become the new "masters of the enterprise as their buying and selling of shares in the market would lead to constant supervision and monitoring of enterprise efficiency" (He Qinglian, 2001, 35).

Instead, what seems to have happened is the liquidation of debts and of trust within the party, as exemplified by the actions of the manager in Chen's labour protest story. Workers who have laboured for many years, accumulating capital within the party by receiving wages below their marginal productivity, and expected that in their senior years they would be compensated for this in the form of a pension and care in their old age courtesy of the 'neo-traditional' paternalistic factory system. Instead, it appears that many managers are in effect appropriating the employees' firm-specific capital. Unlike the Russian case, in the Chinese case, there is economic growth to accompany the corruption. However, even in the Chinese case, it seems that this growth may not benefit the workers. A proper "growth accounting" story would factor in the loss of trust solidarity in the process of asset-stripping, losses as real from the economic point of view as the loss of a building or any other capital asset (Shleifer and Summers 1988). Thus to the extent that the growth has taken place via what might be called the *liquidation of solidarity*, it may not be real. Finally, it may be sowing the seeds of jihad. Indeed some observers claim that nationalism in China appears to be growing extremely rapidly (for example Cooper 2002, 25).

Pitfalls in the Analysis

The argument of the next-to-last section is, in effect, that if a country wants growth, why not try corruption? Before embracing this formula, however, it might be worthwhile to look at some pitfalls. The first is that measured growth via corruption is not necessarily real growth once the losses to the economy from the liquidation of trust or solidarity are factored in. And the distributional consequences are particularly likely to be unfavourable with this style of growth. The stories about what is happening to many employees of state owned enterprises in China provide sobering illustrations of these points.

Secondly, there is an alternative possibility about corruption: that it takes place, and the economy doesn't grow at all, or even declines. Many Arab and African countries are the most outstanding examples. Apart from some of the suggestive ideas referred to in the previous section, no one knows why some corrupt countries grow while others do not. Mauro's oft-cited (1995) evidence is that on balance, corruption is inimical to growth.[34]

The other possibility is that corruption will severely impair the society. In this connection, Lambsdorff (undated) suggests that corruption may be more costly than rent seeking, in that it can motivate the creation of monopolies and regulations to obtain bribes. The capacity for people to cheat each other as corruption grows in China is, on some accounts, growing by leaps and bounds. One possibility is that China is getting stuck in an equilibrium corruption trap. Another is that the practices there are laying the ground for Chinese jihad.

Conclusion

Economic systems can grow, or not, in a variety of ways. The shareholder/transparent system favoured by McWorld and the stakeholder system are two of these. The stakeholder system appears superior in that there is some commitment to equality of treatment, which builds solidarity, and therefore reduces the potential for jihad. The main danger with the solidarity system is that growth may be stymied. The system also has greater potential for corruption, since network exchange tends to be secret and informally enforced.

Moreover, under both systems, one group of actors can appropriate the capital value of mutual trust and destroy the trust in the process. Arguably, this is what took place in the United States under the 'downsizing' phenomenon and again with the recent accounting scandals, with the privatization process in Russia, and appears to be happening now with the process of asset-stripping in China. In the United States, downsizing allowed the executives of the firms to raise their own salaries by firing their employees. In Russia, the privatization of state assets before proper institutions were in place allowed insiders to buy control of the firms at bargain prices and strip them of their assets. In China, the same process of asset-stripping appears to be going on but the result is growth partly because the Communist Party retains overall control over the process. However, there is some evidence that corruption is reaching new heights in the process and there is a danger that the system will fall into a corrupt equilibrium or quagmire.

Globalization demands transparency and thus favours the expansion of the transparent system. The challenge facing the solidarity system is to find ways to promote growth that do not involve corruption. The challenges facing the transparent system are to show that its transparency is not illusory, and to find ways of promoting solidarity within the system apart from the promotion of external enemies. Otherwise the forces of jihad may not be contained.

---

34 Some questions about the magnitude, though not the direction, of Mauro's numbers has been raised by Hongyi Li, Kixin Colin Xu and Heng-Fu Zou, (2000).

References

Alesina, A. and Cukierman, A. (1990), 'The Politics of Ambiguity', *Quarterly Journal of Economics* 105:4, 829-51.

_______, Glaeser, E. and Sacerdote, B. (2001), 'Why Doesn't the United States Have a European-Style Welfare State?', *Brookings Papers on Economic Activity*, 2, 187-279.

_______, and Wacziarg, R. (2000), 'The Economics of Civic Trust', in Pharr, S. and Putnam, R. (eds.).

Auerbach, A. (ed.). *Corporate Takeovers: Causes and Consequences.* (Chicago: University of Chicago Press).

Barber, B. (1995), *Jihad vs. McWorld: How Globalism and Tribalism Are Reshaping the World.* (New York: Ballantine Book).

Barro, R. (1996) 'Democracy and Growth', *Journal of Economic Growth*, Vol.1.

_______, (1998), *Getting It Right: Markets and Choices in a Free Society.* (Cambridge, MA: MIT Press).

Bhagwati, J. (2000), *The Wind of the Hundred Days.* (Cambridge, MA: MIT Press).

Breton, A. and Wintrobe, R. (1982), *The Logic of Bureaucratic Conduct. An Economic Analysis of Competition, Exchange, and Efficiency in Private and Public Organizations.* (New York: Cambridge University Press).

Brown, D. (1991), *Human Universals.* (New York: McGraw Hill).

Bulow, J. and Summers, L. (1986), 'A Theory of Dual Labor Markets with Applications to Industrial Policy, Discrimination, and Keynesian Unemployment', *Journal of Labor Economics* 4, 376-414.

Campos, E. and Root, H. (1996), *The Key to the Asian Miracle: Making Shared Growth Credible.* (Washington: Brookings).

Cerny, P. (1995), 'Globalization and the Changing Logic of Collective Action', *International Organization* 4, 595-625.

Chen, F. (2002), 'Subsistence Crises, Managerial Corruption, and Labour Protests in China', *The China Journal*, 48.

Chong, D. (1991), *Collective Action and the Civil Rights Movement.* (Chicago: University of Chicago Press).

Copper, J. (2002), 'The "Glue" That Holds China Together', *The World And I*, 17:7, 20-5 (Washington: The Washington Times Corporation).

Della Porta, D. and Vanucci, A. (1997), 'The Perverse Effects of Political Corruption', in Hutchcroft, P. (ed).

De Soto, H. (2000), *The Mystery of Capital.* (New York: Basic Books).

Ding, X. (2000), 'The Illicit Asset-Stripping of Chinese State Firms', *The China Journal*, 1-28.

D'Souza, D. (2002), *Culture and Prosperity.* (Washington: Regnery Publishing).

Fiorentini, G. and Peltzman, S. (eds.) *The Economics of Organized Crime.* (New York: Cambridge University Press).

Forbes, H. (1997), *Ethnic Conflict: Commerce, Culture and the Contact Hypothesis.* (New Haven: Yale University Press).

Friedman, T. (1999), *The Lexus and The Olive Tree: Understanding Globalization.* (New York: Farrar, Straus Giroux).

Fukuyama, F. (1995), *Trust: The Social Virtues and the Creation of Prosperity.* (London: Hamish Hamilton).

Furman, J. and Stiglitz, J. (1998), 'Economic Crises: Evidence and Insights From East Asia', *Brookings Papers In Economic Activity* 2, 1-137.

Galeotti, G., Salmon, P., and Wintrobe, R. (eds.) (2000), *Competition and Structure. Essays in Honor of Albert Breton.* (New York: Cambridge University Press).

Gibson, J. (1992), 'The Political Consequences of Intolerance: Cultural Conformity and Political Freedom', *American Political Science Review* 86, 338-56.

Gilpin, R. (2001), *Global Political Economy.* (Princeton: Princeton University Press).

Glazer, A. (1990), 'The Strategy of Candidate Ambiguity', *American Political Science Review* 84, 237-42.

Gordon, D. (1996), *Fat and Mean.* (New York: The Free Press).

Grossman, S. and Hart, O. (1980), 'Takeover Bids, the Free-Rider Problem, and the Theory of the Corporation', *Bell Journal of Economics*, 42-64.

Haggard, S. (1990), *Pathways From the Periphery: The Politics of Growth In the Newly Industrialized Countries.* (New York: Cornell University Press).

Heywood, P. (ed.) (1997), *Political Corruption.* (Oxford: Blackwell).

Hoffman, S. (2002), 'The Clash of Globalizations', *Foreign Affairs*, 104-115.

Huntington, S. (1996), *The Clash of Civilizations and the Remaking of World Order.* (New York: Simon and Schuster).

Hutchcroft, P. (ed.) (1997), *Political Corruption.* (Oxford: Blackwell).

Iannaccone, L. (1992), 'Sacrifice and Stigma: Reducing Free Riding in Cults, Communes and Other Collectives', *Journal of Political Economy*, 100, 271-91.

Johnson, C. (1982), *MITI And the Japanese Miracle: The Growth of Industrial Policy 1925-1975.* (Stanford, CA: Stanford University Press).

Kang, D. (2002a), 'Bad Loans to Good Friends: Money Politics and the Developmental State in South Korea', *International Organization* 56, 177-207.

_______ (2002b), *Crony Capitalism: Corruption and Economic Development in South Korea and the Philippines.* (New York: Cambridge University Press).

Knack, S. and Keefer, P. (1997), 'Does Social Capital Have an Economic Payoff?', *Quarterly Journal of Economics*, 112, 1251-89.

Krugman, P. (2002), 'For Richer: How the Permissive Capitalism of the Boom Destroyed American Equality', *New York Times Magazine.*

Lambsdorff, J. (2002), 'Corruption and Rent-Seeking', *Public Choice* 113:1/2, 97-125.

Lin, Yi-Min (2001), *Between Politics and Markets: Firms, Competition and Institutional Change in Post - Mao China.* (New York: Cambridge University Press).

Li, H., Colin Xu, K. and Zou, H-F. (2000), 'Corruption, Income Distribution and Growth', *Economics and Politics*, 12, 155-82.

Mauro, P. (1995), 'Corruption and Growth', *Quarterly Journal of Economics* 109, 681-712.

Morton, R. (1991), 'Groups in Rational Turnout Models', *American Journal of Political Science* 35, 758-76.

Mueller, D. (1989), *Public Choice II.* (New York: Cambridge University Press).

Murphy, K. (1999), 'Executive Compensation', in Ashenfelter, O. and Card, D. (eds.) *Handbook of Labor Economics,* Vol. 3B (Amsterdam: Elsevier), 2486-557.

O'Meary, P. et al. (eds.) (1999), *Globalization and the Challenges of a New Century.* (Bloomington: Indiana University Press).

Opp, K-D., and Hartmann, P. (1989), *The Rationality of Political Protest: A Comparative Analysis of Rational Choice Theory.* (Boulder, Colorado: Westview Press).

Pharr, S and Putnam, R. (eds.) (2000), *Disaffected Democracies: What's Troubling the Trilateral Countries?* (New Jersey: Princeton University Press).

Posen, B. (1993), 'The Security Dilemma and Ethnic Conflict', *Survival* 35, 27-47.

Qinglian, H. (2000, 2001) 'China's Descent Into A Quagmire', *The Chinese Economy*, Part 1, 33, (May-June); Part 2, 34, (March-April), and Part 3, 34, (July-August).

Rodrik, D. (1997), *Has Globalization Gone Too Far?* (Washington, DC: Institute for International Economics).

Rubin, P. (2002), *Darwinian Politics.* (New Brunswick: Rutgers University Press).

Sachs, J. (1999), 'International Economics: Unlocking the Mysteries of Globalization', in O'Meary, P. et al. (eds.).

_______, and Radelet, S. (1998), 'The East Asia Financial Crisis: Diagnosis, Remedies, Prospects', *Brookings Papers on Economic Activity*, 1-90.

Shleifer, A. and Summers, L. (1988), 'Breach of Trust in Hostile Takeovers', in Auerbach, A. (ed.).

Sinn, H-W. (2002), 'Germany In The World Economy – Hope Springs Eternal', *Supplement to CESifo Forum*, 3.

Stiglitz, J. (2002), *Globalization and Its Discontents.* (New York: Norton).

Uhlaner, C. (1989), 'Rational Turnout: The Neglected Role of Groups', *American Journal of Political Science* 33, 390-422.

Tanzi, V. (1995), 'Corruption: Arms Length Relationships and Markets', in Fiorentini, G. and Peltzman, S. (eds.), 161-80.

Varian, H. (ed.) (1988), 'Symposium on Takeovers', *Journal of Economic Perspectives*, 2:1.

Vishwanath, T. and Kaufman, D. (2001), 'Towards Transparency: New Approaches and Their Application to Financial Markets', *The World Bank Research Observer* 16, 41-57.

Wade, R. (1990), *Governing the Market: Economic Theory and the Role of Government in East Asian Industrialization.* (Princeton: Princeton University Press).

Wang, X. (2002), 'The Post-Communist Personality: The Specter of China's Capitalist Market Reforms', *The China Journal*, 5-21.

Williams, G. (1966), *Adaptation and Natural Selection: A Critique of Some Current Evolutionary Thought.* (Princeton: Princeton University Press).

Williamson, J. (1990), 'What Washington Means By Policy Reform', in Williamson, J. (ed.).

_______, (ed.) (1990), *Latin American Adjustment: How Much Has Happened?.* (Washington, DC: Institute for International Economics).

_______, (2000), 'What Should The World Bank Think About The Washington Consensus?', *The World Bank Research Observer* 15, 251-64.

Wintrobe, R. (1998a) *The Political Economy of Dictatorship.* (New York: Cambridge University Press).

_______, (1998b), 'Privatization, The Market For Corporate Control and Capital Flight From Russia', *The World Economy* 21, 603-13.

_______, (2000), 'Downsizing Trust', in Galeotti, G., Salmon, P., and Wintrobe, R. (eds.).

_______, (2002a), 'The Contest For Power: Human Rights and Economic Efficiency', Paper delivered at the 2002 meetings of the American Economic Association, Atlanta.

_______, (2002b), 'Slobodan Milosevic and the Fire of Nationalism', *World Economics* 3:3. 1-27.

_______, (2006), 'Extremism, Suicide Terror, and Authoritarianism', *Public Choice*, 168 (1-2), 168-95.

Zingales, L. and Rajan, R. (2000), 'The Tyranny of Inequality: An Inquiry Into the Adverse Consequences of Power Struggles', *Journal of Public Economics* 76, 521-58.

PART 3
Corruption

Chapter 6

Invisible Feet and Grabbing Hands: The Political Economy of Corruption and Welfare

Johann Lambsdorff[1]

Introduction

Corruption involves the malfunctioning of some (or all) areas of the public sector. Crucial to this malfunctioning is that individuals or whole units within these sectors are serving themselves, and not the public. Those who study the effects of corruption on welfare are confronted with a multitude of models. Since each has its specific benefits and deficiencies, the adequate choice of a model is complicated and crucial at the same time. This study reviews various different approaches; it aims at providing a guided tour for researchers seeking an appropriate model for their purpose. At the same time this study argues that corruption is always detrimental to welfare, but the precise reason for this impact depends heavily on the model chosen.

This study is organized as follows. First, I discuss the causes of corruption and government malfunctioning. I claim that a sound assessment of the affects of corruption on public welfare remains inconclusive when regulations are considered exogenous to the analysis. This results because corruption and bad regulation are often two sides of the same coin. A principal-agent model is taken as a framework of analysis for the subsequent sections, where four different models are used to analyze the effects of corruption. The first model assumes a self-serving agent and the government taking the role of the principal. Welfare losses result from informational asymmetries. Corruption constrains the contractual space available to agents and principals and disallows agents to commit themselves to honest dealings. A second model builds on the assumption that the principal is himself self-serving. Such principals may be unable to credibly commit themselves to effective policies, discouraging sunk investments. The wish to serve oneself will in reality be an issue for both actors, principal and agent. Instead of an intrinsic motivation to benevolent actions, actors may be extrinsically constrained to serve the public. In a third model,

1 The author is grateful to J. Ahrens, V. De Bonis, C. Schinke, M. Schinke and A. Schmidt for helpful discussions.

the role of competition for the principal's position is investigated. Competition may provide an effective constraint to self-serving. But competition may also bring about waste, as suggested by rent-seeking theory. A fourth model assumes that an agent may be able to obtain a more powerful position. This can also constrain the principal, but other welfare losses are likely to arise. I argue that the agent's self-serving is likely to bring about x-inefficiency, while the principal's self-serving will largely lead to allocative inefficiency. It will be concluded that depending on the role of government the adverse effects of corruption on public welfare can be substantially different. An immediate effect of corruption is that it renders governments unable or unwilling to maximize welfare. But the reasons for welfare losses are different for these types of corruption.

Corruption and Market Distortions

Corruption commonly entails the providing of a service by a public servant or politician in exchange for a bribe. As long as this takes place voluntarily, both actors will be better off, making it arduous to argue that net public welfare suffers. Negative externalities may be imposed on others, for example on unsuccessful competitors that were better qualified than a bribe paying firm. Taking this into account, a common conclusion is that the total effect of corruption cannot be determined *a priori* but depends on the size of externalities. Given circumstances of cumbersome regulation, excessive bureaucracy or market restrictions some economists tended to emphasize the positive effects of corruption (Bayley 1966; Nye 1967; Huntington 1968; Leff 1964; Morgan 1964). Crucial for these effects is the existence of market distortions caused by government intervention disallowing markets to equalize supply and demand and efficiently allocate resources. In such an environment corruption is a symptom of inadequate state intervention (Ades and Di Tella 1999). Externalities arise due to such inappropriate intervention, while corruption helps to open up new contractual possibilities, re-establishing market efficiency. Corruption has even gained recognition in economic textbooks. Mankiw (2000, 123) argues that with regard to state imposed price ceilings on rental fees '... bribes bring the total price ... (including the bribe) closer to the equilibrium price.'

This argument is too brief to be given credibility. In the case of quantity restrictions (for example in import markets) or price ceilings, corruption can be a consequence of state intervention. But as a simple microeconomic analysis suggests, the price that results with corruption is not the initial equilibrium price in an undisturbed market, because bribes act like a wedge between the price suppliers are requesting and the price customers are willing to pay. Due to the artificial scarcity imposed by state intervention, the price (including the bribe) customers must pay is larger than the initial equilibrium price. Equally, the quantity exchanged will not regain its original level. Certainly, assuming pre-existing market distortions to be sufficiently large, it is trivial to conclude that society may be better off with corruption rather than excessive state intervention.

But these arguments require that corruption is caused by superfluous regulation and bothersome government intervention, while, in turn, it helps to overcome these restrictions. No doubt, poor institutional conditions can provide fertile ground for corruption to flourish; however they are often not the basis but themselves a consequence of corruption. Corruption may thus be a cause of distorting regulation, (Rose-Ackerman 1999, 9-17; Lambsdorff 2002b). For example, the investigation of excessive bureaucratic regulation in De Soto (1989) leads the author to conclude that they were largely motivated by the desire to generate corrupt revenues. A vicious circle can exist of inefficient regulation leading to corruption, which in turn cultivates the further spread of troublesome regulation so as to enhance administrative power and the opportunity to exact further payoffs. As expressed by Myrdal (1956, 283):

> In many underdeveloped countries ... the damaging effects [of quantitative controls] have been serious. The system tends easily to create cancerous tumors of partiality and corruption in the very center of the administration, where the sickness is continuously nurtured by the favors distributed and the grafts realized. Industrialists and businessmen are tempted to go in for shady deals instead of steady regular business. Individuals who might have performed useful tasks in the economic development of their country become idle hangers-on, watching for loopholes in the decrees and dishonesty in their implementation.

Bureaucrats and politicians, once bribed, may disregard bothersome regulation. But at the same time they have an interest in keeping such regulation in place and create further bottlenecks. If so, cutting through red tape looses its appeal to economists, because this type of red tape is created for the purpose of being cut. Once considering this vicious circle a welfare analysis of corruption must incorporate the investigation of institutions and regulation and must not consider them exogenous to the analysis. A political-economic viewpoint with endogenous assessment of regulations is required.

Self-Serving Agents

The Principal-Agent Approach

An approach where the creation of rules is considered to be the actual goal of the analysis is provided by principal-agent theory. While this model was initially developed for the relation between private contractual parties such as owners and managers, it has also been utilized to model bureaucracy and public institutions. Its application to the investigation of corruption goes back to Rose-Ackerman (1978, 6) and is meanwhile standard to many economists, (Jain 1998; and Klitgaard 1988, 73).

From a principal-agent approach the design of the regulatory system becomes the actual subject of analysis. A principal (i.e. the government)[2] is assumed to create rules directed at assigning tasks to the agent (e.g. the tax authorities). These are intended to regulate exchange with a client (e.g. the taxpayer). Such exchange relates, for example, to the payment of taxes and customs tariffs, the provision of services and licenses, or the awarding of contracts. This framework is then used to determine an optimal regulatory system. A conflict of interest arises between principal and agent. The principal may be insufficiently skilled or facing time constraints that favour delegation of tasks to the agent. But the agent in turn will have an informational advantage. Either his effort is not observable by the principal (he can hide his true effort from the principal after the contract is negotiated) or he can obfuscate his qualifications before the contract is sealed. An example of the last-named case is that agents may have a certain propensity to behave honestly which is hidden to the principal (Besley and McLaren 1993). This informational asymmetry parallels a situation with limited transparency. Various pieces of information on the agents performance or his quality are unavailable, be it due to purposeful obfuscation or to other influences. This in turn increases the agent's discretion. The lack of transparency limits the principal's capacity to control the agent. In an ideal world, the exchange between principal and agent should be as transparent as possible.[3]

Given this informational advantage, it may not be possible to write contracts contingent on the agent's quality. Likewise a contract that specifies the agent's effort level may not be enforceable because information on effort is not available to the principal or to courts and arbitrators (Furubotn and Richter 1998, 179-80). The principal thus faces problems of moral hazard or adverse selection. One solution suggested for the relationship between private parties is to make the agent partly the residual claimant of the operation. This incentive induces compliance to the terms of the contract. But in reality the role of such economic incentives is lower than predicted by theory (Furubotn and Richter 1998, 202). Not only does the common assumption of the agent's risk aversion restrict the attempt by principals to make agents residual claimants of the operation. But particularly for bureaucracies such incentives play a minor role, because there is no measurable economic surplus accruing to a bureau head, serving as a yardstick for remuneration (Moe 1984, 763). Due to this failure, governments, instead of rewarding honesty, often rather levy a 'tax on honesty' on their citizens. For example, Hart (1970, 875-7) argues that taxpayers have tremendous scope for concealing their true income and may even bribe the revenue agent, so that

2 This study uses the terms principal and government as synonyms. Another approach would be to assign a government the role of the agent, facing the constituency as the principal. Yet, since the power of the constituency is highly limited, this approach does not fit into our analysis.

3 A principal may employ informal sanctions in order to induce efficiency among his agents, and under some circumstances these informal sanctions may be less transparent, (Wintrobe and Breton 1986). This type of informal and non-transparent behaviour is beyond the scope of this model. The focus of this model is on the agent's actions and qualifications and whether these are transparent to the principal.

honesty becomes expensive. Government implicitly taxes it. Instead of providing monetary inducements, principals may try to substitute costly incentives with an appeal to an agent's intrinsic honesty. Or they may attempt to impose psychological barriers against agents' self-serving, for example by encouraging moral conformity through education. Easier to describe in economic terms are attempts by agents to make credible commitments where the resulting signals of honesty are helpful indicators for the principal. While the term 'informational asymmetry' is an "amoral" term that does not include normative assessments, these mechanisms may explain why, in reality, principal-agent relationships are often supported by social norms like customs or professional ethics.

Whether the self-serving behaviour of agents can already be termed corruption is food for debate. There is an unavoidable normative element in the judgment of whether an agent is regarded as being entitled to maximize his self-interest or whether this is a misuse of public funds and a breach of the trust he was given. Particularly when the size of funds involved is small and the agent is simply lazy, the term corruption seems inappropriate. But in the case of large-scale cost padding and embezzlement, some observers may consider this term adequate.[4] Another crucial characteristic of corruption can be seen in the agents' relationship to third parties. A client adds another dimension to the principal-agent approach, because he provides another opportunity for the agent to cheat. Corruption is deemed to take place when an agent trespasses on the rules set up by the principal by colluding with the client and promoting his own benefit. He obtains a bribe that is hidden to the principal. The aim of a bribe is to loosen loyalty between agent and principal and to induce the agent to bend the rules in favour of the client. It is particularly this type of collusion between a client and the agent that distinguishes corruption from simple self-serving behaviour among agents.

Another variant of the principal-agent model emerges when a supervisor/auditor is introduced, who is supposed to monitor the agent and report truthfully to the principal, so as to alleviate the informational asymmetries faced by the principal. But if a supervisor can collude with the agent, he can be induced to falsify his reports. In exchange for a bribe he turns a blind eye on the agent's non compliance. For a review of the relevant literature see Khalil and Lawarrée (1995).

Welfare Implications

Corrupt agents certainly harm their principals. But the overall loss might be less because the agent gains and the principal may adjust. A net loss will result, however,

4 Whether embezzlement represents a type of corruption can be up to dispute because it does not require an exchange between two parties at the cost of others – that is, the existence of a client. But in order to conceal the true costs of a project and to over-invoice, agents often require the cooperation of outsiders. They employ clients who provide fake documents, falsely certify the provision of services and pay kickbacks for obtaining inflated prices in procurement.

if the agent not only makes inroads in the principal's realm, but if decision-making is distorted. This type of distortion is not easy to pin down. A first apparent effect is that corruption will lower the agent's effort. If he colludes with third parties who falsely certify that the agent served them he obtains slack and can devote more time to leisure.

There is also an important impact on the quality of goods. An agent may have to choose between various clients. In case of corruption, his decision would be biased in favour of those clients who pay the largest bribe, instead of those who provide high quality. This can be best illustrated for the case of an auction, where corruption may be a means for inefficient firms to win a public tender. But in perfect markets, those who produce most efficiently can also afford the largest bribes, suggesting that no distortion arises in this regard. This conclusion is even valid when information about competitor's actions is incomplete (Beck and Maher 1986; and Lien 1986). But markets are typically imperfect and competitors will differ in their inclination to offer bribes. For the case of exporting countries this is shown in Lambsdorff (1998 and 2000). This commonly results from the large transaction costs associated with making corrupt deals. Due to the associated risks and the private institutional arrangements required to enforce corrupt deals, the circle of those in a position to make corrupt deals is limited to some insiders (Lambsdorff 2002a). Clearly, those who are most inclined to bribe and best connected for arranging a corrupt transaction are not necessarily the most efficient.[5]

Furthermore, it can be the explicit goal of collusion between agents and clients to create distortions. When clients pay agents for restricting competition by harassing their competitors, distortions are a straightforward consequence of the corrupt dealings (Bardhan 1997, 1322). It may not help in this context that their competitors may do the same and that the most efficient firms may win the battle, because the level of competition suffers. Another apparent example at hand is when clients pay agents (or supervisors) for turning a blind eye to the use of sub-standard material, (Frisch 1999, 92-4; and Klitgaard 1988, 36-48). The creation of a distorting decision becomes the actual intention of the corrupt inducement.

The principal, on the other hand, will seek ways to counter self-dealing by the agent. He will try to induce the agent to reveal his actions truthfully. In case this inducement is unsatisfactory, the principal can anticipate the agent's income from corruption and gain by lowering the official salary. But this will not be sufficient

5 Another position against this 'efficiency' argument arises when a tender is not of a 'winner takes all'-type but instead the less efficient firms are awarded other (smaller) projects. If private firms have exclusive knowledge about their quality, the principal is limited in his capacity to treat each firm differently (according to its capacity), because the efficient firm may otherwise pretend to be less efficient and gain from the slack, the difference between reported and actual effort it has to exert. This suggests that principals treat second best firms 'excessively bad' so as to further deter efficient firms from masquerading. Therefore, adverse selection distorts the principal's decision-making and allows only second-best solutions, (Furubotn and Richter 1998, 202-12). Bribes contribute to this inefficiency by distorting information and increasing problems of asymmetric information.

to avoid distortions. All the principal can achieve are second-best solutions. Losses still arise for all concerned because those types of contracts that would be beneficial to both sides cannot be carried out. Those contracts that require honesty and the absence of corruption will not be sealed when the principal faces an agent who will take advantage of the arising opportunities. The benefits such a contract would provide to both parties cannot be achieved.

Some of the approaches presented in the last section suggest that economic actions are restricted by legislation and regulation, that these restrictions should be assumed to be exogenous to the analysis, and that corruption can enlarge the set of possible actions to be taken by the parties involved. Yet, as seen from an agency perspective, the possibility to behave in a corrupt manner does not enlarge the contractual possibilities. Quite the contrary, contractual possibilities are limited when agents do not adhere to the prohibition of accepting side-payments. When agents cannot credibly promise to reject side-payments from clients, they are not trustworthy when writing contracts that require the absence of such payments. Principals will not offer such contracts in the first place. For example, it may be thought worthwhile to construct good-quality roads but bad quality is expected to result from unavoidable collusive behaviour; in this case, principals may cancel the project and the possible benefits for all parties cannot be achieved. Or imagine that a fair and efficient tax system should be established, but tax collectors cannot be kept from taking bribes in exchange for turning a blind eye to underreporting; the project may fall into disfavour and be terminated by the principal. A related situation arises for the principal's relation to a supervisor. If the supervisor cannot guarantee that he will not fake reports in exchange for a bribe, his contribution looses value for the principal and he may not be hired in the first place – even though an honest exchange would have been favourable to all. Anti-corruption becomes a public good, to be promoted by regulation, detection and sanctions. Already Marshall (1897, 130) argued in this regard:

> Everyone is aware of the tendency to an increase in the size of individual businesses, with the consequent transference of authority and responsibility from the owners of each business to its salaried managers and officials. This would have been impossible had there not been a great improvement in the morality and uprightness of the average man: for even as late as the seventeenth and eighteenth centuries we find the great trading companies breaking down largely in consequence of the corruption and selfishness of their officials.

It must now be noted that the overall level of corruption might be endogenous, depending on actions taken by the principal. Reducing corruption is commonly costly to implement. Costs may arise from detection and punishment, (Klitgaard 1988, 26), from inducing agents to behave honestly, (Kofman and Lawaree 1996; Laffont and Tirole 1993; Olsen and Torsvik 1998; Strausz 1995), from attracting more honest agents for government positions (Besley and McLaren 1993); or reducing corruption may require downsizing government and permitting the persistence of market failure, (Acemoglu and Verdier 2000). The optimum choice of the principal then includes a level of corruption which best balances the advantages from increased honesty among agents against these costs. Lower levels of corruption may not be entirely beneficial if they can only be achieved through excessive expenses for detection, enforcement and incentives or if they go along with an insufficient reduction of market failures. In so far as the principal can effectively influence the level of corruption, one will assume him to choose an optimum level. Living in an optimum should naturally lower our concern for the adverse effects of corruption. But there can be limits to the principal's influence and various other exogenous determinants of levels of corruption may be more important than actions taken by the principal. Nevertheless, as seen from an agency perspective with a benevolent and rational principal, the worries about corruption are substantially limited. Welfare losses are limited to a degree that has been brought to balance other potential costs and losses. Whether this is a convincing viewpoint, certainly, deserves dispute. As I will discuss, factual claims that levels of corruption are at their optimum can easily be undue when the principal's zeal to contain corruption is limited.

Self-Serving Governments

Corruption has been defined as the misuse of public power for private benefit. But the term 'misuse' is open to different interpretations. In the last section it involved the rules set up by a benevolent principal, which were trespassed by a self-serving agent. But a self-serving principal may create an environment where laws do not prohibit his own self-enrichment or that of a ruling class. Corruption can even accompany and underlie the writing and enforcing of rules designed with the intention of furthering the principal's narrow interests. The term corruption may be misplaced when applied to a disobedient agent who is disloyal to rules that are themselves the result of self-serving. Instead, it may be more accurate then to assign this term to the principal's own self-serving behaviour. In this case "misuse" is not clearly related to the trespassing of rules (in the legal sense). Instead, it relates to acts which the general public regards as illegitimate, or which contradict the *public interest*.[6] Corruption in this context is best described as a behaviour of public decision makers where preferential treatment is provided to individuals and where narrow interests are advanced at the expense of the interests of broader segments of society (Lambsdorff 2002b).

The agency approach is primarily concerned with the distortion that results from the principal's limited capacity to control the agent. Such distortions can certainly also arise with a self-serving principal and bring about inefficiencies. But if control is not carried out to benefit the public, it becomes ambiguous whether the limitations faced by the principal are a bad thing. Prerequisite to the agency approach would be that honesty among agents allows for a deal with the principal that also benefits the public. But if the loyal agent serves the corrupt goals of the principal, unusual circumstances must be imagined in which this loyalty also increases public welfare.

6 See (Heidenheimer, Johnston and LeVine 1989, 3-14) for a review of various approaches to defining corruption.

Other approaches are needed to model corruption, and to relate corruption to losses of public welfare. A more promising way to assess the effects on welfare is by a straightforward reference to the goals pursued by the principal and less to the principal's limitations.[7]

Inefficiency by Design

One such approach in which the principal seeks to strike deals which are unfavourable to the general public is provided by representatives of the Chicago School (Stigler 1971; Posner 1974). In their view, lobbying groups and politicians design regulations so as to create rents and promote the narrow interests of individuals or private parties. The welfare losses, it is argued, are different from those arising in an agency model. Posner (1974, 337-9) suggests that governments operate with reasonable efficiency. In contrast to the slackness among agents within agency theory, bureaucrats are considered here to be well motivated, in a way similar to private businesspersons. They are subject to similar supervision as well as competition from colleagues and other agencies. Arguably, there is no x-inefficiency associated with the operation of the bureaucracy. But inefficiencies result from the kind of goal pursued by governments. This comes about as politicians supply protection against troublesome competition by means of subsidies, import quotas, tariffs, tax exemptions and preferential treatment to interest groups paying for this service (Stigler 1971). Governments operate with reasonable efficiency to purposefully attain deliberately inefficient goals, Posner (1974, 337-9).

While the term 'corruption' is not mentioned in this context, the approach by the Chicago School emphasizes that the inefficiency of government operation does not result from its limitations or lacking motivation. As seen by representatives of the Chicago School, it is not even the principal's self-serving behaviour, which is responsible for the inefficiency of laws and regulations, but rather the strong leverage that interest groups have over government operations. The government is not intentionally self-serving, but falls victim to the interests of private actors. This argument suggests the existence of two types of self-serving regimes. Either self-interest brings about a 'predatory government', a 'grabbing hand' regime, (Djankov et al. 2000) – in this case rules and regulations are designed so as to profit the government – or lobbying groups are in a strong position and regulations are created to generate rents for their benefit. In both cases, the problem rests with a government's goals and not its limitations. Since representatives of the Chicago School consider government to strive for inefficient goals, limitations faced by the

---

7 One may defend the applicability of agency theory by arguing that government should be regarded as an agent of the general public. But there is no consistent treatment of this scenario in the literature. The principal is commonly assumed to be benevolent and to have full control over the contract design. If these two characteristics do not fall hand in hand in reality, one may assign the principal's role either to the benevolent party or to the one with the actual power. I pursue the second approach here.

principal may actually be beneficial to the public interest instead of being a source of inefficiency – contrary to the agency approach.

Tullock (1980, 27) and Shleifer and Vishny (1993) extend this analysis by arguing that corrupt structures that are monopolized are superior to disorganized (and corrupt) monopolistic structures. The latter is the case if a businessperson must bribe several departments simultaneously for the operation of his business, for example local legislature, the central ministry, the fire authorities, the police and the water authorities. Each of these institutions acts independently and provides a complementary good because a businessperson needs permission from all. While one may regard such departments as agents, the fact that they are independent (also from superior institutions) suggests that each assumes the role of the principal. As a result of their independent maximization the departments 'overgraze' the market and suffer from the 'tragedy of the commons'. Each public servant does not take into account that the bribe he charges reduces business operations and consequently the bribes all the other departments can pocket. The departments therefore suffer from the lack of cooperation. This case much resembles that of groups of road bandits along a single road. Taking into account that extortion lowers road traffic, each group will determine the optimal 'fee' it charges for using the road. But it does not take into consideration that the fee it charges also reduces the revenues of other road bandits. As a consequence of poor cooperation, the bandits will rob travellers excessively.

Minimizing government may be a straightforward means of reducing its distorting impact. This is a measure that finds support among various economists, see e.g. Becker (1994) and for a critical review Orchard and Stretton (1997). There can be disadvantages to this strategy when much needed government services are insufficiently supplied. Rose-Ackerman (1999, 41-42) argues that budget cutbacks may increase corruption when the underlying government programs have been left intact, because increased competition for the scarce resources may make corruption the dominant strategy. The privatization process that goes along with downsizing government can furthermore provide plentiful opportunities for corruption. Above that, privatized firms may still be exposed to public interference and demands for bribes – even more than their well-connected state-owned competitors (Lambsdorff and Cornelius 2000, 76-7). The argument to downsize government may also be well heard in public debate but less so by a self-serving principal. A self-serving principal may be willing to downsize government where government serves the public but resist such temptations where it benefits himself.

The Kleptocrat's Dilemma

A principal, self-serving or benevolent, always dislikes welfare losses because they absorb what otherwise belongs to him or to the public. A self-serving principal (who disregards his duty of serving the public) will therefore be opposed to welfare losses. For example, corruption resulting in price increases is particularly distorting when it bears on some goods while the prices of others are unaffected. But such a distortion will not arise if prices for all goods and services increase evenly. When the impact of corruption is equal on all economic sectors, resource allocation will not be distorted to favour one sector over another. A self-serving government will thus attempt to organize a corrupt system to operate as smoothly as a tax. Still, bribes will be worse with regard to public welfare than taxes because they must be concealed (Rose-Ackerman 1978, 8; Shleifer and Vishny 1993). Self-serving governments may have to obfuscate their self-enrichment and employ costly mechanisms for gathering bribes. As a result, Rose-Ackerman (1999, 117) notes 'efficient regulatory reforms will be opposed by the kleptocrat if the reforms would convert illegal into legal pricing systems'. On the other hand, secrecy is not an issue when the media and the judiciary can be pressured to play along with political leaders who demand their cut.[8] If a self-serving government equally controls revenues that result from the legal pricing system it does not have to distort allocation to favour illegal pricing systems.

Also the option of discriminating with prices would avoid a distortional allocation. Self-serving governments may want to charge their customers according to their willingness to pay, discriminating with their prices between the needy and the less interested. While this discriminatory power may cause the public to feel uncomfortable and deprived of its consumer's rent, the classic welfare loss does not come about. Instead, a corrupt government can seize the full rent and all deals that are mutually profitable are carried out.

A strong government will even seek to contain low-level corruption among the bureaucracy. This behaviour is already known with regard to laziness. Superiors, even those who are self-serving, will discourage slack behaviour among subordinates because this absorbs 'slack resources' which are otherwise available to them (Moe 1984, 763). A self-serving principal will equally avoid corruption among agents simply because any self-enrichment by the bureaucracy takes away from the resources the principal considers to be his own. Also, a self-serving principal cannot gain from allowing sub-standard quality in public procurement. Either he prefers to embezzle the required funding right away, or he hopes for future economic (corrupt) gains resulting from an improved public infrastructure – which then has to be of good quality. X-inefficiency among the bureaucracy will not be condoned (Posner 1974, 337-9). It appears unlikely that favouring unqualified contractors in tendering procedures is helpful to such a regime. Lobbyists will not be allowed to waste resources and time in an attempt to influence the principal. Also distorting regulation, in contrast to the argument by the Chicago School, may not be an issue for self-serving governments. McChesney (1997, 153-55) argues that such regimes strive for income via extortion but are able to levy the burden equally on all private parties. Governments threaten inefficient regulation, but these are avoided by payments from private parties. Due to this negotiating process, inefficient regulation is commonly

8 Githongo (1997) provides evidence that the Kenyan press was largely free to report on corruption but that its impact was so minor that the government was basically indifferent to widespread revelations of high-level corruption.

avoided. A strong principal will also prevent individual corrupt departments from 'overgrazing' the market because he monopolizes the market for corrupt income.

Clearly, avoiding these distortions requires a corrupt government to be particularly strong. This type of a system is commonly termed a 'kleptocracy' (Grossman 1995). The ruler is sometimes referred to as a 'stationary bandit'. While such a government is in a prime position to acquire large bribes, a negative effect on public welfare is not trivial to proclaim. Quite the contrary, McGuire and Olson (1996) argue that self-serving rulers with complete coercive power have an incentive to exercise this power consistent with the interests of society.

An illustrative example of such a consistency took place in Indonesia. One of the grandchildren of President Suharto attempted to make a cut from taxes on beer that was collected by his private company. But as a result, tourism in Bali was suffering from a shortage of beer and inflated prices, forcing President Suharto to withdraw the tax.[9] *The Economist* presumed that probably some of his relatives were strong in the hotel business. This argument well illustrates the 'encompassing interest' of a strong ruler, who comes to consider how inefficient solutions in one sector spill over to other parts of the economy. If provided with sufficient power a ruler will avoid such consequences. He will keep subordinates from overgrazing the market by taxing excessively and even provide public goods so as to increase future tax income. But whether the principle of the encompassing interest effectively motivates a corrupt ruler to serve the public has been questioned.

Whether there exist reasonable limits on the taxes squeezed out by a predatory regime depends crucially on the elasticity of the tax base. Marcoullier and Young (1995) argue that this elasticity is rather low so that predatory regimes can always rake off a surplus by increasing the rate of taxation. This is why, from a historical perspective, predatory regimes tended to squeeze their citizens without pity. However justified and convincing, this is an aspect that concerns distribution and does not allow for conclusions with regard to economic efficiency, as investigated here. Certainly, there are reasons why a predatory regime may fail to allocate resources efficiently. Even the most powerful kleptocrats have to share power with their subordinates and the resulting coordination problems may produce inefficient outcomes. Kleptocrats may have to assign property rights in exchange for peace with potential contestants, i.e. for buying off competing factions, and not to those who put it to the most productive uses (North 1981, 28). A flourishing economy may threaten a principal's power because it can provide potential competitors with resources to overthrow the ruler (North 1993, 14). A ruler may instead encourage wasteful competition among lobbies, thriftless contests between political factions or violence between ethnic groups as a means to divide and conquer and to bolster his own sway. If the ruler does not have the power to eliminate freelance banditry or collect taxes from bandits, his extortionate taxation imposed on producers will lower welfare by making banditry more attractive than production, (Moselle and Polak 2001). Inefficiency may also result when a ruler has a short time horizon, (McGuire

9 *The Economist* (February 10, 1996), 'Indonesia. When trouble brewed.'

and Olson 1996). The permanent cabinet reshuffles in Zaire, for example, induced ministers to 'run with the loot while they can' and to distort decisions in favour of projects with a short-term kickback potential (Harden 1993, 52).

These caveats imply that a perfectly strong and corrupt government might be utopian. But the resulting conclusions with regard to public welfare remain ambiguous, because losses of public welfare could either be traced to the self-serving of rulers as well as to the constraints faced by the principal. Cynics would conclude that public welfare does not suffer from the principal's corrupt intention but from his deficient powers. In their view, problems do not reside with governments being corrupt but with the fact that they are permanently contested. Society would not have problems with bandits per se but only if they are insufficiently stationary and lacking power. Cynics may thus argue that corruption should not be fought but perfected. Along this line, Murphy, Shleifer and Vishny (1993, 413) argue that the problems with corruption are mitigated when corrupt rulers can collect bribes efficiently. A similar result would apply for society's quest for transparency. Introducing transparency would introduce distortions because the principal would be barred from collecting bribes efficiently. Being forced to conceal his self-enrichment he must prefer those operations that are less easily monitored. Cynics would thus conclude that it is transparency, not corruption, that causes the resulting distortions. But this study argues that such cynical conclusions are easily overemphasized, because a perfectly powerful kleptocrat produces other forms of inefficiencies.

First, citizens will attempt to circumvent the extortionate corruption of its principal. They will invest in techniques to conceal their income and to lower the contribution they must provide to the principal. While this type of tax evasion is not peculiar to a kleptocracy, the corruption of the principal can provide legitimacy to these actions and enhance civic anti-principal cooperation. Both sides may expend resources for improving their position; the citizenry to better evade taxation and the principal to increase his cut. As in the traditional rent-seeking approach, these expenditures do not increase general welfare and are wasteful (Tullock 1971). Also the agent's behaviour may be adversely affected. Given the ruler's precedent, lower levels in the hierarchy may be motivated to seek extra-legal income for themselves instead of being loyal to higher ranks (Rose-Ackerman 1999, 114-7). An even more cogent argument in favour of inefficiencies arises when considering that the strong, corrupt regime faces a credibility problem, a point to which I will turn now.

The Credibility Problem

The most crucial problem with a strong self-serving principal is that he will not be able to credibly commit himself to policies. Such credibility issues have been dealt with in New Institutional Economics (Wiggins 1991; Klein, Crawford and Alchian 1978; and Williamson 1985). This analysis was fruitfully applied to the operation of political institutions and the political economy of dictatorship (North 1993; Weingast 1993; Wintrobe 1998, 24-33 and 38-39; Stiglitz 1998, 8-11).

Investments usually require sunk costs. Once sunk, such resources cannot be transferred or assigned to different tasks. Railroads cannot be removed, power plants cannot be relocated to different countries, and technical know-how cannot easily be used for other purposes. Thus, investors become locked into a particular usage of resources and, being limited in their power to protect their property against rival attacks, they must fear for the expropriation of their rents. Investors are particularly vulnerable where there is corruption because self-serving rulers are not motivated to honour their commitments, nor are they sufficiently constrained to do so, (Ades and Di Tella 1997, 1026; Murphy, Shleifer and Vishny 1993, 413; and Mauro 1995).

The credibility problem resulting from corruption can already be observed with regard to lower level public servants. Corrupt tax collectors can impose capricious tax burdens on investors, corrupt regulators may threaten an arbitrary application of law, and corrupt customs authorities can randomly apply trade regulations. All these actors may be in a position to demand a bribe, while at the same time an investor has lost the outside option of withdrawing the investment decision, having already sunk too many irretrievable assets into the project. Corrupt judges are another issue at hand. Predictable laws are necessary to defend investments against rival attacks and to make contracts between private parties enforceable. But corrupt courts will not necessarily enforce these contracts and may favour the party that offers the largest bribe. This implies that corruption also inhibits the enforcement of contracts between private parties, discouraging the sinking of resources that are specific to a private party (Acemoglu and Verdier 1998). In a survey of business people in Karnataka, India, it was found that the high level of corruption among the local administration less affected the software industry. This results from the minor role of immovable assets for the software industry, at least as compared to the construction and manufacturing industries. This lower dependency seems to have reduced extortionate demands for bribes among public officials and rendered aspects of credibility less pressing.[10]

Problems of poor credibility are likely to multiply when not only bureaucrats but whole governments are self-serving. In case of extortion among lower ranks an effective threat is to involve those higher up in the hierarchy. But if extortion becomes the actual object of government, superiors will not discipline their subordinates but optimize a corrupt system so as to benefit themselves. There are no effective complaints mechanisms and no legal recourse available to investors. In this case the principal will fail in making credible commitments. As argued by (North and Weingast 1989, 803-4):

> The more likely it is that the sovereign will alter property rights for his or her own benefit, the lower the expected returns from investment and the lower in turn the incentive to invest. For economic growth to occur the sovereign or government must not merely establish the relevant set or rights, but must make a credible commitment to them. A ruler can establish such commitment in two ways. One is by setting a precedent of 'responsible behavior,' appearing to be committed to a set of rules that he or she will consistently

10 See *The Hindu* (October 1, 2000), and later (March 28, 2001).

enforce. The second is by being constrained to obey a set of rules that do not permit leeway for violating commitments.

In order for commitments to be credible the respective person must be motivated or forced to honour them (North 1993, 13). But a corrupt ruler is devoted primarily to personal enrichment and lacks the motivation for honouring commitments (Rose-Ackerman 1999, 118). Corruption implies that a government is unscrupulous when it comes to taking advantage of arising opportunities. On the other hand, the (utopian) autocrat with full control faces no legal restrictions and can quickly overturn constitutional obstacles if this becomes favourable to his or her corrupt goals, eliminating any external constraints. While such a principal may be in a position to avoid some of the inefficiencies mentioned before, he has lost the option to commit himself to trustworthy policies. A government's strength helps in avoiding some inefficiency. But a government so strong can quickly confiscate the wealth of its citizens. Thus, a kleptocrat cannot avoid welfare losses, even when these threaten his own income.[11]

The common approach to overcome the credibility problem is by constraining the principal.[12] As soon as such restrictions are imposed, the credibility problem will be overcome. In so far as transparency can contribute to constraining the principal it contributes to increasing the credibility of government commitments. But constraining a self-serving principal also disallows a perfect system of bribery, bringing about other forms of welfare loss. There emerges a trade-off where welfare losses are inescapable. I will return to this issue in the last substantive section of the chapter.

---

11 One may conjecture that adverse effects on public welfare can temporarily be eliminated when a kleptocrat finds a credible means of sharing power with bribe-paying investors. This may be what Wedeman (1997) has in mind when he argues that the 'rent-sharing' type of corruption that he observes in South Korea has been less detrimental to development than the 'looting' type that prevailed in former Zaire. Indeed, if such means of sharing power can be found, this type of corruption may provide fertile ground for large-scale investments. But unless some benevolence exists among the principal, conditions for less powerful investors and innovators may even further deteriorate due to the strong position of a leading industry that takes over the principal's role (Murphy, Shleifer and Vishny 1993, 413). Another conjecture could be that the fear of loosing one's reputation might effectively induce a kleptocrat to honour sunk investments. But it seems unlikely that investors provide unconstrained kleptocrats' with the possibility to establish such a reputation in the first place.

12 A strong parliament can effectively limit the powers of kings or presidents, as was the case with the 1688 English revolution, limiting the Crown's legislative and judicial powers and disallowing a 'confiscatory government' (North and Weingast 1989). A strong high court can provide limitations to a principal and enforce previous political commitments (Landes and Posner 1975). Another of the many possibilities for restricting the power of principals is by delegating decisions to autonomous bureaucrats (Furubotn and Richter 1998, 421). The requirements within a principal-agent model would be to insulate agents from the principal's direct orders. Agents must be required to respect the law and not to follow the opportunistic interests of the principal.

The Contested Principal

A principal with full control is a utopian assumption that has been subject to criticism (Moe 1984, 765-72). One reason for existing constraints is the competition for the principal's position, created by potential entrants. The principal must fear to be ousted, be it through election, coups, revolution, or by powerful rival factions within the government. While this is a realistic assumption, it is largely alien to the agency approach, which assumes the existence of an uncontested principal who has full control over government operations (Kofman and Lawarrée 1996; Laffont and Tirole 1993; Olsen and Torsvik 1998; Strausz 1995). Those holding official positions are faced with competition and must exert effort to remain in power and seek support from outside. This type of competition imposes important constraints on the principal's actions. At the same time, there are a variety of welfare conclusions originating from competition. While competition may help to get rid of self-serving principals, it may provoke other types of welfare losses.

Competition and Benevolence

The assumption of benevolence seems overemphasized and has been criticized on a variety of grounds. Politicians may not be primarily motivated by productive efficiency or the public interest and they are not even seeking an optimally balanced set of hierarchical controls and monitoring mechanisms (Moe 1984, 761-2). As expounded in the last section, principals may even be purely self-serving. If an intrinsic motivation to serve the public is rare, competition may be all societies have to induce some basic level of benevolence.

At first, competition for the principal's position should enable societies to get rid of those performing particularly poor. Principals who care little about public welfare are unlikely to stay in power for long. An active opposition may thus discourage bribery among politicians (Rose-Ackerman 1978, 28). Transparency can easily increase political competition because incumbents can better be held accountable for their actions and voters can better identify and sanction self-seeking behaviour. This argument in favour of competition becomes particularly important when principals strive for their own corrupt goals. Competition may thus operate like an invisible hand, substituting a possible lack of benevolence among politicians with a mechanism that makes sure that public welfare is pursued. This is a standard argument in political economy at least since Schumpeter (1942).

Competition may not only limit self-seeking among the principal but force him to tightly control the agents. A contested principal may be effectively pressurized to secure that the agent serves the public (Breton and Wintrobe 1975). The contested principal will be held responsible for the agent's corrupt actions. Those principals who are least able or willing to contain corruption at lower ranks may fear to be ousted. Principals are thus likely to monitor how well their agents contribute to public welfare, disallowing shirking, laziness and corruption among lower ranks.

Yet, the power of competition should not be overestimated. Moe (1984, 762) argues that it does not guarantee that inefficient programs are eradicated and that dishonest politicians are disposed of. One reason for this arises when corruption is used to subvert the selection process. Politicians with control over corrupt income may spend these resources in return for staying in power. Corruption and the power to allocate rents to supporters can be a helpful instrument for guaranteeing political survival. Honest politicians have fewer such resources at their disposal and may perish as a result of competition for political positions (Buchanan 1993, 69). Those who can trade in most political assistance are in a prime position for survival. Even benevolent principals may trade in some of their generous motivation for political support. Competition alone may be insufficient to ensure that benevolence among the leadership prevails. In addition to that, it may directly trigger another type of welfare loss, namely, waste.

Waste

Competition among self-serving politicians can have direct welfare consequences, as argued by rent-seeking theorists. For a review see Rowley (1988) and Coate and Morris (1994). The rent-seeking models assume that governments create distorting laws and regulations but do not overlook its consequences and do not control to whom the resulting stream of incomes accrues. They lack clearly defined goals. They are too naïve to understand the vested interests that are behind the measures they are requested to support. Tullock (1993, 26) posits that politicians are mere brokers for the interests of others. Unlike traditional welfare analysis, rent-seeking theory is not concerned with the resulting inefficient allocation of resources in the product market. Rather, it is concerned with the problem that most types of regulation create artificial rents. These invoke competition in the attempt to influence regulation to one's own behalf and to seize these rents. Private parties invest in lobbying. Costly campaigns are organized and lawyers are hired to increase one's chances. A marketplace emerges for preferential treatment by public decision makers, and private parties are requesting these services and investing resources for this purpose. Equally, politicians strive to obtain lucrative government positions. They do so by transparent public debate and elections, but also by lobbying and other wasteful expenditures. Such expenses may influence recruitment and improve their position in the government's internal promotion. If principals must compete against potential rivals, they cannot be sure whether to remain in power.

Expenses for lobbying, while wasteful to the public, may prove helpful to principals, for example when they include donations to finance election campaigns or to harass rivals. These resources are not used to serve consumers and the public by increasing the cake, but rather to battle for a larger slice of the given cake for oneself. Welfare losses in this case arise because there is initially a zero-sum game, but given the costly resources invested into influencing the outcome, this transforms into a negative-sum game. These expenses represent a form of waste because they go along with effort but not with increasing overall public welfare (Lambsdorff

2002b).[13] Brock and Magee (1984) have introduced the term 'invisible foot' for this effect of competition among rent-seekers.

Paying bribes instead of lobbying is an alternative type of rent-seeking. Ironically, rent-seeking theory predicts that bribes are less wasteful because, as opposed to molesting lobbying, they benefit the recipient. Lambsdorff (2002b) argues that this conclusion is one-sided, because bribes, as opposed to lobbying, are more effective in inducing large artificial rents. A politician's chances of getting re-elected deteriorate with the creation of artificial rents and he must obtain a net benefit from doing so, which cannot be achieved by pure lobbying. While waste may be lower in the case of bribes, the allocative distortions will exacerbate.

Another argument put forward by rent-seeking theory is that waste is largest in case of competition and lowest where favours are provided in the absence of competition, particularly in case of nepotism and cronyism. This arises because a monopolist can avoid wasteful expenditures spent on staying ahead of rivals. But once considering that the rent is the monopolist's private good, he will attempt to increase this rent with the help of lobbying and bribes. To the contrary, for competing firms the artificial rent is a public good where little incentive is given to expend resources for increasing it (Lambsdorff, 2002b).

Waste arises when the principal is indeterminate, particularly with regard to who should receive the income resulting from artificially created rents. It results when a principal is merely a 'passive broker among competing private rent seekers' (McChesney 1987, 102). Strong leadership and little competition for the principal's position may contain welfare losses. But at the same time, a strong leader may be tempted to serve himself. Thus, whether the waste argument suggested by rent-seeking theorists is strong enough to tip the balance against the useful role of competition remains ambiguous. If principals were perfectly benevolent and corruption would not be an issue, certainly, societies might prefer less competition. This, in turn, would allow them to minimize the welfare losses that go along with wasteful rent-seeking.

The Powerful Agent

Realistically, self-serving is an option for both, principal and agent. If so, the optimal strategy for them might be to collude. Jointly, they would behave like a perfect kleptocrat and share the proceeds from exploiting the public. Yet, it can be questioned whether this strategy is individually optimal for two reasons. First, any agreement between the two actors may not be enforceable and be subject to opportunism from either side. Individual optimization may lead them to depart from joint maximization. Second, an independent agent may act as an effective constraint on the principal's actions. This may signal to outsiders that policies enacted by the principal are credible and will not be changed at will. The existence of an independent agent

13 While the existence of this form of waste appears plausible, it is not clear how it can be avoided. North (1984, 39) argued that the form of waste identified by traditional rent-seeking theory may simply be a form of unavoidable transaction cost in political decision-making.

serves as a yardstick for the credibility of political commitments. This credibility can be advantageous to the principal and deters him from colluding with the agent. Political opponents who contest the principal may also chastise such collusion as illegitimate (or even corrupt) and request the agent's independence.

Agents constrain the principal. They can obtain a powerful position vis-à-vis the principal. Niskanen (1975), for example, has been prominent in arguing that the bureaucracy has a strong position vis-à-vis Congress. Politicians face restrictions from countervailing powers and they may have to seek the support of their agents to secure their own survival. Also, due to a division of power there might be multiple principals in place who all want to control the agent. The agents, in turn, may be in a position to favour one principal over another and obtain a stronger bargaining position. One further reason for the agent's power arises with principals who are contested and must fear to be ousted from their position, be it through election, coup, revolution or by powerful rival factions within the government. Agents become more powerful when their principals are contested. For example, they can inform (or misinform) the public about a corrupt act of the principal or they can provide political support to the principal's rival. Support by the agent may therefore be helpful to the principal in securing his power and the agent can effectively demand some leeway in return. As I will argue here, self-serving among the agent in this case is likely to cause x-inefficiency, while the self-serving activities of the principal will bring about allocative inefficiency.

X-inefficiency

An agent may be intrinsically motivated to serve the public. But he may equally misuse his position to pursue his own benefit. A suitable approach to model the resulting welfare effects has been offered by the theory of x-inefficiency. While this approach was modelled for different purposes it has also been utilized for describing the adverse impact of corruption and government operations on public welfare (Isham and Kaufmann 1999; Button and Weyman-Jones 1994, 91-2). In contrast to allocative inefficiency, this type of inefficiency is defined as one that originates from a lack of effort and motivation among the workforce, resulting in productive units not operating on the production possibility frontier. The original approach to x-inefficiency as developed by Leibenstein aimed at explaining the efficiency losses resulting from a lack of competition in private goods markets. Leibenstein (1966, 398-402) argues that monopolistic firms do not minimize costs for a given production level. In a competitive environment, inefficient producers are put under pressure from competing firms, but monopolies can maintain their market position with a modicum of effort and little motivation among its workforce and managers. The market selects those firms that are able to efficiently use their factor inputs. But such a selection process does not exist in the case of a monopoly. This absence of pressure results in a lack of motivation and effort among the workforce and an inefficient organization of production (Leibenstein 1973). Competition provides a mechanism for processing information and discovering the best alternatives. Rationality is not an *a priori* condition for making decisions but it emerges *ex post* when the inferiority of alternatives is detected (De Alessi 1983, 74). Monopolies resist the testing of alternatives. High-cost firms can survive, while neither managers nor shareholders become aware that other technologies could be tested and prove superior.

This parallels the situation faced by public institutions. Principals are not mainly devoted to public welfare, just as managers of monopolies are not primarily interested in maximizing a firm's profit. In pursuing their own benefit, they observe that agents are in a strong position, too. The principal may be neither willing nor able to instigate competition between agents, select the best qualified and highest motivated and to constantly induce highest effort. As seen in this perspective, principals may be neither willing nor able to fight corruption and contain the self-enrichment of their subordinates. In return for the political support provided by agents, principals may allow some bureaucratic slackness, some x-inefficiency, and, ultimately, some bribe taking among lower levels in the public service. Self-serving among the bureaucracy will not be contained as predicted by formal principal-agent analysis and corruption exceeds its optimal level.

It has been questioned whether x-inefficiency represents a net loss of resources, because what the superior looses is won by the subordinate. The slackness among the workforce (in our case the bureaucracy) can be regarded as a non-monetary form of income. This income may outbalance the losses to the manager (in our case the government) (Stigler 1976; Parish and Ng 1972). But x-inefficiency is likely to aggravate agency problems, (Button and Weyman-Jones 1992, 440 and 1994, 92-3). As noted in the discussion of the 'welfare implications' of the presence of 'self-serving' agents above, profitable projects that require a commitment to honesty cannot be carried out. The lack of honesty is now additionally driven by the principal's indifference.

An application of this model relates to speed money, which a benevolent principal may permit as long as it induces his agents to exert higher levels of effort and to process cases according to urgency (Lui 1985). But a non-benevolent principal may want to profit from the speed-money given to his agents. He may demand a share in return for prolongating bureaucrats' labour contracts instead of closing down a non-performing civil service. Or he may turn a blind eye to the agent's malfeasance in exchange for political support. This provides an argument why speed money is likely to slow down bureaucracy (Myrdal 1968, 952-3; Rose-Ackerman 1978, 90).

Allocative Inefficiency

As a result of the restrictions faced by the principal, his self-serving is likely to cause allocative distortions. This can be traced to the impact of corruption on prices. Where private firms have to pay bribes to public officials, they will add these costs to the prices of their goods. The price paid for government services will increase (Klitgaard 1988, 39; Rose-Ackerman 1999, 28-9). Supply and demand of these goods will not be at their optimum level. Prices may already increase with agents demanding kickbacks. But an even stronger impact will arise when the principal takes advantage of his power in a systematic way. He may impose tariffs in favour of domestic firms who share part of their income with him. A corrupt government can restrict the amount of necessary permits and licenses so as to create artificial scarcity. Or demand and supply for public utilities, such as gas, water or telecommunications, will be distorted when politicians take kickbacks in exchange for contracts. Another example is when private firms can obtain a monopoly position with the help of government protection in exchange for favours.[14] A self-serving principal controls the regulatory system and can follow his corrupt goals in a more systematic way. This is the reason why the prices of whole sectors are distorted and allocative inefficiencies arise.

Politicians can use their coercive power to create monopolies, form cartels or deter entry into markets (Stigler 1971; Posner 1974). Corruption provides a motivation for public decision makers to impose market restrictions, because they can pocket parts of the rents for themselves (Lambsdorff 2002b). Imposing restrictions may already be an option to agents.[15] But principals can impose such restrictions in a more forceful way by making them part of law. The notion of corrupt public decision makers as monopolists, creating market restrictions and rents, suggests the application of a classical instrument of welfare economics to the analysis of corruption – the Harberger triangle. The governments' monopoly position implies that the bribes demanded (and the prices in sectors affected by corruption) are inefficient. The reason for this inefficiency is that mutually profitable exchange is impeded because the large price forces those out of the market whose willingness to pay falls short of the monopolistic market price. This is harmful to public welfare because marginal costs of producing the product are lower than the monopoly price, and an exchange which is beneficial to both sides does not take place because the monopolistic government takes into account that lowering its 'fees' reduces the revenues obtained from other corrupt deals it undertakes.

There is one crucial limitation faced by the principal. His self-enrichment must be kept confidential, avoiding that political opponents in their zeal for power acquire delicate pieces of information. Even at the end of a political career this imperative may apply when keeping one's ill-gotten gains requires a political ally as a successor. As a result of the necessity to conceal payments, some goods are preferred to others. Customized goods present better opportunities to arrange for hidden payments than off-the-shelf products. Shleifer and Vishny (1993) report on a bottle-making factory in Mozambique that needed a new machine for fixing paper labels onto the bottles. A simple machine could have been bought for US $ 10,000, but the manager wanted a

14 There are also examples of corruption lowering prices, particularly when it accompanies fraud. Customs officials may collect only the bribe rather than a more costly official duty. Tax collectors may lower the amount owed in exchange for a cut (Shleifer and Vishny 1993). At the legislative level tariffs can be lowered for favoured sectors or tax privileges be given to industries in exchange for bribes.

15 For example, police officials may offer to harass competing firms in exchange for a bribe. Or license authorities may restrict market entry when paid bribes from insiders.

more sophisticated version for ten times that price. Since there was only one supplier of this machine, this provided sufficient room to over-invoice and pay a kickback to the manager. The loss to the factory would in this case have been substantial. Winston (1979, 840-1) argues that the risk associated with corruption increases with the number of transactions, the number of people involved, the duration of the transaction and the simplicity and standardization of the procedure. Because the risk does not clearly increase with the value of a transaction, large, one-shot purchases create a more efficient base for a kickback. This biases the decisions made by corrupt public servants in favour of capital intensive, technologically sophisticated and custom-built products and technologies.

At the same time, some areas or input factors are unattractive to those seeking a corrupt income. Investments may present a better opportunity to extract money as opposed to smaller labour contracts, (Mauro 1997; Tanzi and Davoodi 1997). In extreme cases, public investments fail to meet public demand, resulting in 'white-elephant projects'. As pointed out by Alesina and Weder (1999, 8), this distortion does not only arise in the case of public investments but is also relevant to private investments once investors belong to the inner circle of those profiting from bribery. Capital input will exceed its efficient level while labour input will fall short of it. Education is an area where corrupt principals find few opportunities to extract income for themselves. Mauro (1998) declares that expenditure levels will be too low, arguing that other expenditures offer public servants better opportunities to collect bribes. Similar considerations suggest that expenditure on maintenance is too low, particularly when a corrupt government can better extract bribes from new investments, (Tanzi and Davoodi 1997). Military spending seems to provide a good base for kickbacks and is preferred by a corrupt principal, (Gupta, de Mello and Sharan 2001).

Conclusions

Society will commonly dislike the distributional consequences of corruption, where it seems fair to assume that the rich and powerful are able to enrich themselves at the expense of the poor. But these aspects of distribution are not the subject of this study, which linked corruption to public welfare. Four models have been expounded, one with a self-serving agent, another with a self-serving principal, a third with a principal restricted by competition and a final model where the principal faces a powerful agent.

An immediate effect of corruption is that it renders governments unable or unwilling to maximize welfare. But the reasons for welfare losses are different for these types of corruption. With self-serving agents, welfare losses result from informational asymmetries, which constrain the contractual space available to agents and principals. Those contracts, which require the absence of corruption, cannot be sealed. The welfare effects will largely relate to principals omitting economic transactions because agents cannot credibly commit themselves to honest dealings.

A self-serving principal may attempt to design a perfect bribery system that operates as smoothly as a tax. But in order to do so, he must be able to set aside constitutional and legal restrictions. But this cripples his chances to make believable commitments to long-term policies. The private sector will not risk sinking resources where corrupt governments do not commit themselves to honouring and defending property rights. Potential investors will justifiably fear opportunism and governments will be unable to attract investors and private capital. The welfare effect will largely be felt by investors who are discouraged from sinking their investments, leading to reduced capital accumulation.

Competition for the principal's position may provide a constraint to self-serving. But the effectiveness of this mechanism may be up to dispute. Above that, competition may also provoke waste, as suggested by rent-seeking theory. This type of waste may take the form of disproportionate expenses for lobbying and public campaigns and excessive wining and dining. Absence of corruption would allow societies to live with less competition and less associated waste.

A contested principal may provide scope for an agent to obtain a more powerful position. Given this powerful position, the agent may get away with shirking, self-serving and petty corruption. This is likely to bring about x-inefficiency. The principal's self-serving, on the other hand, will now be contained by the agent's power. It can be carried out only secretly in areas where the principal has control. Since these areas are preferred over others, allocative inefficiency will arise.

Assigning specific types of welfare losses to certain models is certainly stylized, as pointed out in the study. Corrupt agents may also deter investors and bring about allocative inefficiency. Corrupt principals may also trigger x-inefficiency. Yet, I provided reasons why the predominant effect should be the one predicated.

Fruitful avenues for research might seek to empirically assess to what extent differences in types of corruption exist in reality – for example utilizing survey data on the performance of countries and comparing one country to another. Relating these results to data on capital productivity and capital accumulation may provide a way of testing the hypothesis that different forms of corruption have different effects on public welfare.

References

Acemoglu, D. and Verdier, T. (1998), 'Property Rights, Corruption and the Allocation of Talent: A General Equilibrium Approach', *Economic Journal* 108, 1381-403.

_______, (2000), 'The Choice Between Market Failures and Corruption', *American Economic Review* 90, 194-211.

Ades, A. and Di Tella, R. (1997), 'National Champions and Corruption: Some Unpleasant Interventionist Arithmetic', *Economic Journal* 107, 1023-1042.

_______ (1999), 'Rents, Competition, and Corruption', *American Economic Review* 89, 982-93.

Alesina, A. and Weder, B. (1999), 'Do Corrupt Governments Receive Less Foreign Aid?', *Working Paper No. 7108* (Cambridge, MA: *National Bureau of Economic Research*).

Bardhan, P. (1997), 'Corruption and Development: A Review of Issues', *Journal of Economic Literature* 35, 1320-46.

Bayley, D. (1966), 'The Effects of Corruption in a Developing Nation' *Western Political Quartely* 19:4, 719-32. Reprinted in Heidenheimer et al. (eds) (1989), 935-52.

Beck, P. and Maher, M. (1986), 'A Comparison of Bribery and Bidding in Thin Markets', *Economics Letters* 20, 1-5.

Becker, G. (1994), 'To Root Out Corruption, Boot Out Big Government', *Business Week*.

Besley, T. and McLaren, J. (1993), 'Taxes and Bribery: The Role of Wage Incentives', *Economic Journal* 103, 119–41.

Breton, A. and Wintrobe, R. (1975), 'The Equilibrium Size of a Budget-Maximizing Bureau: A Note on Niskanen's Theory of Bureaucracy', *Journal of Political Economy* 83:1, 195-208.

Brock, W. and Magee, S. (1984), 'The Invisible Foot and the Waste of Nations', in Colander, D. (ed.), 177-86.

Buchanan, J. (1993), 'Public Choice after Socialism', *Public Choice* 72, 67-74.

Buchanan, J., Tollison, R., and Tullock, G. (eds.) (1980) *Toward a Theory of the Rent-Seeking Society* (College Station: Texas A&M University Press).

Button, K. and Weyman-Jones, T. (1992), 'Ownership Structure, Institutional Organization and Measured X-Efficiency', *American Economic Review* 82, 439-45.

_______ (1994), 'X-Efficiency and Technical Efficiency', *Public Choice* 80, 83-104.

Coate, S. and Morris, S. (1994), 'On the Form of Transfers to Special Interests', *Working Paper 94/21* (University of Pennsylvania, Center for Analytic Research in Economic and Social Science).

Colander, D. (ed.) (1984), *Neoclassical Political Economy. The Analysis of Rent-Seeking and DUP Activities.* (Cambridge, MA: Ballinger).

De Alessi, L. (1983), 'Property Rights, Transactions Costs, and X-Efficiency: An Essay in Economic Theory', *American Economic Review* 73, 64–81.

De Soto, H. (1989), *The Other Path.* (New York: Harper and Row).

Djankov, S., La Porta, R., Lopez-de-Silanes, F., and Shleifer, A. (2000), 'The Regulation of Entry', *National Bureau of Economic Research Working Paper No. 7892*.

Edgeworth, F. (1903), 'The Tariff Problem by W.J. Ashley', *Economic Journal* 13:52, 571-5.

Fiorentini, G. and Peltzman, S. (eds.) (1995), *The Economics of Organized Crime.* (Cambridge, MA: Cambridge University Press).

Frisch, D. (1999), 'Entwicklungspolitische Gesichtspunkte der Korruption', in Pieth, M. and Eigen, P. (eds.).

Furubotn, E. and Richter, R. (1998), *Institutions and Economic Theory. The Contribution of the New Institutional Economics* (Ann Arbor: University of Michigan Press).
Githongo, J. (1997), 'Independency, Investigation and Denunciation of Corruption from the Press – The Case of Kenya' Eight International Anti-Corruption Conference, Lima, Peru.
Grossman, H. (1995), 'Rival Kleptocrats: the Mafia versus the State', in Fiorentini, G. and Peltzman, S. (eds.), 143-56.
Gupta, S., de Mello, L., and Sharan, R. (2001), 'Corruption and Military Spending', *European Journal of Political Economy* 17:4, 749-77.
Hafner, O. (1998), 'The Role of Corruption in the Misappropriation of Tropical Forest Resources and in Tropical Forest Destruction', *Transparency International Working Paper,* (Berlin: Transparency International); www.transparency.org/documents/work-papers/index.html.
Harden, B. (1993), *Africa. Dispatches from a Fragile Continent.* (London: Harper Collins Paperback Edition).
Harrison, G. and Riley, S. (1998), 'The Evolution of Corruption in Mozambique', (Unpublished manuscript).
Hart, A. (1970), 'Fiscal Policy in Latin America', *Journal of Political Economy*, 78:4, Pt 2, 857-89.
Heidenheimer, A., Johnston, M. and LeVine, V. (1989), *Political Corruption – A Handbook.* (New Brunswick: Transaction Publishers).
Huntington, S. (1968), 'Modernization and Corruption', in *Political Order in Changing Societies* (New Haven: Yale University Press), 59-71. Reprinted in A. Heidenheimer et al. (eds.) (1989), 377-88.
Isham, J. and Kaufmann, D. (1999), 'The Forgotten Rationale for Policy Reform: The Productivity of Investment Projects', *Quarterly Journal of Economics*, 114, 149-84.
Jain, A. (1998), 'Models of Corruption' in Jain, A. (ed.) *Economics of Corruption.* (Boston and London: Dordrecht), 13-34.
Khalil, F. and Lawarrée, J. (1995), 'Collusive Auditors', *American Economic Review*, 85:2, 442-6.
Klein, B., Crawford, R. and Alchian, A. (1978), 'Vertical Integration, Appropriable Rents, and the Competitive Contracting Process', *Journal of Law and Economics*, 21, 297-326.
Klitgaard, R. (1988), *Controlling Corruption.* (Berkeley: University of California Press).
Kofman, F. and J. Lawarrée (1996), 'On the Optimality of Allowing Collusion', *Journal of Public Economics*, 61, 383–407.
Laffont, J-J. and Tirole, J. (1993), *A Theory of Incentives in Procurement and Regulation.* (Cambridge, MA: MIT Press).
Lambsdorff, J. (1998), 'An Empirical Investigation of Bribery in International Trade', *European Journal of Development Research* 10, 40-59. Reprinted in Robinson, M. (ed.) (1998) *Corruption and Development.* (London: Frank Cass Publishers).

_______, (2000), 'De la propension des exportateurs à verser des pots-de-vin – l'impact sur les échanges', *Revue Tiers Monde* 41:161, 89-116.

_______, (2002a), 'Making Corrupt Deals – Contracting in the Shadow of the Law', *Journal of Economic Behavior and Organization*, 48:3, 221-241.

_______, (2002b), 'Corruption and Rent-Seeking', *Public Choice*, 113:1/2, 97-125.

_______, and Cornelius, P. (2000), 'Corruption, Foreign Investment and Growth', *The Africa Competitiveness Report 2000/2001* in Schwab, K. and Sachs, J., et al. (eds.)., Joint Publication of the World Economic Forum and the Harvard Institute for International Development (Oxford: Oxford University Press), 70-8.

Landes, W. and Posner, R. (1975), 'The Independent Judiciary in an Interest-Group Perspective', *Journal of Law and Economics*, 18, 875-901.

Leff, N. (1964), 'Economic Development Through Bureaucratic Corruption', *American Behavioral Scientist*, 8:3, 8-14. Reprinted in A. Heidenheimer A. et al. (eds.) (1989), 389-403.

Leibenstein, H. (1966), 'Allocative Efficiency vs. X-Efficiency', *American Economic Review* 56, 392-415.

_______, (1973), 'Competition and X-Efficiency: Reply', *Journal of Political Economy* 81, 765-77.

Lien, D. (1986), 'A Note on Competitive Bribery Games', *Economics Letters* 22, 337-41.

Lui, F. (1985), 'An Equilibrium Queuing Model of Bribery', *Journal of Political Economy* 93, 760-81.

Mankiw, N. (2000), *Principles of Economics*, 2nd Edition. (Forth Worth: Harcourt College).

Marcoullier, D. and Young, L. (1995), 'The Black Hole of Graft: The Predatory State and the Informal Economy', *American Economic Review*, 85:3, 630-46.

Marshall, A. (1897), 'The Old Generation of Economists and the New', *Quarterly Journal of Economics* 11:2, 115-35.

Mauro, P. (1995), 'Corruption and Growth', *Quarterly Journal of Economics* 110:3, 681-712.

_______, (1997), 'The Effects of Corruption on Growth, Investment, and Government Expenditure: A Cross–Country Analysis', *Corruption and the Global Economy*, (Washington DC: Institute for International Economics), 83–107.

_______, (1998), 'Corruption and the Composition of Government Expenditure', *Journal of Public Economics* 69, 263-79.

McChesney, F. (1987), 'Rent Extraction and Rent Creation in the Economic Theory of Regulation', *Journal of Legal Studies* 16, 101-18.

_______ (1997), *Money for Nothing. Politicians, Rent Extraction, and Political Extortion.* (Cambridge, MA: Harvard University Press).

McGuire, M. and Olson, M. (1996), 'The Economics of Autocracy and Majority Rule: The Invisible Hand and the Use of Force', *Journal of Economic Literature*, 34, 72-96.

Moe, T. (1984), 'The New Economics of Organization', *American Journal of Political Science*, 28:4, 739-77.

Morgan, T. (1964), 'The Theory of Error in Centrally-Directed Economic Systems', *Quarterly Journal of Economics* 78:3, 395-419.

Moselle, B. and Polak, B. (2001), 'A Model of a Predatory State', *Journal of Law Economics and Organization* 17:1, 1-33.

Murphy, K., Shleifer, A. and Vishny, R. (1993), 'Why is Rent-Seeking so Costly to Growth', *American Economic Review* 82:2, 409-14.

Myrdal, G. (1956), *An International Economy.* (New York: Harper).

_______, (1968), *Asian Drama.* Vol. II. (New York: Random House).

Niskanen, W. (1975), 'Bureaucrats and Politicians', *Journal of Law and Economics* 18, 617-43.

North, D. (1981), *Structure and Change in Economic History.* (New York and London: Norton).

_______, (1984), 'Three Approaches to the Study of Institutions', in Colander, D. (ed.) (1984), 33-40.

_______, (1993), 'Institutions and Credible Commitment', *Journal of Institutional and Theoretical Economics* 149, 11-23.

_______, and Weingast, B. (1989), 'The Evolution of Institutions Governing Public Choice in Seventeenth Century England', *Journal of Economic History* 49, 803-32.

Nye, J. (1967), 'Corruption and Political Development: A Cost Benefit Analysis', *American Political Science Review* 61:2, 417-27. Reprinted in A. Heidenheimer, A. et al. (eds.) (1989), 963-83.

Olsen, T. and Torsvik, G. (1998), 'Collusion and Renegotiation in Hierarchies: A Case of Beneficial Corruption', *International Economic Review* 41:2, May, 413-38.

Orchard, L. and Stretton, H. (1997), 'Public Choice', *Cambridge Journal of Economics*; 21:3, 409-30.

Parish, R. and Ng Y-K, (1972), 'Monopoly, X-Efficiency and the Measurement of Welfare Loss', *Economica*, 39, 301-8.

Pieth, M. and Eigen, P. (eds.) (1999), *Korruption im Internationalen Geschäftsverkehr: Bestandsaufnahme, Bekämpfung, Prävention.* (Basel und Frankfurt am Main: Luchterhand).

Posner, R. (1974), 'Theories of Economic Regulation', *Bell Journal of Economics and Management* 5:2, 335-58.

Rose-Ackerman, S. (1978), *Corruption – A Study in Political Economy.* (New Haven: Academic Press).

_______, (1999), *Corruption and Government. Causes, Consequences and Reform.* (Cambridge: Cambridge University Press).

Rowley, C. (1988), 'Rent-Seeking versus Directly Unproductive Profit-Seeking Activities', in Rowley et al. (eds.), 15-25.

Rowley, C., Tollison, R. and Tullock, G. (eds.) (1988), *The Political Economy of Rent-Seeking.* (Boston: Kluwer Academic Publishers).

Schumpeter, J. (1942), *Capitalism, Socialism and Democracy.* (New York: Harper).

Shleifer, A. and Vishny, R. (1993), 'Corruption', *Quarterly Journal of Economics* 108, 599-617.

Stigler, G. (1971), 'The Theory of Economic Regulation', *Bell Journal of Economics and Management Science* 2, 3-21.

_______, (1976), 'The Xistence of X-Efficiency', *American Economic Review* 66, 213-6.

Stiglitz, J. (1998), 'Distinguished Lecture on Economics in Government: The Private Uses of Public Interests: Incentives and Institutions', *Journal of Economic Perspectives* 12:2, 3-22.

Strausz, R. (1995), 'Collusion and Renegotiation in a Principal-Supervisor-Agent Relationship', *Center for Economic Research Discussion Paper, No. 9548* (Tilburg University, Netherlands).

Tanzi, V. and Davoodi, H. (1997), 'Corruption, Public Investment, and Growth', *International Monetary Fund Working Paper*, 97-139.

Tullock, G. (1971), 'The Cost of Transfers', *Kyklos* 24, 629–43.

_______, (1980), 'Rent Seeking as a Negative-Sum Game', in Buchanan, J. et al. (eds.) (1980), 16-36.

_______, (1993), *Rent Seeking, The Shaftesbury Papers, 2.* (Cambridge, MA: Cambridge University Press).

Wedeman, A. (1997), 'Looters, Rent-Scrapers, and Dividend-Collectors: Corruption and Growth in Zaïre, South Korea, and the Philippines', *The Journal of Developing Areas* 31, 457–78.

Weingast, B. (1993), 'Constitutions as Governance Structures: The Political Foundations of Secure Markets', *Journal of Institutional and Theoretical Economics*, 149, 286-311.

Wiggins, S. (1991), 'The Economics of the Firm and Contracts: A Selective Survey', *Journal of Institutional and Theoretical Economics*, 148, 603-61.

Williamson. O. (1985), *The Economic Institutions of Capitalism. Firms, Markets, Relational Contracting.* (New York: The Free Press).

Winston, G. (1979), 'The Appeal of Inappropriate Technologies: Self-Inflicted Wages, Ethnic Price and Corruption', *World Development* 7:8/9, 835-45.

Wintrobe, R. (1998), *The Political Economy of Dictatorship.* (Cambridge, UK: Cambridge University Press).

_______, and Breton, A. (1986), 'Organizational Structure and Productivity', *American Economic Review*, 76:3, 530-38.

Chapter 7

Information, Corruption, and Measures for the Promotion of Manufactured Exports

Glenn P. Jenkins and Chun-Yan Kuo

Introduction

There has been a growing emphasis in many developing countries on export-led growth policies that attract both domestic and foreign investment into activities that will increase exports. Many countries, however, have not achieved the desired response. Among other problems, investors often face foreign exchange controls, tariffs on imported inputs, and a costly system for the exemption or refund of sales taxes on inputs used to produce exports. These factors have frequently impeded the inflow of foreign investment and prevented the expansion of export production and sales.[1] This chapter addresses two issues related to the design and administration of the fiscal provisions that affect the competitiveness of a country in the production of manufactured exports.

The first issue is how to design a system that allows exporters to sell their output free of the burden of domestic sales taxes. The second issue is how to relieve exporters from the burden of import tariffs levied on inputs used in the production of exports.

The value-added tax (VAT) is the most common form of general sales tax, having been implemented in more than 120 countries.[2] Under this system, in order for exports to be sold free of tax, they are generally taxed at a zero rate and the exporters are allowed to claim a refund for the taxes paid on input purchases. The refund procedures of many VAT systems, however, do not function well. Refunds are either not paid in a timely fashion by the government or are overstated by exporters. In short, the procedure seldom works as it should.

---

1 The effectiveness of the institutional arrangements to promote exports is equally important for success in investment and economic growth. See Rodrick (1999).

2 The situation in India is worse. In India, with its central excise tax system and its state level sales taxes, a situation is created where it is virtually impossible to determine the amount of sales and excise taxes embodied in the cost of producing exports. See Maxwell (1999, 6).

Import duties on intermediate inputs can be prohibitive for manufactured exports, especially if the rates are high. The mechanisms to remove this export impediment include tax free zones, duty drawback systems, duty exemption systems, bonded warehouses, and duty free factory systems. All these systems have some limitations and are not equally effective in achieving their intended objectives.

In terms of their importance in the design of tax policies to promote exports, these two forms of border tax adjustments often turn out to be several times as important as income tax holidays and accelerated depreciation allowances (Jenkins and Kuo 1997; Le 2002).

In this chapter, we provide a synthesis of how a number of developing countries have tried to address these issues.[3] We identify the elements of the administrative systems needed to deliver effectively the VAT input tax credit refunds and to eliminate the burden of import duties on inputs used in exports. Emphasis will be placed on the informational needs for their effective administration. These findings might prove helpful to policymakers who are faced with the development of institutions to administer such border tax adjustments.

Tax relief for exporters under VAT

Basic input tax credit system

Under the credit invoice method, all VAT registrants are obliged to collect and remit VAT on their taxable supplies. These registrants are allowed to recover the tax paid on their purchases. For each reporting period, registrants need to calculate the tax collected on sales and remit to the tax authority the amount that is in excess of the taxes they paid during that period on purchases. If the difference is negative, the registrants may be able to claim the difference as a tax refund.

In certain situations, a registered vendor may be involved in supplying both taxable and tax-exempt goods and services. In these cases, the input tax credits are allowed only to the extent that the business inputs are used in the taxable supply of the vendor. In other words, when a vendor is involved in both taxable and exempt supplies, the credit is only available for purchased inputs considered reasonable for use in the taxable supply. To deal with this situation, apportionment rules for the input tax credits are required to allocate the tax credits among the different supplies of a business operation. If the exporter is also engaged in exempt supplies, an apportionment in input tax credit must be applied to ensure that no excess input tax credits are granted for the exempt business.

In theory, a correctly designed and administered VAT system completely removes such taxes from the cost of exported goods, thereby making a country's exports more competitive.

3 These countries include Ghana, Kenya, Malawi, and South Africa in Africa; Indonesia, Korea, Malaysia, Sri Lanka, India, Pakistan, Taiwan and Thailand in Asia; and Argentina, Chile, Dominion Republic, Mexico and Uruguay in Latin America.

Tax refunds to exporters

A VAT system cannot operate effectively in the absence of a well-functioning input tax credit and refund system. To facilitate the administration of the VAT system and to protect the government revenue, registrants are required to maintain records to substantiate their entitlements for the taxes paid on the purchase of production inputs. In other words, registrants must be prepared to provide the tax authority a satisfactory invoice or other document reporting the amount of taxes paid on business inputs.

Since the VAT on imported inputs is normally payable at the time of importation, it is included as part of the registrant's input tax credit entitlement. In most countries, the proportion of VAT collected at Customs is generally very high. For example, the ratio is about 50 percent in Mexico (Kuo 1996), 40 percent in Indonesia, 55 per cent in North Cyprus (Jenkins 2001) and 75 percent in Canada. Since exports are generally zero-rated, exporters can claim the taxes paid on their inputs as a refund. Hence, most exporters are in a chronic position of waiting for tax refunds because of excess tax credits.

Most VAT jurisdictions allow taxpayers to file tax returns more frequently than the legal requirement. For example, a business can opt to file monthly, even if it is only required to file its tax returns quarterly. Because exporters are claiming refunds rather than paying tax, they have an incentive to file their tax returns more often in order to get their refunds earlier. This exacerbates the problem of administrative congestion because of the increase in the volume of refund requests.

To ensure that goods are exported to qualify as a zero-rated supply, exporters must have shipped the goods out of the country and obtained some proof of the validity of the export. If this information is not easily verifiable, the length of time the government takes to refund the excess tax credits to the legitimate exporters will increase. This is financially damaging to exporters, since they must tie up substantial amounts of cash by paying input taxes. Obviously, they would like to receive a refund as quickly as possible to restore their cash flow. In a number of countries it was common for exporters to wait for up to one year to obtain a refund for the VAT taxes paid on inputs. An extreme case is found in the development and exploration of mining activities. In this case large VAT input tax payments are incurred years before these mines become operational and their sales of production begin.[4] In a number of countries no VAT refunds are actually paid to the "potential" exporter until the mine starts to make sales.

The difficulty of accurately making refunds of excess tax credits to exporters is an important weakness of the value added tax system. Countries, such as Canada, Bolivia, Korea and Thailand, experienced a heavy volume of fraudulent claims for refunds of input VAT payments in the years following the introduction of their VAT systems (Khadka 1999).

---

4 This issue was raised by tax practitioners for Canadian mining companies, which were involved in several mining projects in Latin America.

Issues and potential solutions

In the case of suppliers to the domestic market, most countries specify that the VAT input tax credits are to be used immediately to offset taxes due on sales; or if there is an excess of credits, they are to be carried forward to offset taxes due in the future. If the tax credits continue to be in excess of taxes owed for a specified period of time, then usually a provision is available to refund the excess tax credits in cash. For businesses selling to the domestic market, the need for cash refunds of excess credits is a relatively infrequent event. The situation is very different in the case of major exporters. For example, in Uruguay, which exports very few manufactured items, the refunds given to exporters accounted for over 0 percent of all refunds (Barreix 1999b). Here the excess credits will exist from before start-up and will accumulate. In order to avoid placing the exporters at a competitive disadvantage, they need a mechanism to turn quickly the tax credits from input purchases into cash.

Some people target the refund system to engage in fraud. For example, firms claiming to be exporters may apply for excessive refunds on the basis of fake invoices of input purchases, and fake documentation of export sales, including customs verification of exports. This has been a serious problem in the administration of the VAT system in Thailand. Cases of such fraud have been reported in Uruguay, Mexico, and Indonesia (Flatters 1996). The administrative issues become even more complicated and fraud is made easier in the regional duty-free trading zones, such as the Common Market for Eastern and Southern Africa (Glenday 1996), and Mercosur (Barreix 1999b).

Most of the exporters would like to get their refunds quickly from the government in order to reduce their net cash outflows and thereby lower their cost of doing business. The government may also have a policy to help businesses by speeding up the payment of refunds. In such a situation, the tax refund administrators find themselves facing a dilemma. Will they process the refunds quickly and face the risk of approving fraudulent claims? Or will they audit every claim and, as a result, delay the payment of refunds to everyone?

A computerized VAT administration information system with data on both the taxes paid on inputs and the volume of domestic and export sales is essential to give the tax refund administrators comfort that they are not sending a check to someone engaged in fraud. In many developing countries, such an information system does not exist or it focuses on the amounts of tax collected and not on the amounts of tax credits being claimed. The result is often the worst of all possible scenarios. Due to a lack of information the refund administrators hesitate to approve the payment of refunds. Delays result and the legitimate exporters start to bribe or 'tip' the tax officials to receive the refunds due to them. If they take bribes to speed up the administrative processing of refunds to true exporters, the tax administrator faces little risk of rebuke. However, if he processes a fraudulent claim there is a risk that eventually it will become known. For example, in the case of Thailand the amount of reported exports was not consistent with the foreign exchange position of the country.

However, the process of making bribes to speed up the administration process, attracts the dishonest bureaucrat who is more willing to accept bribes for processing fraudulent claims as well. Because of this lucrative administrative situation, a substantial number the tax auditors generally are assigned and/or are attracted to managing the export refund system. The end result is that the tax administrators receive substantial amounts of side payments, they pay more fraudulent refund claims, and the legitimate exporters get far less than they are entitled to. In this case the lack of information by the tax administration creates the conditions for the incubation of bribery and corruption. Both the legitimate exporter and the fraudulent claimant have an incentive to bribe both honest and dishonest tax administrators to get payments from the government. Our research examines current practice in a wide range of countries to see how they cope with this problem. Three 'innovations' are found that show considerable promise, and at least one that appears never to work.

The innovation that shows little or no promise is creating a new agency separate from the VAT and customs administrations, such as an export promotion agency, to administer refunds. Massive fraud is the usual result. The Philippines has recently experienced such fraud; and Indonesia with its B4KPM office experienced similar difficulties in the early 1990s. These agencies never had the necessary information or technical skills to determine whether a claim was legitimate or fraudulent. Furthermore, such agencies do not have the safeguarding of the integrity of the fiscal system as their mandate; they exist primarily to promote exports. Even fraudulent export documentation often improves the short run official statistics on export growth.

In contrast, our studies revealed that requiring fiscal bonds from those claiming export refunds has speeded up the payment of refunds. With this innovation, the government requires taxpayers who apply for tax refunds to obtain a customs bond, or deposit some percentage of the amount in a special bank account until the tax authority has decided if it is going to audit the claim. The claims, however, are paid immediately after the request is made. The tax authority is required to give final approval or conduct an audit within a prescribed time period.

This scheme can apply to exporters as well as local firms requesting tax refunds. Firms that have developed a proven track record of honesty might be allowed to maintain a bank guarantee for a smaller percentage of the outstanding claims. This innovation places a tighter degree of control on excess input tax credits under the VAT system. Such a system was implemented in Taiwan during the early years of export expansion with great success (Kuo 1998). The government of Mexico has been implementing a similar but not so tightly structured scheme since 1999 (Kuo 1999). While this system has resulted in a much faster refund of the input tax credits, it does cost the exporter an extra amount to obtain either a bond or a bank guarantee. These costs will offset some of the benefits of obtaining the tax refunds faster and with fewer administrative hassles.

Another innovation with demonstrated success in speeding up the payment of refunds is to have tax refunds claims certified by chartered accounting firms or certified public accountants. This allows taxpayers to use the recognized accountant firms to verify the financial statement and a claim for input tax credits, thereby placing the responsibility of tax liability on both the taxpayers and accountants. This option should eliminate most of the fraudulent claims and, hence, reduce the government's administrative costs. After Kenya introduced this system, the number of export tax credit refunds for VAT dropped by over 40 percent (Terkper 1999b). Clearly, many firms had been submitting refund claims for VAT that did not stand up to the scrutiny of financial auditors. Such a system also frees foreign-owned firms from dealing with local tax officers,[5] thereby reducing their compliance costs. Although the local accounting firms charge for their services, the service charge is well worth the cost, especially for large claims. In order not to place a financial burden on those requesting small refunds, a size threshold for the claims should be given to allow small claims to be made without the certification from an accounting firm.

The third innovation for speeding up payment of refunds is not to impose VAT on business purchases at the time of importation. Historically, Taiwan has implemented this practice.[6] More recently a version of this approach also has been introduced in Singapore (Jenkins and Khadka 1998). The tax is automatically deferred until either the imported goods are resold or until the goods produced by using the imported inputs are sold. As no VAT is paid on imported inputs when they enter the country (Kuo 1998), the tax refunds for manufactured exports will be reduced. Hence, making imported inputs for export production VAT-exempt, or taxed at a lower rate at the time of importation, can substantially reduce the VAT input tax credits and claims for refunds by exporters. In Mexico, the government taxes import transactions at a lower rate when they are destined for the industrial zones along the Mexico-USA border. This has lowered the financial burden of the cumulated excess tax credits (Kuo 1999b).

This option, however, may also create other problems. If the importers cease operation or no longer file tax returns after bringing a consignment of goods into the country, then the government may never collect the taxes due on their domestic sale. This can be significant in less developed countries where the informal sectors are relatively large. It may also increase the administration costs for the government by breaking the invoice-tax-credit chain in the production and distribution process under the VAT. However, under a tightly administered VAT system, these untaxed imports should be subject to VAT on their first sale within the country.

To reduce the incentive for fraud and to increase the compliance in the tax withholding system for the income and social security tax systems, a country might wish to issue tax credit certificates to the exporting firms instead of cash payments to cover the VAT refunds. This system is being used in Uruguay with considerable

5 For example, some foreign firms in China have experienced a great deal of difficulties in getting input tax credits. These firms often have to deal with local authorities that have different interpretations of the tax laws.

6 In the case of goods imported by individuals or non-registrants, the VAT is collected at the Customs in Taiwan (Kuo 1998).

success, although some fraud still has taken place (Barreix 1999b). Virtually all firms will have withholding tax obligations that are substantial in the area of payroll and social security taxes. It is likely that the VAT tax credits that need to be refunded to exporters will be less than those withholding obligations that these same firms should be paying. Hence, by integrating the administration of the refund system for VAT with the withholding tax system for wages and salaries, both systems might be strengthened.

Nothing in tax administration is automatic. The government needs to audit the tax credit certificates to determine if they are legitimate. However, at least the completely fraudulent claimant is likely to be restrained, because the tax credit certificate has value only if the firm also has employees and wage withholding obligations. There may be cases where the firm's withholding obligations are less than its excess VAT input tax credits. Provisions are necessary to issue cash refunds in these cases; however, the number of such cases will be few as compared to the total that would exist if the tax credit certificate system were not employed.

The tax credit certificates should not be tradable (at least initially) between enterprises in order to avoid the fraudulent duplication of certificates. If the trading of tax certificates is allowed then the purchaser of the tax credit must be made liable if the tax certificate is not legitimate. In this case it is likely that the major purchasers of the tax credit certificates will be major firms who have the technical capacity to determine at the lowest cost if the tax certificate is legitimate or not (Barreix 1999b). The cost of this audit by the purchaser of the tax certificate will be reflected in the amount that the certificates are discounted when traded.

Three of the four administrative innovations described above are using a market mechanism rather than the information maintained by the tax administration to separate the legitimate claimants for a VAT refunds from fraudulent ones. As compared to bona fide export firms, it is relatively costly for crooks to get a large accounting firm to certify the legitimacy of their claims, particularly if the auditing firm is going to be held liable when the fraud is discovered. It is also relatively costly for them to obtain a bank guarantee, if most of their transactions will be fraudulent. Similarly, tax credit certificates are not of much use to them as they are unlikely to be paying significant amounts of other taxes. If they try to sell tax certificates that were obtained fraudulently, it is less likely that they will get them past the scrutiny of the due diligence undertaken by the purchasers of the tax credit certificates.

These proposed institutional changes to the normal VAT administration can help to increase the effectiveness of the VAT systems, but they do not make a complete solution. Although the auditing requirements are greatly reduced, the auditing function of the tax administration needs to be built and maintained. When this component of the tax administration is weak, then it is unlikely to be able to police even its private agents. For example, Uruguay, which has a fairly good VAT tax administration, has approximately 50,000 VAT taxpayers and 70 full time auditors. By comparison, Sri Lanka, which has 15,000 VAT taxpayers, has only 12 auditors (Barreix 1999a). Sri Lanka is trying to operate with about 60 percent of the auditing strength of Uruguay. Hence, we should not be surprised when we find that Sri Lanka has experienced both delays and fraud in its VAT refund system (Barreix 1999a).

Relief of trade taxes for exporters

Conceptual framework

Experience has taught us that the expansion of manufacturing exports is one of the most important vehicles for economic growth in developing countries. To be successful in international markets, exported goods must be competitive in terms of both quality and price. In order to achieve this objective, governments need to pursue a general public policy to ensure that their exported goods and services are free of indirect domestic and trade taxes. As discussed above, if exports are zero-rated under the consumption type VAT, all exported goods or services can, in theory, be sold free of domestic value added taxes.

To get the same result for trade taxes, the government should either exempt or refund the import duties imposed on business inputs. This would, in effect, remove the tax burden that is embodied in the cost of inputs used to produce exports. For this to happen, the government needs to remove import duties not only from goods directly imported and used in the production of exported goods, but also from the cost of local goods that, in turn, use imported inputs in their production (Maxwell 1998; Glenday and Ndii 1999). The government should credit or refund the import duties embodied in the cost of the domestic inputs in order not to penalize exports that use such goods.[7] Unfortunately, in order to refund these hidden taxes, the administration must perform a series of calculations that involve tracing through the backward linkages of the production process, and are extremely difficult to estimate.

In theory, imported machinery and equipment, if they are to be used in the production of exports, should also enter the country duty free in the same manner as raw materials. Since capital goods are often used to produce both taxable (including exported and domestically taxable goods) and exempt products, the government may find it once again administratively cumbersome to separate the two uses in order to estimate the correct amount of rebate. In addition, manufacturers use capital goods over a long period of time and it is very difficult to forecast whether firms will continue using the capital items to produce for export into the future. Again it is often cumbersome to calculate the portion of import duties levied on capital goods used only in the production of exports.

The entire process of calculating and verifying the amounts of import duties that should be exempted or refunded is greatly facilitated by a simple set of tariff rates. The ideal for this purpose is single rate of tariff. Chile was the first country to implement such a single rate tariff system. It is the only country in our study where

7 As demonstrated by Maxwell, there always exists some kind of hidden tax on exports so long as there are duties imposed on imported goods for the purpose of protection. See Maxwell (1998).

we found a duty drawback system working reasonably well. In the case of Chile most of its exports are of an agricultural or agro-processed nature, so the problem of tariff refunds on imported inputs is much smaller for exporters as compared to the situation with export oriented manufactured products.

Alternative schemes and operations

If it is the government's objective to provide tariff relief for imported inputs used to produce exports, several alternative approaches are available to deal with this issue. They include systems for duty drawback and duty exemption (or suspension) of import duties, and export-processing zones.

Duty drawback system The duty drawback system is the classical and the most common method of providing relief from import duties imposed on goods used for the production of exports. Virtually all countries that provide incentives to export-oriented firms have a duty drawback system. Because the duties are paid upon importation, importers, exporters, or manufacturers of exported goods may claim refunds. In general, firms must meet several conditions before the government can refund duties. First, the firms must have paid the import duties. Second, the firms had to have exported the final products. Third, an estimate needs to be made of the amount of duty drawback paid on the imported inputs used in export production. The imported goods eligible for duty drawback are usually only raw materials. Sometimes the list of eligible inputs may be extended to include fuel, packaging materials, machinery and equipment.

Similarly, domestic manufacturers who produce goods and services used by exporters should also be eligible for the duty drawback on the tariffs they pay for imported inputs. These producers are indirect exporters. A difficult question arises as to the number of prior stages of manufacture that should be allowed before the final export is made.[8] Korea, Taiwan, Mexico and Kenya are all examples of countries which have allowed indirect exporters to claim duty-exempt imports (Kuo 1998; 1999a; 1999b). The most difficult issue becomes calculating the refund on import duties to indirect exporters. In the case of Taiwan, a sophisticated input-output coefficient was developed and calculated for each line of production. This ensured the precise amount of hidden tax in the exported goods but it was undoubtedly cumbersome and the government had to employ a great number of personnel to deal with this program.[9] In the other extreme, Kenya adopted a single fixed coefficient for all goods for the sake of simplicity. But inequities among goods became obvious and it was eventually forced to change its system.

8 In the case of Kenya, the back linkage may go back two stages of production.

9 When the duty drawback system involves parties such as importers, exporters and manufacturers of exports, the applicant for tax refunds in Taiwan has to obtain a letter of consent from the other parties who are involved and do not file for refunds. This makes the system even more cumbersome administratively.

The system of duty drawbacks is the most information intensive system available to provide exporters relief from duties on imported inputs. The process is triggered by the act of exporting with the information being assembled by moving backward through the production and input purchasing stages of the activity. First, it requires knowledge of the input-output technical coefficients that are used in the production of the export to identify and quantify the types of inputs used. Second, it requires information on the sources, quantities, prices, and tariffs paid on the inputs used for each specific set of exported goods or services. Finally, it requires information on the financial transactions of the business in order for audits to be conducted of the payments made through this scheme.

Corruption is a universal theme surrounding the administration of a duty drawback system in almost every country. The nature of the problem that a duty drawback is supposed to address, and the administrative procedures it entails, incubates corruption. There are several reasons for this. First, when the goods are first imported, there is no information recorded by the Customs Administration that these items will be used to produce exports and that a duty drawback is expected in the future. Hence, in most countries it is difficult for Customs to trace the actual import entry of the items that are embodied in the items being exported. Generally, the duty drawback administration will have to rely on customs documents that the exporter provides at some later date. Hence, there is usually an ample opportunity for the exporter, perhaps with the collusion of some customs officers, to exaggerate the amount of duties actually paid at the time of importation.

Second, only the exporters know the quantities of materials used in the production processes. Due to differences in models, sizes, and quality of the items being produced, the duty drawback administration will have to either take the exporters' values for the inputs used, negotiate the quantities, or specify arbitrary (and usually inaccurate) input-output coefficients for each item produced. These input-output coefficients are derived on an ad hoc basis through a process of negotiations between the producers and customs officials in the presence of a few engineers.

In the industrialized countries, the solution to the above two problems is to have a system of professional audits of the books and records of the exporting firm, combined with sound technical information on the manufacturing processes. Unfortunately, the usual recommendation made by advisors from advanced industrialized countries for such a detailed auditing system for the duty drawback administration in developing countries is not implementable. Developing countries do not have the available professional auditors, nor is the government able to pay wages competitive with the private sector for such skills. Even if they could obtain professional auditors, they would most likely be needed in areas of greater priority. When one finds professional auditors working in the duty drawback area, it is often because they are attracted to the area by the amount of bribes they expect to receive.

The third reason for the failure in implementation of duty drawback systems is because there is a great reluctance on the part of Customs to return the duties paid.

The revenue administrators, and especially Customs, have no incentive to refund duties in a timely fashion, since refunding this money makes it harder for them to meet their revenue targets. As a consequence, many governments do not treat duty drawbacks as a reduction in revenue, but as an explicit expenditure item in the budget. Unfortunately, this procedure puts the duty drawback refunds under the same constraints and uncertainties as all other discretionary budgetary expenditures.

Due to the likely disputes over the amounts of drawback refunds that are to be properly refunded, and the risk of error that might prove embarrassing to the administration, the usual reaction is to delay payments. In order to overcome the reluctance of the bureaucracy to actually make the refunds legitimate, exporters make side payments to the duty drawback administrators. Once the payment of bribes by legitimate exporters become a 'normal' operating procedure in order to obtain tax refunds, then the administration of the duty drawback system usually becomes an arbitrary process. All aspects of the duty drawback refund system, from the amount of inputs used, the amount of tariffs paid on the imported input, and the amount of goods actually exported, is subject to the influence of bribes and negotiation.[10]

Duty exemption system Sooner or later, as the compliance costs mount, it becomes obvious that the duty drawback system is not an effective way to relieve exports from the duties paid on their imported inputs. As a consequence, other ways of providing duty relief need to be substituted for a duty drawback system. A common characteristic of these alternative methods is that exporters make no payment to Customs at the time the imports initially enter the country and no refund is made later.

In the duty exemption schemes, the government sets up an account-offset system so that import duties can be held in suspense as a liability. The liability is then cancelled upon export. Because the specific importer accounts for the liability, the importer himself can only claim the account-offset. Usually, an importer applies for such an account to be set up for his firm with the Department of Customs even before the inputs are imported. Upon the exportation of the finished products, the refundable amount is credited to the payer's account. In order to make this offsetting entry with accuracy the relationship between the use of inputs and the amount of exports must be established.

Both the duty drawback and the exemption systems operated concurrently in Taiwan, but the exemption scheme has been the instrument that has been more important since the 1970s. This is also the case in Malawi where the duty drawback program did not work well because the government delayed refunding the import duties and surtax imposed on imported and domestically purchased inputs, creating a cash flow problem (Gray 1999).

10 In Vietnam is has been calculated that the present value of the costs of the delays in the refund of taxes and tariffs on leather shoe exports was equal to 17 percent of the initial investment costs in setting up the facilities. For the apparel manufacturing sector it was equal to 77 percent of the initial investment costs. These values were significantly greater than any of the other hidden costs associated with operating in that country (Le, 2002, chapter IX).

With the duty exemption system, the administration's problem of determining what has been imported, and what duties have been suspended, is usually solved by the normal entry procedures of customs. The abuses of the system occur when exporters do not export the goods produced by the inputs and at the same time are not prepared to pay the duties that were suspended. Alternatively, they may resell the inputs in the domestic market without paying the tariffs. To prevent this form of fraud under the suspense system, the importer is normally required to supply the government with a guarantee. Common forms of such a guarantee are the purchase by the exporter of government bonds or negotiable securities approved by the Ministry of Finance, or bank drafts issued by a financial institution in the amount equal to the duty payable. In this way, the government is assured of receiving the revenues it is owed, while at the same time the firm will receive an interest rate on the amount of funds it invests in government bonds. Alternatively, if the firm purchases a bank guarantee usually, it will incur its cost which is a percentage of the amount of the bond. This was the system undertaken in Taiwan and became very popular especially for large businesses (Kuo 1998).[11] Taiwan has carried this system one step further and has accepted promissory notes from companies with a proven track record of compliance. As a result most of Taiwan's exports are produced under such duty suspense schemes.

In Mexico, the suspense or exemption system was adopted but it was widely abused initially because there was no requirement for customs bonds or bank guarantees. As a result, the government of Mexico introduced a system of Customs Bank Accounts in 1999. Under this new system, the direct and indirect exporters are required to deposit an amount of funds equal to the taxes under suspense in interest bearing accounts in banks. The Customs Authority will release the funds back to the firms upon approval of claim for duty remission on the inputs used to produce exports.

A duty exemption scheme was adopted in Korea in specific locations such as export processing zones and bonded warehouses or factories (Kuo 1999a).

Corruption has been much less prevalent in duty exemption systems. This is due to the fact that a record of the transaction is captured by customs for the purpose of the duty exemption system, right at the point when the imported inputs enter the country. At this point the information can be captured for future use in an almost costless fashion. When an accounting entry is made by both the firm as well as the customs system at the beginning of the process, without money having to change hands, the purpose of the importation becomes much more transparent. Often the duty exemption is given only if the firm already has an export order for the items being produced. The interest bearing bank deposits or guarantees reduce the incentive and scope for the private sector to pay bribes to the administration officials to condone fraud. At the same time, the involvement of the banks that are often

11 In late 1970s, the amount of tax relief using the suspense scheme accounted for approximately 80% of all duties on imported inputs used to manufacture exports in Taiwan (Kuo 1998).

working with the businesses in much more important ways, such as the financing of a firm's investments, reduces the incentives for the firm and the government officials to engage in corrupt practices. Simply put, the duty exemption system drastically reduces the power of the government officials over the resources of the firm, and also reduces the financial stakes for the firm and its incentive to pay facilitation payments.

Export processing zones Use of export processing zones (EPZs) to promote export has been quite popular in many developing countries around the world. These include Taiwan, Dominican Republic (Campanella 1999) and Kenya (Glenday and Ndii 1999). Some countries have been successful, but not all.

EPZs are a type of free trade zones established to process goods for exports exclusively. The zones are usually located in the vicinity of harbours or other forms of international transportation. A physical wall to ensure that goods will be taxed when leaving the tax free zones areas for domestic markets surrounds them. The administrative operations in this bonded area are theoretically simple, straightforward and all trade-related activities can be handled in the zones. As such, foreign investors do not have to deal with the domestic bureaucracy's specific regulations, rules, foreign exchange transactions, etc. and thus business transaction costs are greatly reduced.

If Customs officials attempt to delay or slow up the importation of inputs or exportation of the final goods, it is the obligation of the EPZ operator to solve the problem. In this case the negotiations tend to be carried out with higher levels of customs where the problem tends to be solved more quickly, even if facilitation payments are made. As Customs is not holding any funds of the exporters, then they have much less leverage to extract facilitation payments for their services.

With the EPZ, no import duties are levied on materials and other intermediate inputs, nor are equipment parts and components used to produce exports within the EPZ. The EPZs in Taiwan and the Dominican Republic are regarded as being successful and important vehicles for promoting exports. It is important to note, however, that the share of total exports from Taiwan that originated from the EPZs, reached a peak of only nine percent in the 1970s. Thus other institutional arrangements to provide duty relief, such as its accounts based duty exemption system, has been much more important in the promotion of exports (see Table 7.1).

It is also interesting to observe what has been happening in Kenya with respect to EPZs. Although they have been built at great expense they have been characterized by excess capacity (Glenday and Ndii 1998). The fundamentals of international trade such as the small size of the regional Common Market for Eastern and Southern Africa, inadequate infrastructure in Kenya, and appreciation of the domestic currency and rising labor costs, have kept international trade flows much smaller than anticipated.

In a situation where a country has very high tariffs, inadequate infrastructure for modern industries to function, and a full blown rent seeking bureaucracy, the use of EPZs may be the only way that reform minded policy makers can get an export oriented growth strategy started. However, the traditional concept of public sector EPZs with their high fences and customs officials riding trucks going in and out of the premises is an idea whose time has passed. EPZs are expensive to build and usually only match the needs of footloose industries, such as garment and shoe manufacturing, and some forms of electronics. They also make it expensive for local manufactures to get into the business of exporting if they have to relocate their export manufacturing activities to the EPZ in order to get themselves free of indirect taxes and a rent seeking bureaucracy. With the rapid fall in the cost of information technology to capture the information on imported inputs and exports on-line when the transactions occur at the border, the bonded factory or warehouse that is not tied to a specific location seems to combine the best features of the EPZ and the duty exemption schemes.

Bonded factory or warehouse Unlike the EPZs, the customs bonded factories or warehouses can be set up anywhere at the convenience of the producers. The functions are essentially similar to those of EPZs so that the bonded factory can reduce congestion in the EPZs and also offer some flexibility for firms to be close to resources used in their production. Like the EPZs, the bonded factory is usually allowed to get imported raw materials and intermediate inputs duty free. However, the government may levy tariffs on equipment or parts used for maintenance of the factories. This is due to the dual function of such production facilities.[12]

To reduce the level of fraud caused by the selling of duty free imported inputs out of the bonded warehouse, it is usually necessary for the firms to post some type of guarantee bond, or bank guarantee or government security. In some countries, such as Taiwan and Indonesia, the firms that have a clean compliance record are allowed to post only a promissory note using collateral from the firm.

Although the bonded factories were set up for exports, the products may also be sold to domestic customers. When this occurs, the factories in countries such as Taiwan are required to pay duty only on the imported materials used to make the goods sold domestically (Kuo 1998). This places the bonded factories on an equal footing with other domestic manufacturers. Because these firms are able to be competitive enough to export these items, the prices of these goods when sold on the domestic market will tend to get bid down to their world prices, plus the tariffs paid on imported inputs. Hence, the tariffs associated with this export commodity become pure revenue tariffs, without any direct production inefficiency.

Korea and Kenya's system for equalizing the playing field is very different. Instead of disallowing tax exemption for imported materials, they impose final goods tariff rates on any of the final products sold in their domestic market (Kuo 1999a; Terkper 1999b). This provides these firms with the same level of effective protection as a pure domestic supplier selling in the local market. As a consequence

---

12 In some countries such as Belize, many export promotion facilities are called export processing zones. However, they function and are administered in a manner very similar to the way other countries treat bonded factories.

the economic efficiency cost of domestic protection is much higher with the system used in Korea and Kenya as compared to the system used in Taiwan.

The bonded factory has proven in most countries to be a largely self-administered system. In order to function properly, each factory must account for imported materials, finished products and provide information on the amount of materials required to produce each unit of finished good. Imported materials taken out for the manufacturing process need be recorded. The system operates in such a way that detailed, but simple, records of the quantity of imported materials are kept. When the firms export finished products, they reduce in the account the corresponding amounts of imported materials used in the production.

In addition to the customs bonds and government guarantees, there is an informal automatic policing mechanism built into the bonded factory or warehousing system that reduces the incentive for firms to leak duty free imported inputs without paying duties. If such sales should occur, competing suppliers who have already paid import duties will complain immediately, since it places their livelihood in jeopardy. The most common form of sanction against the operator of the bonded warehouse or factory is to have the license to operate such a facility revoked. This is a severe economic punishment, and one that the operator of the bonded warehouse facility is usually very reluctant to risk. Furthermore, if they are in the business of manufacturing for export and domestic sales, a sideline of smuggling is not particularly appealing when the probability is high that competitors whose silence is difficult to purchase will catch them. The formal process of applying for bonded factory status with its bond or bank guarantee requirements discourages those planning to engage in fraud. This informal policing system no doubt goes a long way toward explaining why, in countries such as Indonesia, Malaysia, Malawi and Ghana, a very low incidence of the sale of duty free imports exists, despite the fact that in the case of some of these countries the level of surveillance or auditing done by Customs of these in-bond facilities is rather rudimentary.

The number of bonded factories is large in countries such as Malaysia, Taiwan, Mauritius (Radelet 1999), Korea, Kenya and Pakistan (Maxwell 1998). They have been quite successful in promoting exports.

The concept of the bonded factory was extended to the science-based industrial parks in countries such as Taiwan in order to promote the development of science and technology in the island. The tax incentives provided to the parks are in fact the same as those in the EPZs but focus on computer, automation, and scientific research (Kuo 1998). The firms in the parks appear to have made a significant contribution to the recent economic growth in Taiwan, especially in electronics and other high-technology goods.

Institutional arrangements

Removing duties on imported inputs for use in the production of exports is very important for developing countries to be able to compete in selling their products in international markets. In fact, the duty remission systems have been shown to be the most important policy measure for the promotion of Taiwanese exports in the 1970s and 1980s (Jenkins and Kuo 1997). However, development of the mechanisms and institutional arrangements to implement this policy is equally essential for a successful export promotion and economic growth. Without an administrative system that minimizes the opportunities and incentives for corruption, positive results are unlikely to follow.

The most common mechanism to eliminate duties from inputs is the duty drawback system. The administrative complexity of this mechanism is a major deterrent to its use. It can relieve import duties paid and embodied in the production of indirect exporters for small exporters or irregular exporters. It is a necessary, but far from sufficient, mechanism to provide relief to exporters from the burden of import duties on inputs.

In administering either the exemption or suspense system, it is important for the government to develop simple computerized systems for recording the importation of inputs where duties have been suspended and export sales. With this system, the proper accounts and records in terms of imports, duties payable and re-exports that have taken place must be maintained. In addition, the importer should be required to supply the government with government bonds or securities issued by a financial institution in the amount equal to the duty payable. The interest rate associated with these bonds or securities should be payable to importers. This would minimize the cash flow cost to importers as well as protect the tax revenues for the government. Customs should administer the duty exemption system as information from customs transactions can be captured at almost no cost at the time when the goods are imported. The system implemented in the Philippines whereby an independent One Stop Shop authorized and issued Tax Credit Certificates is not one to be emulated. It is extremely difficult to keep track of imported inputs and their re-exports and as a result the implementation of such systems often results in major fraud.

The EPZs may in theory appear to be conceptually good, but they have proven to be expensive and inappropriate for many industries, particularly for those that already have a domestic operation. The bonded factories or warehouses are much more efficient as they can be located individually anywhere in the country, so long as Customs carefully maintains records on import duties payable and credits claimed for inspection by Customs personnel. The system has a fair amount of self-policing built into it but randomly targeted inspections by government officials will always be required.

Conclusions

A clear conclusion of this analysis is that the administration of the indirect tax on the inputs used by exporters is a critical determinant of the ability of producers of a country to be internationally competitive. Examples of successful administrative systems for these types of border tax adjustments are not plentiful. More can be said with certainty about what will not work than about what will be successful.

We know that One Stop Shops for the refund of VAT credits that are divorced from the administration of the VAT and Customs are a prescription for massive fraud. The evidence is also overwhelming that traditional duty drawback systems are almost always the catalyst for corruption, and are costly and ineffective at relieving exporters from the duties they pay on imported inputs.

Creative administrative designs that rely on markets such as bonds, bank guarantees, or accountants' professional reputations to provide an incentive for compliance and honest tax administration have been used effectively in a number of countries. There is no single prescription for the efficient and accurate refunding of excess VAT tax credits, or a single way to bring about the exemption of trade taxes on imported inputs for exporters that fits the needs of all countries. However, we find that systems that reduce the need for such refunds, or rely on easily obtained information that can be used in audits are much more likely to be successful than procedures that rely on physical inspections and bureaucratic approvals.

None of these innovations will guarantee that a county will be a successful exporter of manufactured goods. The factors and policies that bring about this result go well beyond the focus of this chapter. The existence of an administrative system to insure that border tax adjustments are made in an efficient manner should be viewed as a necessary but not sufficient condition for the realization of this larger objective.

Table 7.1 The Relative Importance of Exports in Export Processing Zones in Taiwan (millions of US dollars)

Year	Kaohsiung	Nantze	Taichung	Total EPZs Exports	Total National Exports	Ratio (Percent EPZ)
1967		n/a	n/a	7	641	1.09
1968	27	n/a	n/a	27	789	3.42
1969	62	n/a	n/a	62	1,049	5.91
1970	109	n/a	n/a	109	1,481	7.36
1971	156	2	5	163	2,060	7.91
1972	196	16	16	228	2,988	7.63
1973	282	54	40	376	4,483	8.39
1974	348	92	69	509	5,639	9.03
1975	290	92	71	453	5,309	8.53
1976	393	146	137	676	8,166	8.28
1977	417	166	167	750	9,361	8.01
1978	473	227	206	906	12,687	7.14
1979	602	325	278	1,205	16,103	7.48
1980	685	402	337	1,424	19,811	7.19
1981	821	432	426	1,679	22,611	7.43
1982	724	493	408	1,625	22,204	7.32
1983	750	475	396	1,621	25,123	6.45
1984	938	629	470	2,037	30,456	6.69
1985	872	635	365	1,872	30,726	6.09
1986	949	1,010	444	2,403	39,862	6.03
1987	1,244	1,400	530	3,174	53,679	5.91
1988	1,356	1,773	637	3,766	60,667	6.21
1989	1,397	1,948	664	4,009	66,304	6.05
1990	1,026	1,921	578	3,525	67,214	5.24
1991	1,094	2,198	678	3,970	76,178	5.21
1992	1,217	2,279	674	4,170	81,470	5.12
1993	1,107	2,628	591	4,326	85,092	5.08
1994	1,156	2,956	668	4,780	93,049	5.14
1995	1,447	4,025	800	6,272	111,659	5.62
1996	1,484	4,579	834	6,897	115,942	5.95
1997	1,545	5,421	969	7,935	122,081	6.50
1998	1,280	4,122	692	6,094	110,582	5.51

Sources: Ministry of Economic Affairs, Export Processing Zones, *Monthly Statistical Reports*, (1998); Council for Economic Planning and Development, *Taiwan Statistical Data Book*, 1999.

References

Bachracharya, R. and Flatters, F. (1999), 'Ghana's Trade Policies: Exemptions from Import Duty' (Paper prepared for Sigma One Corporation).

Barreix, A. (1999a), 'Promoting Export-Oriented Foreign Direct Investment: Tax and Customs Issues – The Case of Sri Lanka' (Background paper prepared for Harvard Institute for International Development).

_______, (1999b), 'Promoting Export-Oriented Foreign Direct Investment: Tax and Customs Issues – The Case of Uruguay' (Background paper prepared for Harvard Institute for International Development).

Campanella-Amenta, J. (1999), 'Tax Incentives in Developing Countries: Dominican Republic', Background paper prepared for Harvard Institute for International Development.

Flatters, F. (1999a), 'Export Facilitation in Malaysia' (Background paper prepared for Harvard Institute for International Development).

_______, (1999b), 'Export Facilitation in Indonesia' (Background paper prepared for Harvard Institute for International Development).

Glenday, G. (1996), 'Customs and Trade Facilitation: Challenges and Opportunities in Sub-Saharan Africa' (Paper prepared for the Symposium on 'Innovations in Trade Administration: Customs in the 21st Century', Harvard Institute for International Development and the International Tax Program).

_______ and Ndii D. (1999), 'Export Platforms in Kenya' (Background paper prepared for the Harvard Institute for International Development).

Gray, C. (1999), 'The Effectiveness of Tax Measures to Promote Export Growth in Malawi' Paper prepared under the Malawi Economic Management and Reform Project, funded by the USAID.

Jenkins, G. (2001), 'Review of the Value Added Tax in the Turkish Republic of Northern Cyprus' (Department of Economics, Eastern Mediterranean University).

_______ and Chun-Yan Kuo, C-Y. (1997), 'Which Policies are Important for Industrialization: The Case of Taiwan' (International Tax Program and Harvard Institute for International Development).

_______ and Khadka, R. (1998), 'Value Added Tax Policy and Implementation in Singapore', *International VAT Monitor* 9:2, 35-47 (Amsterdam: IBFD Publication).

Khadka, R. (1999), 'A Survey of the Customs and Tax Facilities in Thailand' (Background paper prepared for Harvard Institute for International Development).

Kuo, C-Y. (1998), 'Tax Incentives in Taiwan' (Background paper prepared for Harvard Institute for International Development).

_______, (1999a), 'Tax Incentives in Korea' (Background paper prepared for Harvard Institute for International Development).

_______ (1999b), 'Tax Incentives in Mexico' (Background paper prepared for Harvard Institute for International Development).

Le, T. (2002), *Foreign Direct Investment in Vietnam* (Ph.D. Dissertation in Public Policy, Harvard University).

Maxwell, T. (1998), 'Modernizing Pakistan's Export Policies' (Paper prepared for the World Bank).

_______ (1999), 'Making India a World Class Exporter' (Paper prepared for the World Bank).

_______ (2000), 'Incentive Reform in Sri Lanka' (Paper prepared for the World Bank).

Radelet, S. (1999), 'Manufactured Export, Export Platforms, and Economic Growth' (Paper prepared for Harvard Institute for International Development).

Rodrick, D. (1999), *The New Global Economy and Developing Countries: Making Openness Work* (Washington, DC: Overseas Development Council).

Snodgrass, D. and Rajah R. (1995), 'Malaysia's Experience in Promoting Export of Manufactures and Its Potential Relevance to Indonesia' (Paper prepared for the Ministry of Trade, Indonesia).

Terkper, S. (1999a), 'Tax Incentives in Ghana' (Background paper prepared for Harvard Institute for International Development).

_______ (1999b), 'Tax Incentives in Kenya' (Background paper prepared for Harvard Institute for International Development).

_______ (1999c), 'Tax Incentives in South Africa' (Background paper prepared for Harvard Institute for International Development).

PART 4
Government Behaviour

Chapter 8

Cases For and Against Transparency/ Obfuscation in Intergovernmental Relations

Giorgio Brosio

Introduction

This chapter explores a main area of possible non-transparent/obfuscating practices in intergovernmental relations; namely, intergovernmental transfers.

International financial organizations, such as the World Bank and the IMF, and the normative theory on fiscal federalism prescribe that the allocation of transfers should be made according to transparent formulas, accessible to all stakeholders, and inserted into a well defined legal framework, that specifies the duties and the entitlements of each layer of government. Otherwise, wide avenues are open to misuse of funds and/or straight corrupted practices.

However, while recommending transparency experts cannot but sometimes question among themselves the general validity of their recommendations. For example, in deeply divided countries with a huge potential of regional conflicts, one wonders if some obfuscation of whom gets how much would not help soothing conflicts, and/or postpone their occurrence to a future time, when it is hoped that political and socio-economic conditions will have improved and regional conflicts will be better managed.

Obviously, the recommendations in favour of transparency and non-obfuscation are usually resisted by government officials, especially in transition and developing economies, who point to the merits of using discretionary, less than transparent methods, particularly so in the early phases of a decentralization process.

Although intergovernmental transfers are not a vast topic, dealing with the impact of transparency is a quite complex issue. The aims of this chapter are rather limited, however. In the first section, I define the notion I use here of the terms transparency and obfuscation and the asserted pros and cons of them. I then proceed to show, in the second section, how transparency, or better non-obfuscation, is necessary to avoid misuse of funds and petty corruption. In other words, non-obfuscation is necessary to achieve local efficiency.

The achievement of broader aims of general/national efficiency and of regional redistribution may be associated with some level of obfuscation in the allocation of transfers. While non-obfuscation does not represent a necessary condition for achieving these broader goals, there is an evident trade-off between the achievement of these broader aims assigned to the transfer system and local efficiency. This is shown in the fourth section. Finally, I argue in the fifth section how centralized systems offer more scope for obfuscating practices and thus a greater potential for inefficient use of funds.

Transparency and obfuscation, relationships between the two concepts

Given the huge number of definitions of political and institutional transparency and their variance, making clear what I mean here by transparency and obfuscation is not a pedantic exercise. It helps to avoid possible misunderstandings in the remaining of the chapter.

We have transparency when all stakeholders to an issue have access to exactly the same information concerning it. On the other hand, we have obfuscation when the information provided to the stakeholders leads them to interpret in a different way the issue – that is, to give a different meaning to it. Obfuscation is thus compatible with omitting information, transmitting information beyond the possibility of using it or, clearly, transmitting false information.[1]

Transparency is not equivalent to the lack of obfuscation. We can have at the same time transparency and obfuscation. (And also lack of obfuscation and non transparency[2]). This is because stakeholders have different abilities to use information. An example referred to transfers may clarify this statement. Suppose that a central government utilizes for the allocation of its transfers a sophisticated and complex formula based on a host of indicators and that it makes this formula available to everybody. Surely, that government is following a transparent procedure. This does not exclude, however, the possibility of some obfuscation. In fact, while the beneficiary governments will have no problems in understanding the implications of

1 By distinguishing between transparency and obfuscation the definitions suggested here are somewhat more elaborated than those currently used when dealing with fiscal and budget transparency. For example, Lipford (2001, 575-6) defines transparency 'as the ease with which the public can interpret spending and budgetary figures, measures current and future tax liabilities, and evaluates the benefits of government programs'. Another, widely referred to definition is provided by Kopits and Craig (1998, 1): 'Fiscal transparency is defined … as openness toward the public at large about government structure and functions, fiscal policy intentions, public sector accounts, and projections. It involves ready access to reliable, comprehensive, timely, understandable, and internationally comparable information on government activities…'. The International Monetary Fund Code of Good Practices on Fiscal Transparency (www.imf.org.) is based on four principles: (1) clarity in government's role in the economy and responsibilities; (2) readily available budgetary information for the public; (3) open budget preparations, execution and reporting; and (4) independent assurance of integrity. The meaning given here to obfuscation is similar to that of Hojman (2002).

2 This happens when every stakeholder interprets in the same way the issue and the message sent to each of them has been differentiated intentionally to ease its understanding.

the formula and behave consequently, citizens, more specifically ordinary citizens, may find it difficult to grasp all its implications. In other words, they will interpret the formula in a different way.

There are a few immediate implications from these definitions. The first one is that, to eliminate the possibility of obfuscation, the message sent to different stakeholders may have to differ, thus impinging on transparency. Secondly, that messages – formulas in the case of transfers – have to be simple and immediate, if one wants to combine transparency and lack of obfuscation. Consequently, there is a trade off between the clarity of the message that is required to avoid obfuscation, and the sophistication of the instrument that may be required to obtain its stated goals.

I am tempted to suggest that transparency has, in this context, mostly a nominal value, while on factual grounds obfuscation and its lack are crucial.

The arguments used by international organizations and by the normative theory of fiscal federalism to support transparency (or better, non-obfuscation) are based mainly on the fact that it can nurture slack, that is, misallocation of funds by beneficiary governments, when not outright corrupt practices. To avoid these dangers the use of clear 'transparent' formulas is suggested. Obviously, the more fragile are democratic institutions, the more urgent becomes the suggestion[3]. Misuse of funds and corruption can concern not only the beneficiary governments, but also the payer, that is, the central government. When the method of allocation is obscure – the argument goes – government officials at the central level may keep in their coffers (pockets) some of the funds officially allocated to subnational governments.

There is no scarcity of arguments for central governments, on the other hand, to counter the recommended transparency and to prefer a discretionary, somewhat obfuscated, system. First, appropriate socio-economic data is missing. This is especially true in developing and in transition economies.

Secondly, a formula that uses available data may not fit the perceived needs (and capacity) factors of beneficiary governments. It is thus much better – is the frequent argument of officials – to use a discretionary, incremental method. For example, a method where the allocations of the previous year serve, each year, as the basis for the determination of the transfer to each distinct subnational unit.

The main arguments used to support obfuscation are, however, regional cleavages and the threat of secession. These arguments are mostly found in countries that are experiencing a decentralization process, such as the transition economies. During the previous centralized system, it is argued, uniformity of levels of service provision (by itself the main merit of centralization) implied a substantial redistribution of resources from richer to poorer areas. After decentralization a system of transparent transfers, that would ensure the same regional uniformity of levels of service provision, would not be accepted by the richer regions, and could foster secession. On the other hand,

3 This is because, also according to the literature (see for example Alt, Lassen and Skilling 2001) fiscal transparency acts as a substitute of competition, improving the fiscal behaviour of governments.

the same transparent system with a lower intensity of redistribution could nurture separation aspirations in the poorer regions.

Both regions, the argument proceeds, make faulty calculations of the gains and losses of staying united. Or, which amounts to the same, the transfer system may be used by separatist movements to inflame followers and voters exploiting their myopia and their lack of information. It is thus much better to use some obfuscation until separatist trends subside and the mutual advantages of staying together become clearer.

Local efficiency and obfuscation: an analysis based on horizontal competition

Let us consider the allocation of a general-purpose transfer, whose main aim is to fill vertical and horizontal imbalances in subnational government finances. For simplicity, the way this transfer is financed is left entirely out. That is, taxes, or opportunity costs are not introduced in the analysis. We also leave out of the discussion the criteria that can be used for its allocation and, finally, we assume that the total allocation of the transfer is entirely disbursed to subnational governments. In other words, no retention for improper use is made at the central level.

Consider a country with a national government and two local jurisdictions, *i* and *j*. For simplicity's sake, potential crowding and congestion effects are also excluded and the analysis is conducted in terms of the representative household served by a given local jurisdiction. In deciding whether or not to re-elect their local incumbents, voters use the relative performance criterion, that is, the well-known Salmon mechanism (Salmon 1987) which consists in making inter-jurisdictional comparisons of performance.[4]

With this starting-point, the question arises whether or not it is possible to increase local efficiency by reducing obfuscation. To answer this question, it is necessary to specify the meaning of local efficiency.

In this economy, local jurisdictions choose the level of local public good to be provided to each resident. The aim of these jurisdictions is to maximize the difference between the central transfer and the cost of production. This represents the local inefficiency, that can be reduced by inducing local governments to compete with each other in implementing their respective policies. In fact, despite the lack of information on the value of costs, the expansion of the discretionary budget is bounded via the re-election constraint faced by the incumbents.

Assume that X_i and X_j, are the outputs observed by the voters of local jurisdiction *i* and *j*, such that:

$$X_i = X(E_i, G + e_i)$$
$$X_j = X(E_j, G + e_j)$$

4 See also the theory of yardstick competition (Besley and Case 1995; Ashworth and Heyndels 1997).

from which it follows that:

$$(X_i - X_j) = (E_i - E_j) - (e_j - e_i)$$

where E represents the incumbent's effort, G is the central government transfer (assumed to be equal across jurisdictions, if these latter have the same population), and e is a random variable, which represents an observation error, tied to the size of the transfer.

Since voters are interested only in the relative performance of their government, the probability for an incumbent to be re-elected in jurisdiction i, P_i, derives, apart from variables such as environmental characteristics, etc., from his/her performance relative to the performance of the local government of reference. It is easy to observe that the smaller the difference associated with the errors, the higher the possibility for the voter to infer the level of effort by observing the output level. Hence, it follows that the probability of winning depends on the fact that the difference in errors is smaller than the difference in efforts, i.e.

$$P_i (X_i - X_j) = P[\mathrm{E}_i - E_j < e_j - e_i]$$

Obviously, there are a few additional conditions for the proper working of this model of horizontal competition. Firstly, incumbents should not collude; secondly, they have to be interested in their re-election, thus not looking for a corner solution. I assume that these conditions are satisfied.

The problem may appear oversimplified and devoid of analytical, or of policy interest. However, a simple example can illustrate its relevance. It could be in fact the case of a developing country, where a donor agency has allocated a certain amount of money for assisting local governments. The donor does not intend to intervene in the criteria for allocation, these being typically a duty of the central government of the beneficiary country. Its only worry is to minimize misuse, or petty corruption and it can only intervene on the issue of transparency. The donor is also able to monitor the actual disbursement of funds to local units. Nothing will be left to central government (or, more likely, to its officials). In this case, it is easy to show that the best course of action is to impose transparency, if there some room for horizontal competition.

A graphic illustration may help to make the argument clearer. The level of perceived and effective effort is reported on the vertical axis, while the observed output lays on the horizontal one. Lines OU and OL define the level of effort that voters perceive observing the level of output.

Suppose that point E represents the real effort. Point E^i illustrates the case where voters perceive a level of effort higher than the real one, because the information they have understates the amount of the grant received by their local government. They will be induced, if the perceived level is higher than that of the local government of their reference, to vote for the incumbent. Point E_1 illustrates the opposite case. Here the perceived level of effort is lower than the real one, because on the basis of the information they have voters tend to overstate the level of the grant. They will thus be induced to vote for the challenger. In neither case, their voting decision stimulates efficient behaviour from their local government.

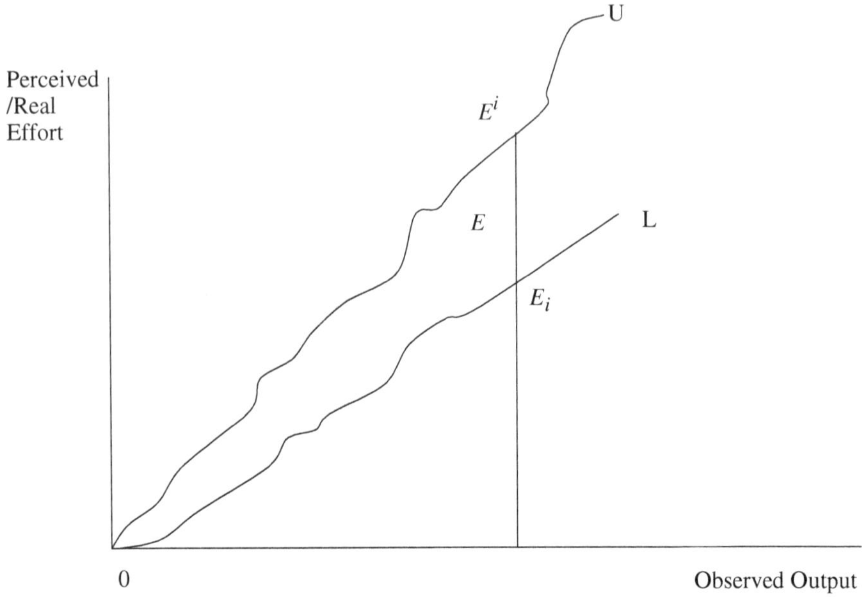

Figure 8.1 Errors of Information and the Performance of Governments

General, inter-jurisdictional, efficiency and obfuscation

According to the arguments made in the preceding section, non-obfuscation when coupled with horizontal competition ensures local, that is, intra-jurisdictional efficiency. Given the transfer allocation it receives from the central government, each distinct jurisdiction will be induced to exert an efficient amount of effort (or, at least, the level of effort that allows it to win elections).

What is important to stress is that every criterion that can be used for the allocation of the total transfers will avoid misuse, if competition works. This local, intra-jurisdictional, efficiency will be reached whatever the criteria chosen for the allocation of the transfer, such as the number of the elderly, or the number of young on the total population, the fiscal capacity, or the inverse of fiscal capacity, etc.

Provided that citizens are satisfied with the amount of their transfers and do not consider wider issues – such as the possibility that a different system of allocation would attain a higher level of inter-jurisdictional or global efficiency, as opposed to local intra-jurisdictional efficiency – we will have coincidence between the goal of the donor (central government) and that of the citizens of each distinct jurisdiction.

In this sense there is no politics, or political game outside each distinct jurisdiction, because basically there are no opportunity costs involved by the choice of the distinct method of allocation.

Again a simple example may help to illustrate this point. Let us suppose that the transfer is allocated according to the number of local public employees, as it is done in many parts of the world. This can happen because this number is easily available, or because wages are the single most important item of local expenditure.

Horizontal, non-obfuscated competition will put a brake on misuse of funds and corruption in every jurisdiction. But surely a personnel-based transfer is not allocated in a way that ensures its most efficient use from an inter-jurisdictional/global point of view. This is because all local jurisdictions will be induced to increase the number of their employees to get a larger transfer and the production function of local governments will be distorted in favour of excessive labour input. Hence, the criterion used for the allocation will impinge negatively on allocative inefficiency. But still each local jurisdiction will be induced to make the best use of its resources, that is compatible with this distortion.

When the opportunity costs from the use of a given formula are introduced, the choice of the criteria for the allocation of the transfer is no more irrelevant and citizens will not stay indifferent to whatever criterion is chosen. Each of them knows that he/she will gain if a larger share of the grant is allocated to his/her jurisdiction, by using an appropriate formula.

The issue to be explored here is if obfuscation can help to reach goals that have a broader aim than avoiding local misuse and corruption.

There is, to my knowledge, no attempt in the literature on the allocation of intergovernmental transfers to show that practicing obfuscation – meaning using methods for the allocation whose working is interpreted in different ways by the distinct stakeholders – produces efficiency gains non attainable by using non obfuscated methods. In fact, all the literature suggests the use of objective, non-controllable by the beneficiary, indicators of need and fiscal capacity.[5]

Obviously, the more complex and sophisticated becomes the formula for allocation, the more difficult it will be for the stakeholders – particularly for the general public – to have a correct understanding of it. In other words, the (sudden) introduction of a complex system for the allocation can create, at least initially, some obfuscation. This can be done on purpose or incidentally by the central government, but there is nothing structural in it. Overtime, stakeholders will have a better grasp of the formula, and obfuscation will disappear (unless the central government persists in its efforts to make things complicated).

---

5 Even the argument used in the theory of rank order tournaments (O'Keefe, Viscusi, and Zeckhauser 1984) about the role played by some lack of precision in the measurement of effort to induce all players to take part actively to the competition does not fit the present case. In fact in this case there is no obfuscation in meaning used in this chapter, because errors in measurement do not provide different information to distinct stakeholders.

The same effect provided by a complex, sophisticated formula can be obtained by using a set of distinct grants instead of a single, non-conditional one. This is a common practice in intergovernmental relations. To achieve national objectives, such as the implementation of national/minimum standards in distinct sectors, or to encourage infrastructure building, governments use a vast array of specific transfers[6]. Some are allocated by means of specific formulas, some are allocated on a negotiated basis, and some are totally discretionary, as it frequently happens with capital transfers. An increasingly popular technique is of matching, that is, of co-financing schemes, that should foster fiscal accountability by recipient governments. Again, the intended (or non-intended) result of these practices is obfuscation. Citizens, and even local governments and the different branches of the central government as well, have no clear perception of who gets what. Misuse and corruption can ensue.

The use of complex formulae and/or a huge number of distinct transfer programs may exert a negative impact on the political and fiscal accountability of countries. Or, more generally, this use may act as an indicator of non-fully-fledged democratic systems.[7]

A third system of obfuscation can consist in allocating transfers in instalments. For example, the central government makes an initial allocation and then supplements it with subsequent allocations, using the same, or a different formula. The rationale for this method may be to restrain the growth of local expenditure, or to enforce a hard budget constraint.

The financing of health care – that is the main expenditure responsibility of regional government – in Italy provides an illustration of this technique (see Bordignon and Mapelli 2002). Health care has been funded until recently by central government transfers, calculated according to some measure of regional needs. However, since the beginning the amount of these transfers was recognized by all parties to be inadequate to finance the level of service provision prescribed by the central government. These transfers have then been followed by supplementary ones, which have in fact been paid with a delay of more than a year. It is doubtful whether the system has helped to put a brake on the growth of health care expenditure. It is much less open to doubt that the system has introduced a huge degree of obfuscation in the financing of health care. In turn, this may be responsible for the widespread

---

6 In fact, one could even argue that the number of distinct grants to subnational governments could be used as a rough measure (indicator) of obfuscation.

7 This observation can be contradicted by the observed use of sophisticated formulae for the distribution of general transfers in countries with long lived democratic traditions, such as Denmark and the United Kingdom, where some parameters of the formula are estimated according to regression analysis, by itself a less than transparent method. There is possibly another explanation to the use of complex formulas by countries with long lived traditions of democratic and accountable government. Namely, that governments want to make clear that they are entirely rules bound. That is, that there is no discretion in their behaviour. In other words, they are sending a signal about their political and administrative integrity. This observation amounts to the argument put forward by Alt, Lassen, and Skilling (2001) according to which transparency is a substitute for fully-fledged, that is competitive systems.

occurrence of misuse of funds that characterizes the working of health care provision in Italy.

A remark has to be made concerning the relation between obfuscation and the number of subnational units. Since ecological variance is larger, the smaller is the average area of local jurisdictions – for example, municipalities show higher variance in their socio-economic structure than regions – a formula for the allocation of grants will have, *ceteris paribus*, to be more articulated for lower than for higher level jurisdictions. For example, altitude may be a relevant indicator of need for municipalities in France or Italy, but a much less relevant one for their regional governments, in view of its presumable lower variance at this level of territorial government. There are clearly some policy implications from this consideration. It is, for example, an argument for reducing the number of local units.

Equity (regional redistribution) and obfuscation

Obviously, from an analytical point of view one could not disentangle efficiency from equity issues. This applies also to transfers. However, frequently in the real world issues concerning the regional equity aspects of the allocation of transfers dominate efficiency concerns and may require a separate consideration.

The argument frequently made by officials in favour of obfuscation is that it allows to attain a level of regional redistribution higher than the level obtainable with an open system. This is because of lamented greediness of voters of the richer jurisdictions, or because of their myopia, or their imperfect calculation of the costs and benefits of staying together.

To explore the validity of the argument one has to make at least two distinct cases. The first one assumes a median voter framework. That is, the policy of the central government – namely, the level of interregional redistribution – reflects closely the preferences of the median region/voter. In this case, obfuscation is used to hide a degree of redistribution that non-median regions/voters consider as inappropriate[8]. For example, the median region/voter is poorer than the average and he/she wants to maximize regional redistribution, or *vice versa*. She/he supports obfuscating procedures because he/she believes these turn to her/his advantage, by reducing opposition to the transfers system. In this case it is hard to find a general argument in favour of obfuscation. Its merits or demerits are context specific. Its effects will last until obfuscation can stay hidden, or resentment against it does not grow.

Italy, in the post World War II period, represents a convenient example. The system of grants paid to local and regional government has always had a number of elements of obfuscation. They included a complex formula for the allocation of non-conditional transfers, a huge number of specific grants, some of them allocated

8 In fact, the intensity of the redistribution may be lower or greater than that desired by non-median voters/regions. It is a fact of everyday life, that a donor may use obfuscation to induce the beneficiary to accept a donation that the latter would consider excessive.

with complete discretional decision-making power and transfers in kind, such as the allocation of public works, equipment and personnel.

This obfuscation has possibly allowed a level of redistribution from richer to poorer areas greater than that would have prevailed without it. The intensity of the redistribution is also correlated with the gradual moving of the median voter/region to the South of the country that took part during this period. Obfuscation may have delayed the rise of the protest of the richest regions against this (for them) excessive redistribution. The electoral success of the 'Northern League' may be attributed to the vanishing of the obfuscation effects. It is also likely that the feeling of having been cheated by the central government contributed to exacerbate the protest.

A more successful example of a set of somewhat obfuscated transfers is provided by the French DOM and TOM (Overseas Departments and Territories). These jurisdictions are heavily subsidized (see Belorgey and Bertrand 1994). Part of the subsidies return to the 'Métropole' through special wage allocations for civil servants dispatched on these jurisdictions, and other instruments. The small share of their population on the total French population clearly attenuates the impact of these subsidies on the national public finances. However, obfuscation may contribute to the perceived wide acceptance among the French voters of the peculiar fiscal arrangements of these territories.

The second case refers to the case where the central government can decide the allocation on its own, departing if it deems it necessary from the preferences of the median region/voter. In the fiscal literature this is referred to as the case of a benevolent government, or to the merit goods argument (although it could equally be the case of a malevolent government, or of the demerit goods argument). This can take place, for example, in a situation of strong regional strife, where regions, that are in a deep mutual conflict, accept to delegate the central government to find an agreed upon by all solution. Obfuscation could be chosen in this case by the central government if it believes that it can help to reach an agreement, or at least to put a break on the strife between the contending regions. Nigeria (ChiiChii 1986; Federal Republic of Nigeria 1980; Ikein and Briggs-Anigboh 1998) could provide a testing ground of the suitability of obfuscation to solve apparently non-resolvable situations. Even before independence, politics and economics in this country have been totally dominated by the issue of the allocation of oil revenue among the states that form the Nigerian federation. Civil wars, secessions and the coming to power of brutal dictatorships have been the result of the inability to reach an agreed upon solution about the division of the oil spoils. A number of Commissions (some of them headed by prestigious British economists, such as Hicks and Prest) have been appointed to propose transparent formulas for the allocation, but to no avail. While oil producing regions claim that a fair federal system has to based on the principle of derivation, the other areas of the country pretend that fairness requires a redistribution of oil revenue. One can be tempted to suggest to experiment an obfuscated approach by which the total pool, that is, the total amount of open transfers to distinct states is reduced, and is replaced by a number of distinct programs, particularly transfers in kind, managed directly by the central government. This would amount surely to the same recentralization of the system. At the same time, the obfuscation associated with this solution could temporarily attenuate the regional strife. There are, however, two dangers in this approach. Firstly, one has to consider that, although the central government has an obvious incentive to keep the country together, its uniting action could be seriously endangered by the pressures coming from the states that are more influential at the central level. Secondly, obfuscation could increase the level of corruption and misuse of funds, which (in the case of this specific country) is already one of the highest in the world according to all sources.

Obfuscation and the degree of decentralization

From the preceding arguments it emerges that there is a greater potential for non-transparent/obfuscating practices in centralized systems, while when systems decentralize the potential (perceived need) for these practices diminishes. The reason is because in a centralized system the national government is more involved, than in a decentralized system, in what local governments do and in their mutual relationships. To make this point clearer, I propose a political/electoral definition of the degree of centralization/decentralization in democratic systems, that refers to the probability of re-election of each unit of government. This definition is presented in the Appendix and can be summarized as following. In every system there are national goods and local goods, referring to areas of impact of their benefits and costs. In a completely centralized system of government the probability of re-election of the central government depends of the level of provision of both national and local goods, while in a completely decentralized system, the central government is electorally responsible only for the provision of national goods. The degree of decentralization can thus be inferred from the impact of the provision of local goods on the re-election prospects of the central government.

If this definition works, then in a centralized system the central government is induced for electoral sake to intervene in local affairs. For example, to promote global/national efficiency and/or to determine and implement national standards. The central government may be also induced to promote uniformity of service provision. In fact, historically, the most important justification for the choice of a centralized system has been, until recently, keeping the country together by equalizing the level of services.[9]

Obviously, centralization is not the only way of keeping countries together, as shown by a host of recent examples. However, once the choice of centralization is made, the involvement of the central government in local affairs is amplified. The central government acts as a principal *vis à vis* the local governments, trying to influence their behaviour towards the attainment of the goals it has set up. This has an impact on transfers, increasing their number, using transfers in kind in addition

9 Italy after unification provides a good example and also Spain in the Eighteenth century.

to financial transfers, increasing their complexity, and increasing the extent of obfuscation, as it has been argued in the previous sections.

If a centralized system has a higher potential for misuse of funds, this potential is surely expanded in those local jurisdictions that are the main beneficiaries of (obfuscated) transfers. Usually, these are the more backward and poorer areas. In part, misuse and corruption are a reflex of the greater importance of transfers in their sources of finance (this is the usual argument made against transfers from the point of view of fiscal accountability). Working on top of the relative importance of transfers, obfuscation may explain the higher incidence of misuse and corruption frequently observed in these jurisdictions. Since the number of distinct programs of transfers is a possible cause of obfuscation, an immediate policy recommendation would be to reduce the number of distinct transfers. That is, to reduce the guidance provided by the central government, lowering the number of its instruments (specific transfers) and to substitute it with increasing reliance on local responsibility and control.

Decentralization implies, on the other hand, less central government involvement in local affairs, because of the perception of a lesser responsibility of the central government in the provision of local goods. This implies that the relationship between the central and the local governments is not shaped in a typical contractual way, but rather according to mutually agreed rules of the game. For example, in decentralized systems the total amount of general grants is predetermined[10] by law leaving little room for year to year negotiations between the central and the local governments. The allocation of this total amount is made according to formulas. In other words, there is much less room for obfuscating practices.

Some evidence about the different role of obfuscation in centralized versus decentralized systems is provided by the evolving function of auditing agencies. In every democratic system the performances of local government units are audited by specialized agencies, such as the *Court des Comptes* in the French tradition, or the *Audit Commission* in the UK. In centralized system the main function of these bodies was to check the legal basis of the decisions taken by local governments. In fact, in such a system the rules are dictated by the central government and auditing bodies serve to check the conformity of local government decisions to the laws, the regulations and the decrees issued by the central government. Centralization amplified the role played by these auditing bodies, which was also compatible with obfuscating practices, since the reports of these bodies were intended for central government use, only. The more recent evolution of these bodies, paralleling the decentralization of government systems, shows a change in their activity that privileges the checking of the effective performances of local government units, thus providing benchmarks that help citizens to evaluate carefully the action of their local jurisdiction. In other words, they have become a main instrument against obfuscating practices, by enabling voters to have a clear grasp of what they get and what they pay

10 The methods may vary. The most frequent is to make reference to a share of total tax revenue or to the collections of a single broad-based tax.

to get them. Thus, the simple existence of auditing agencies makes debating the pros and cons of obfuscation practically irrelevant.

Conclusions

If the preceding analysis is correct, there is not much room for suggesting obfuscation in a normative theory of intergovernmental transfers. This is because the existence of obfuscation opens the door to misuse of funds and/or petty corruption. On the other hand, the possible pretended benefits from obfuscating practices are context specific. Thus, no generalization is sustainable.

In general, centralized systems present higher levels of obfuscation than decentralized systems. They have thus a higher potential for local inefficiency.

A final point has to be addressed. It concerns how to ensure transparency and non obfuscation in intergovernmental transfers. In addition to the usual instruments suggested by international organizations such as transparency manuals and codes of conducts, the use of independent commissions or of autonomous bodies is increasingly recommended (see for example: Ahmad 1998; Ahmad and Mansoor 2002). Independent commissions are fundamental to work out clear formulas and their implementation with honestly collected and treated information, especially for countries with few mechanisms of checks and balances. In fact, the implementation of the formulas for allocation is surely one of the crucial steps for ensuring transparent and non obfuscated practices.

References

Ahmad, E. (1998), 'The Reform of the Fiscal Transfer System', in Brean (ed.).

_______ and Mansoor, A. (2002), 'Indonesia: Managing Decentralization', in Ahmad and Tanzi (eds.).

_______and Tanzi, V. (eds.) (2002), *Managing Fiscal Decentralization* (London: Routledge).

Alt E., Lassen, D. and Skilling, D. (2001), *Fiscal Transparency, Gubernatorial Popularity, and the Scale of Government: Evidence from the States* (Mimeo).

Ashworth, J. and Heyndels, B. (1997), 'Politicians' Preferences on Local Tax Rates: An Empirical Analysis', *European Journal of Political Economy* 13:3, 479-502.

Belorgey, G. and Bertrand, G. (1994), *Les DOM-TOM* (Paris: La Découverte).

Besley, T. and Case, A. (1995), 'Incumbent Behavior: Vote-Seeking, Tax-Setting, and Yardstick Competition', *American Economic Review* 85, 25-45.

Bordignon, M. and Mapelli, G. (2002), 'Can We Fit a Square Object in a Round Hole? Fiscal Federalism and the National Health Service in the Italian System of Government', *Paper Presented at the ISAE Conference 'Monitoring Italy', Rome.*

Brean, D. (ed.) (1998), *Taxation in Modern China* (London: Routledge).

ChiiChii, A. (1986), *Fiscal Federalism in Nigeria* (Canberra: Australian National University).

'Federal Republic of Nigeria', (1980), *Report of the Presidential Commission on Revenue Allocation: Main Report* (Apapa: Federal Government Press).

Hojman, D., (2002), 'Obfuscation, Inequality and Votes. A Model of Policy Choice under Rent Seeking' (*Liverpool Research Papers in Economics, Finance and Accounting)*.

Ikein, S. and Briggs-Anigboh, C. (1998), *Oil and Fiscal Federalism in Nigeria*, (Aldershot: Ashgate).

'International Monetary Fund', *Code of Good Practices on Fiscal Transparency* www.imf.org.

Kopits, G. and Craig, J. (1998), 'Transparency in Government Operations', *IMF Occasional Paper No. 158.*

Lipford, J., (2001), 'How Transparent is the U.S. Budget?' *The Independent Review* 5:4, 575-91.

O'Keefe, M., Viscusi, K. and Zeckhauser, R. (1984), 'Economic Contests: Comparative Rewards Schemes', *Journal of Labor Economics* 2, 27-56.

Salmon, P. (1987), 'Decentralization as an Incentive Scheme', *Oxford Review of Economic Policy* 3:2, 24-43.

Appendix

A definition of the degree of (de) centralization based on political/electoral interrelations

The degree of centralization/decentralization can be defined in political/electoral terms by referring to the probability of re-election of the central government.

Suppose a country with a central government, *C*, subdivided in two distinct regional jurisdictions, *i* and *j*. There are only two publicly provided goods, namely, defence, *D*, a purely national one, and health care, *H*, a mainly local and mixed one. These goods can be provided under different institutional arrangements.

The probability of re-election depends only on the level of service provision for the publicly provided goods, that is, $P_c\ \alpha D,\beta H)$, where P_c is the probability of re-election of the central government and α and β are the discount factors, assigned to the arguments, with $0 \leq \alpha,\beta \leq 1$. This probability is related to the probability that each voter will grant his/her consent to the incumbent politician. In turn, this probability is a function of the utility of each voter (Muller, 1989, provides a good summary of, and references to, the literature on voting under conditions of uncertainty). For simplicity, we assume that voters' utility function has only two arguments, namely defence and health care provision.

The degree of decentralization can be inferred – according to this approach – from the value of α and β When $\alpha = \beta$ the system is completely centralized, since voters consider that the central government only is responsible for both goods. In fact, in a purely centralized system the two arguments are discounted equally by the central government. This is because, independently from constitutional and/or other legal regulations voters consider that the central government has the full and exclusive responsibility for their provision. When $\alpha > \beta$ the system is decentralized. When β equals zero, the system is completely decentralized and the central government bears no responsibility whatsoever for the provision of the local good. A completely decentralized system implies that the probability of re-election depends for each unit of government from the single good for which the voters hold them responsible. The probability of re-election will depend for each layer of government on the level of service provision for a single good.

An essential point has to be made. The degree of decentralization defined here does not depend on equalization (regional redistribution) issues. In other words, according to our definition the central government is evaluated by citizens in the areas assigned to the responsibility of subnational government independently of equalization issues. This means that even in those jurisdictions, which do not benefit from equalization grants, voters consider the central government has a role to play. For example, providing insurance against possible failures in the service provision by their regional government.

Chapter 9

Transparency in the Budget Process of a Bureaucratic Organisation: A Principal-Agent Model of Budgeting

Louis M. Imbeau

Introduction

Transparency has to do with the flow of information among the participants to a decision-making process. As suggested by Webster's definition, a transparent process is frank (i.e. 'free from pretence or deceit'), obvious (i.e. 'easily detected or seen through'), and clear (i.e. 'readily understood'). In the budget process, transparency is most often looked at from that normative standpoint. For the International Monetary Fund (IMF), for example, 'transparency in government operations is widely regarded as an important precondition for macroeconomic fiscal sustainability, good governance, and overall fiscal rectitude' (Kopits and Craig 1998, 1). In other words, budgeting is more efficient in a transparent setting. This is what the IMF argues when it pressures public administrations in developing countries to adopt explicit budgetary rules. This is the assumption behind much of the empirical research that tends to show that public deficits are lower when budget rules are more stringent (Alesina and Bayoumi 1996; Haan and Sturm 1994; Hagen and Harden 1994). But things are not that simple. Obviously, there are situations where frankness, obviousness, or clearness may have unwanted effects. In a parliamentary system, for example, budgetary secrecy is often seen as necessary if the corruption of the whole process is to be avoided. In a bureaucratic organisation, a superior must often hide information from subordinates to protect the integrity of her plans. A more moderate normative position, then, would be that complete transparency in a budget process is generally impossible to reach and, sometimes, undesirable, as bureaucratic organisations are characterized by uncertainty.

Indeed, adopting a positive perspective, many observers of decision-making processes have looked at the role of information and have concluded that uncertainty or information asymmetry and delegation of responsibility are fundamental characteristics of bureaucratic organisations, if not of any organisation. For Max Weber, politicians confront uncertainty as bureaucrats derive power from their control over information: 'Under normal conditions, the power position of a fully developed bureaucracy is always over towering. The "political master" finds himself in the position of the "dilettante" who stands opposite the "expert", facing the trained official who stands within the management of administration. This holds whether the "master" whom the bureaucracy serves is a "people", equipped with the weapons of "legislative initiative", the "referendum", and the right to remove officials, or a parliament, elected on a more aristocratic or more "democratic" basis and equipped with the right to vote a lack of confidence' (Weber, in Gerth and Mills 1946, 232). In other words, we can observe a tendency of politicians to use authority-based budget control and of bureaucrats to use expertise-based budget manipulation (Bendor et al. 1987). But as Bendor, Taylor and Van Gaalen (1987, 797) argued, 'the Weberian emphasis on the uncertainty confronting politicians must be complemented by an analysis of the uncertainty confronting bureaucrats'. Indeed, they showed that a legislature may find it advantageous deliberately to increase the uncertainty that a bureau faces: 'if the legislature makes it harder for a risk-averse bureau chief to predict demand or penalty, the bureau will restrain its deception' (Bendor, Taylor and Van Gaalen 1985, 1041). In short, information asymmetry is pervasive in bureaucratic organisations. It appears when some participants to a process have control over information that others lack. Subordinates have access to information that is unknown to their superiors concerning the characteristics of the goods and services they produce or the needs of the population they serve. Lacking that information, a superior may find it difficult to make efficient budgetary allocations.

One way to compensate this information asymmetry is through the delegation of responsibility. Indeed, budgeting decisions, or decisions regarding spending allocations, may be delegated or not. Where there is no delegation the budget is entirely decided by the superior for every level of her organisation. Subordinates have no budgeting decision to make. They are mere executants. This situation is typical of small or highly centralized public administrations where a few persons make all budgetary decisions. In larger or more decentralized organisations, the superior delegates part of her budgeting responsibilities to subordinates thus creating two sets of spending allocation decisions, or two budgets: 1) the superior's budget in which the superior decides the share of her total financial resources each subordinate will receive; 2) the subordinate's budget in which he allocates funds within his sub-division to executants. The superior delegates part of her responsibility to subordinates in large part because of uncertainty. But this method does not go without risks. As Robert Dahl (1967, 21) observed 'there are decisions that require me to delegate authority to others ... but if I delegate, may I not, in practice, end up with a kind of aristocracy of experts, or even false experts?' Roberto Michels (1915) had expressed the same idea concerning political parties in his famous Iron law of oligarchy: 'Organization gives birth to the domination of the elected over the electors, of the mandataries over the mandators, of the delegates over the delegators. Who says organization says oligarchy'.

When information asymmetry and delegation of responsibility combine, a unique situation is created, coined as the 'agency relationship' in the literature of neo-institutional economics and political science. Indeed, at the most general level, Stiglitz (1987, 967) suggested that a principal-agent situation arises 'whenever one individual's action has an effect on another individual'. More specifically, Gilardi (2001, 3) defines the principal-agent relationship as 'a social transaction, or interaction, in which one actor, the agent, carries out actions that are intended to fulfil the interests of another actor, the principal'. In the specific situation where one considers the process of allocating financial resources to programs and activities in a bureaucratic organisation, I argue that a principal-agent relationship appears when both information asymmetry and delegation of responsibility are present.

In this chapter, I propose a theory of budgeting based on the principal-agent theoretical framework. First, I provide an institutional description of the delegation structure and information asymmetry in a public university, as an example with which to substantiate the following theoretical discussion. In the section that follows this description, I explore the dynamics of a simple principal-agent relationship where both actors can play either transparency or opacity with regard to the budget information each one controls. I show that the outcome of this relationship varies according to the presence or absence of built-in incentives aimed at modifying the agent's preferences. In the third section, I develop a more complex model where the principal delegates part of her responsibilities to a supervisor. I show that the budget outcome depends on the supervisor's collusion behaviour which in turn varies with the incentive structure in place. In the last section I discuss several implications of the model, both normative and positive.

Delegation and information asymmetry in a public university: An illustration

To illustrate the workings of delegation and information asymmetry in budgeting, let us look at the budget process in a public university as an example. Following Bergman, Muller and Strom (2000), let us conceive of the budgetary process in a democratic society as a 'chain of delegation' going from the electorate to budget executants. For example, the most important delegation nodes in the budget process in the higher education system in the province of Quebec could be depicted as follows:

Electorate – Provincial Legislature
President of the Treasury Board – Departments
Minister of Education – Universities and Colleges
Finance Vice-rector – Faculties
Dean – Departments

The electorate delegated to the provincial Legislature the responsibility to spend or otherwise allocate the equivalent of 24 percent of provincial GDP, a total of $43,480. million for the 1999-2000 budget. The provincial Treasury Board then allocated this amount among the various government programs and services, of which $9,676. million were allocated to the ministry of education which in turn allocated $278 million to the university I use as an example here. At each one of these levels, a subordinate receives an amount of money from his superior and reallocates it among his own subordinates. The same process continues within the university. At this level, the central budgeting question is: how are monetary resources allocated to university activity? I limit the discussion to this part of the university budget that is used to staff and operate faculties and departments (mainly salaries for teaching, administrative, and support personnel, as well as material resource expenditures). In the university annual financial statement, these expenditures are included in the Operating fund under the heading 'Teaching and free research'. Expenditures in 'Teaching and free research' for fiscal year 1999-2000 totalled $217.7 million. There is no need to say that the largest part of this amount was already committed when the University prepared its 1999-2000 budget. Permanent employees (professors, secretaries, technicians, and professionals) directly involved in teaching and free research functions consumed around $195 million[1] which left about $23 million for annual allocations. In this description, I ask two questions regarding the annual allocations for 'teaching and free research' expenditures: Is there a delegation of responsibility in the budgeting process? Is there information asymmetry?

Delegation of responsibility

There is delegation of budgeting responsibilities for both the auxiliary teaching personnel budget ($14.9 million) and the material resource budget ($4.9 million). Using a complex formula based on a weighted volume of activities (number of students, courses, diplomas, etc.), the vice-rector allocates these amounts among the 16 faculties. In single department faculties (Dentistry, Law, Music, Theology, Philosophy, Pharmacy, and Nursing) the delegation stops there. In the other nine faculties, the dean allocates the amount received among the departments after having extracted the amount necessary for faculty operations. In those cases, the delegation stops at the department level, the chair being responsible for allocating the money received among various spending areas under his responsibility. Therefore, we have a two-level structure of delegation within the university: Vice-rector to Dean and Dean to department Chair. This process has been working with only minor modifications for at least the last 20 years.

Things are similar with the decisions to hire new permanent (or likely to become permanent) personnel (tenure-track professors, secretaries, technicians, and professionals) but they used to be quite different. Indeed, up until 1997, the delegation structure in this area was a one-level delegation. The decision to 'open a position' was taken by the vice-rector after a request by the department chair channelled through the dean. Once the decision was made, it was left to the department to choose in which specific sector the hiring would take place and what would the hiring requirements be (completed PhD or not, postdoctoral experience or not, etc.). The dean only made formal interventions in those decisions in multiple-department faculties. However, in 1997, as part of a scheme aimed at reducing the University

1 This is an approximation.

budget deficit hiring decisions were decentralised to the faculty level. Though the vice-rector kept the authority to authorize each position, he delegated to the dean the responsibility to allocate teaching positions among departments while leaving to the department its traditional role in choosing the candidate. In short, after 1997, the delegation structure for hiring decisions was also a two-level structure. This change in the delegation structure raises the issue of its impact on overall spending. Is it possible that the decision to delegate, made to foster the objective of eliminating the university deficit, actually increased costs? In order to answer that question, one also has to consider the role of information in the budget process.

Information asymmetry

There is quite an important amount of information that is available to the participants in the university budgetary process: information concerning revenue and spending in previous years (in particular, detailed information concerning each transaction recorded by the university Finance service), and information concerning the level of activity of each unit in previous years (number of students taught, number of diplomas, number of courses, etc.). This information is controlled by the vice-rector. Therefore, there is information asymmetry in favour of the vice-rector. There is, however, information asymmetry in favour of the dean against the vice-rector and of the department chair against the dean when actual needs are considered. Indeed, each faculty is a 'black box' to the vice-rector (except maybe his or her own faculty) and each department to the dean. The culture of a faculty or a department, as well as the quality standards for research and the training requirements for students, are, to a certain extent, unique to each unit. A vice-rector (dean) may observe the inputs and the outputs of a faculty (department) but may find it difficult to understand what goes on in-between. Therefore, when it comes to making allocation decisions, the vice-rector (dean) is somewhat dependent on the information provided by the dean (department chair). The information asymmetry here is in favour of subordinates over superiors. If the superior relies on the information she has (information about past activity) she runs the risk of making the wrong choices in establishing institutional priorities, thus over funding faculties or departments that have less development potential and under funding those that have more.

One way to solve this problem is to get involved in a long and costly process of consultation to gather appropriate information. The other way is to let subordinates (deans and department chairs) make the decision and bear the consequences. This problem is particularly acute when it comes to cutting expenditures, as was the case in this university in 1997. How does one go about choosing which department or which faculty should have less personnel? On the one hand, one may want to spread spending cuts equally across the board, a potentially inefficient decision since some units may be already overstaffed while others are in need of additional personnel. One may also want to scatter the resistance to budget cuts, or to deviate toward others the criticism one's budget policy may cause. In this case, the solution is to delegate the responsibility to make cuts to lower tier decision-makers in the organisation.

This is what the university did in 1997: delegating the responsibility to make hiring decisions actually meant delegating the responsibility to decrease the number of teaching, administrative, and support personnel positions. As long as faculties and departments were to compete against each other, the university spared the resistance its budget policy could have provoked.

Therefore delegation is a way for superiors to solve the problem of uncertainty caused by information asymmetry in favour of subordinates. It may also be a solution to the opposition or resistance of subordinates to difficult budgetary decisions. But what is the effect of delegation on spending level if it has any? Let us see what a principal-agent theory treatment of this issue can tell us.

A theory of budgeting in a bureaucratic organisation

I assume that actors are rational, i.e. they are utility maximizers. Their utility function includes three arguments:

- money, a short cut for 'things of value' like trips abroad, cars, comfortable houses, good food, nice offices, big spending accounts, etc.
- power, i.e. influence over others or the capacity to make others do what they would not otherwise; this capacity is generally linked to authority positions in the organisation;
- esteem, the assurance of being recognized as knowledgeable, efficient, intelligent, etc. by others, i.e. actors value the fact of having their opinion taken into account in the allocation of resources.

The maximization of one argument often coincides with the maximization of others. Positions of authority, for example, generally come with higher wages, higher influence over others and higher possibility of seeing one's ideas incorporated into the content of decisions. However, it may happen that the search for one of these objectives is incompatible with another. For example, one may resign from office on a question of principle. This amounts to giving up money and power to protect one's (self) esteem. Choosing a career in the private sector may be seen as giving more importance to money than to power since wages are higher for private than public servants, yet authority may be seen as lower for the former. Hence, actors in the budget process want a budget that provides them with money, power, and esteem. They want a budget that includes monetary advantages for themselves (big spending account, high salary, etc.), leverage over their subordinates (high discretionary budget to distribute among subordinates), and characteristics that correspond to their idea of a good budget and that help them implement the ideas they have about a good policy.

Actors are further assumed to be involved in a relationship characterized by delegation of authority and information asymmetry, a principal-agent relationship. The principal delegates part of her authority to an agent who controls an information that is not available to her. To decrease her level of risks, the principal may make a formal contract with the agent in which is imbedded a set of incentives for the agent to divulge the information he has. The principal and the agent may also indulge in informal transactions (Breton and Wintrobe 1982) in which efficiency behaviour is exchanged for trust (to be immediately consumed as 'esteem' or to be capitalized in view of a future use). Here I concentrate on this part of the informal transactions between the principal and the agent that concerns information. Two types of information are particularly relevant: uncompressible expenditures and total revenue.

Agents control the information concerning uncompressible spending. Indeed they have a better knowledge of the amount that is necessary to maintain at their actual level the outputs of their units: for a university department chair, for example, how many lecturers are needed to keep a given program running or how many secretaries are necessary to maintain efficiency. From the principal's point of view, the difference between the total budget allocated to an agent's unit and this unit's uncompressible spending may be seen as superfluous expenditures –the 'discretionary surplus' (Migué and Bélanger 1974) that the agent tries to maximize. Information about the level of uncompressible spending is necessary for the principal to make an efficient allocation of resources (i.e. an efficient budget) among the services she is heading. Having that information, the principal can better distribute her budget among agents and avoid the risk of free riding (one agent getting a higher proportion of the budget than necessary) and of adverse selection (over funding one service while under funding another). This is why the principal tries to convince the agent to be transparent, that is to relay the information he controls to her so as to increase her own efficiency. This efficient behaviour on the part of the agent is what I call '*upward transparency*' (T_U), which I define as the behaviour of the agent that provides the principal with the information she needs to make efficient budget allocations.

Total revenue is an important information controlled by the principal. Revenue sources at each budgeting level are numerous and complex enough for a superior to have the capacity to hide part of that information from her subordinates. In the university budget process, for example, the subsidy given by the ministry of Education and voted on by the provincial legislature represented only 55 percent of total university budget in 1999-2000, the rest coming from various other sources. Likewise, revenue given to departments through the general allocation scheme is supplemented by other sources – like compensations for professors assigned to administrative duties or funds for graduate student support – and these supplementary revenue sources could make up a substantial part of a department revenue. The multiplicity and the complexity of revenue sources thus create an asymmetry in favour of the principal who knows her total revenue whereas the agent does not. From his point of view, the difference between his superior's total revenue and her (the superior's) uncompressible spending may be viewed as her room to manoeuvre of which the agent wants to get a part. The agent needs the information concerning the principal's real room to manoeuvre in order to set his budget requests at the most appropriate level. If his requests are too far below the principal's capacity, he gets a budgetary allocation that is inferior to the one he would have gotten had he asked for more. If his requests are too far above the principal's capacity, they could be seen as unrealistic and his evaluation of costs and needs as non credible, thus eroding his capital of trust with the principal. The agent can save the cost of finding out about the principal's real manoeuvre room and, most importantly, the cost of cheating (that is of artificially inflating service costs and clients' needs) if the principal adopts a '*downward transparency*' (T_D) behaviour, the behaviour of the principal that provides the agent with a clear picture of her real room to manoeuvre.

Thus, using a game theory presentation in normal form, we have two actors, the principal (P) and the agent (A), with two strategies, transparency (T) and opacity (O) (or, equivalently, more or less transparency), the combination of which yields four budget outcomes (Figure 9.1):

A Delegation-Success Budget (DSB): appears when the agent is more transparent and the principal less. Here the principal gets to know everything she needs in order to make an efficient budget while preserving her freedom of action by not revealing her real room to manoeuvre. This budget is called a delegation-success because it corresponds to the situation depicted by Arthur Lupia and Mathiew D. McCubbins (2000) where the delegation of authority yields a budget that is better than it would have been without delegation.[2]

Blind budget (BB): when none of the actors cooperate. This type of budget corresponds to the outcome the principal would have realised had she not delegated to her agent. Indeed, since all the information controlled by the agent is kept from the principal, this budget corresponds to the budget the principal could have achieved by herself.

Cooperative budget (CB): is the result of both actors adopting a cooperative strategy of 'more transparency'. This outcome also improves the principal's welfare relative to BB but less so than DSB.

Delegation-failure budget (DFB): when the agent is less transparent and the principal is more. In this case, the agent keeps for himself the advantages of being the one informed while drawing profits from the principal's transparency. The information provided by the principal is used by the agent to increase his share of the budget.

It is reasonable to assume that the actors' preference scales are the following ones, given their utility maximizing propensity:

---

2 'We say that delegation succeeds when an agent's actions improve a principal's welfare relative to the status quo, where the status quo is the outcome that the principal would have realized had she not delegated to her agent. We say that delegation fails when an agent's actions reduce a principal's welfare relative to the status quo' (Lupia and McCubbins 2000, 296).

Principal: DSB > CB > BB > DFB
Agent: DFB > CB > BB > DSB

Hence the game depicted in Figure 9.1:

		P	
		T_D	O_D
A	T_U	CB 3,3	DSB 1,4
	O_U	DFB 4,1	BB* 2,2

* Nash Equilibrium

Figure 9.1 Budget outcomes and payoff matrix of the basic budget relationship (RG#12: Prisoner Dilemma)

The budget relationship depicted in Figure 9.1 is a typical prisoner dilemma game (game #12 in Anatol Rapoport's and Melvin Guyer's (1966) taxonomy) with Blind Budget as the natural solution and Nash equilibrium. Assuming a one-shot game, the likely outcome of the interaction between a principal and an agent maximizing their utility is a blind budget. Allowing for long term learning through experience, the theory of meta-games shows that Cooperative Budget is an equilibrium if both actors adopt a strategy of reciprocal response: I will cooperate if you do, I won't if you don't (Brams 1975). Therefore the Blind Budget outcome may be avoided through personnel stability. If both the principal and the agent stay in office long enough for them to learn from repeated interactions, they may end up at a Cooperative Budget.

Another way of avoiding the blind budget outcome is through the modification of the preference scale of one actor (or of both). This is possible through a structure of incentives that increases the costs and the benefits of a given strategy for an actor. This solution is typical of normative applications of the principal-agent theory Imagine that the principal links specific benefits to upward transparency (a financial bonus, a symbolic recognition (esteem) or a promotion for the transparent agent) and specific costs to upward opacity (a financial penalty, or indifference, or the demotion, for an opaque agent) so as to change the agent's preference scale to this one: CB>DFB>DSB>BB. We would then have a new game, depicted in Figure 9.2.

		P	
		T_D	O_D
A	T_U	CB 4,3	DSB* 2,4
	O_U	DFB 3,1	BB 1,2

* Nash Equilibrium

Figure 9.2 Budget outcomes and payoff matrix of the budget relationship when incentives are built in (RG#21)

The game depicted in Figure 9.2 corresponds to game #21 in Rapoport and Guyer's taxonomy, a 'class I game with a single threat-vulnerable equilibrium' (Rapoport and Guyer 1966: 207). Both players have a dominant strategy: Opacity for the principal and Transparency for the agent. Assuming that both players follow their dominant strategy, the natural outcome is DSB which is also a Nash equilibrium.

What is the implication of this section? In the absence of a long term relationship with the agent, the principal may modify the outcome of the basic principal-agent budget model by building incentives into the relationship in order to convince the agent to be more transparent. This outcome is an improvement over the non cooperative solution of the basic model without incentives and over the status quo the principal would have realised without delegation.

Now, how can we take into account the fact that budgetary processes often involve multi-layer principal-agent relationships? There are two ways of theoretically dealing with a chain of principal-agent relationships. One may assume that the effect of each relationship adds up into a combined effect of the process on the budgetary outcome. In such a case, there is no need to go any further in terms of theoretical development than a two-actor relationship. However, following Tirole (1986), I argue that there is an interaction between two overlapping principal-agent relationships because the same actor plays the agent in the upper relationship while playing the principal in the lower one. Therefore we need to go a step further in the theoretical construction to take this interaction into account. I suggest to use Tirole's concept of 'supervisor' to represent the actor who plays the role of agent in a relationship while playing the principal in another one.

Let P stand for the principal and A for the agent, in a principal-agent relationship. Let the following expression stand for a two-level nested relationship:

$$\begin{array}{lll} P_1 \rightarrow & & A_1 \\ \underline{\qquad\qquad} & P_2 \rightarrow & A_2 \end{array}$$

where A_1 and P_2 represent a single actor playing different roles in a two level chain of agency relationships. The actor playing the roles A_1 and P_2 in the two-level nested agency relationships becomes S_T (the "supervisor" in Tirole's agency relationship):

$$P_T \rightarrow \qquad S_T \rightarrow \quad A_T$$

The strategy A_T has at his disposal is to increase or reduce the distortion in the bottom-up flow of information (upward transparency or opacity) whereas S_T has two sets of strategies at his disposal: downward transparency or opacity in his relationship with A_T and upward transparency or opacity in his relationship with P_T. P_T is assumed to be the first principal in a series of principal-agent relationships. As such, she is assumed not be involved as an agent in a higher level relationship.

In general, a principal faces several supervisors and a supervisor faces several agents. Therefore a more accurate representation of a Tirole's agency relationship is the following one:

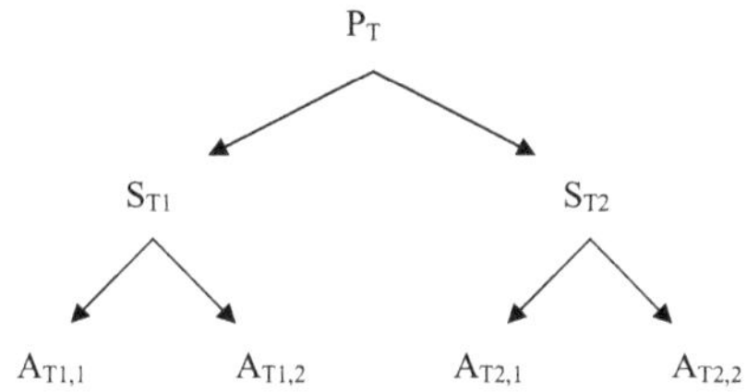

Tirole has shown the importance of collusion in such a setting. There may be 'horizontal collusion' among supervisors against the principal or among agents of a given branch against the branch supervisor. This possibility of collusion may be theoretically treated within the single principal-agent relationship presented in the previous section. Supervisors (agents) may collude to modify the principal's (supervisor's) preference scale thus making the principal (supervisor) adopt a more transparent behaviour. To avoid horizontal collusion, the principal (supervisor) has two strategies: downward opacity (i.e. confer with each supervisor (agent) separately and share with each one a different information along the old principle 'divide and conquer') or downward transparency (i.e. building trust through the sharing of information).

A vertical collusion takes place between a superior and his immediate subordinates in order to deceive the third party in the three-tier relationship. There may be a collusion between a principal and his supervisors in order to increase the quality of the information coming from the field in spite of the resistance of agents (principal-supervisor collusion) and there may be a collusion between a supervisor and her agents to deceive the principal (supervisor-agent collusion). The principal has two types of instruments to avoid the building of a supervisor-agent collusion or to counter the effects of such a collusion when it exists: monitoring (v.g. close control of spending down the line in order to know what is actually going on, appointment of trusted individuals as supervisors, regular switching of supervisors in order to prevent the building of trust within a division) and incentives (v.g. bonus or promotion linked to upward transparency on the part of the supervisor).

To see the impact of collusion on the dynamics of the basic principal-agent game, lets consider two nested principal-agent relationships where the supervisor plays the role of agent in the upper relationship and the role of principal in the lower one (Figure 9.3).

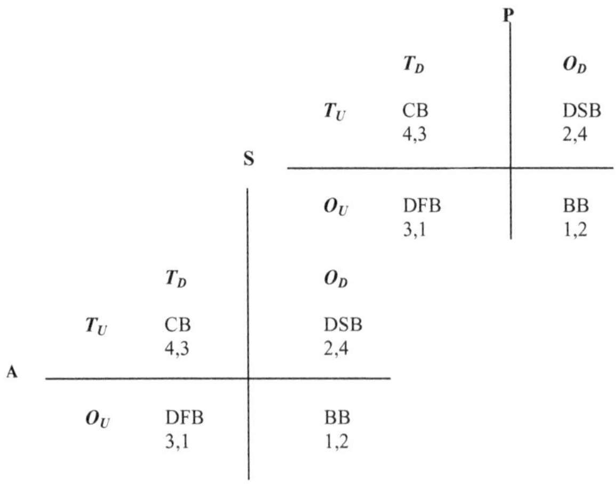

By assumption, a principal-supervisor (P-S) collusion implies that both the principal and the supervisor adopt a cooperative strategy in the upper budget and that both the supervisor and the agent adopt a maximizing strategy in the lower budget. A supervisor-agent (S-A) collusion implies cooperative strategies in the lower budget and maximizing strategies in the upper budget. Collaboration (Co) stands for an agreed cooperative behaviour on the part of all three players.

Table 9.1 gives the outcomes and the payoffs of four collusion scenarios (No: no collusion; P-S: principal-supervisor collusion; S-A: supervisor-agent collusion; Co: collaboration) under four incentive structures (IS1: no incentives in either budget; IS2: incentives in both budgets; IS3: incentives in lower budget only; IS4: incentives in upper budget only). The collusion scenario preferred by the supervisor and the ensuing outcome is determined by the addition of the payoffs to the supervisor. For example, consider the payoffs when there is no built in incentive (IS1). Each collusion scenario yields a unique outcome in each budget. No collusion (No) implies that the outcomes of the games correspond to the natural solution, each player adopting a maximizing strategy: BB in both budgets. A P-S collusion implies that players adopt cooperative strategies in the upper budget (outcome: CB) and a maximizing strategy in the lower budget (outcome: BB). Conversely, in a S-A collusion, players adopt maximizing strategies in the upper game (outcome: BB) and cooperative strategies in the lower game (outcome: CB). Finally, a collaboration scenario implies that all players adopt the cooperative strategy of more transparency, yielding the outcome CB in both budgets. Given these results, the supervisor prefers a collaboration scenario to a collusion scenario since his total payoff is 6 (3+3) under this scenario as opposed to 5 (3+2 and 2+3) 4 (2+2) under the two collusion scenarios P-S and S-A. Applying this reasoning to all combinations of incentive structures and collusion scenarios, we find that total payoffs to the supervisor are higher when she colludes with the principal, except under IS-1, where no incentive exists, and IS-4, where there are incentives only in the upper game. In those cases, the supervisor prefers to collaborate with both the principal and the agent thus maximizing her gains. But what about costs? Don't these choices have an impact on agency costs and overall spending?

Three types of costs can be identified in the budget relationship: information-search costs, efficiency costs, and incentive costs. Three assumptions about cost distribution can help assess them:

1. A player's opacity results in information-search costs for the other player. In other words, resources – money, time, and energy – are devoted to looking for the information obfuscated by the other player. Therefore, information-search costs vary from one budget outcome to another; they are higher when both players are opaque (outcome: BB) and they are lower when both players are transparent (outcome: CB). Hence an ordinal scale that, can be represented by an interval scale for computing purposes:

BB	>	DFB	=	DSB	>	CB
4		2		2		0

2. Some budget outcomes are more efficient (i.e. closer to a situation that cannot be improved for one individual without deteriorating the situation of another) than others. Efficiency is improved when the principal is better informed or, equivalently, when the agent is transparent. There is also a gain in efficiency when the principal can keep a certain latitude by being opaque. Considering a loss in efficiency as a cost, we have the following ordinal scale of efficiency costs with their associated cardinal values:

DFB	>	BB	>	CB	>	DSB
4		3		2		1

3. The implementation of incentives and controls aimed at modifying an agent's preferences is costly. Assuming that the 'no incentive' structure (IS1) bears no cost, assuming equal costs for incentives in the upper (IS4) or the lower (IS3) budgets, and assuming that these costs add up when incentives are implemented at both levels (IS2), we have the following distribution of incentive costs:

IS2	>	IS4	=	IS3	>	IS1
4		2		2		0

Table 9.1 Budget outcomes, payoffs, and agency costs resulting from various collusion scenarios and incentive structures

Incentive Structure #1

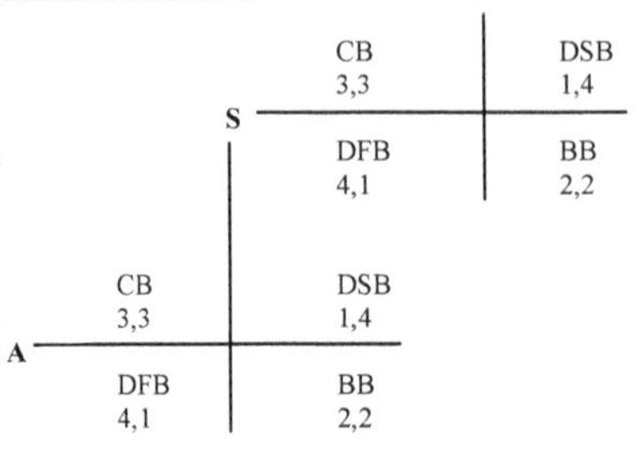

Collusion scenarios:	No	P-S	S-A	**Co**
Upper budget				
Outcome:	BB	CB	BB	**CB**
Principal's Payoffs:	2	3	2	3
Supervisor's Payoffs:	2	3	2	**3**
Lower budget				
Outcome:	BB	BB	CB	**CB**
Supervisor's Payoffs:	2	2	3	**3**
Agent's Payoffs:	2	2	3	3
Agency Costs	11	7.5	7.5	2

Incentive Structure #2

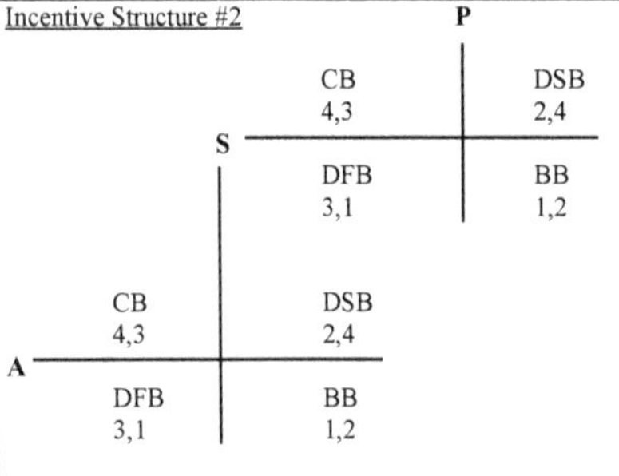

Collusion scenarios	No	**P-S**	S-A	Co
Upper budget				
Outcome:	DSB	**CB**	BB	CB
Principal's Payoffs:	4	3	2	3
Supervisor's Payoffs:	2	**4**	1	4
Lower budget				
Outcome	DSB	**DSB**	CB	CB
Supervisor's Payoffs	4	**4**	3	3
Agent's Payoffs	2	2	4	4
Agency Costs	13	12.5	15.5	10

Incentive Structure #3

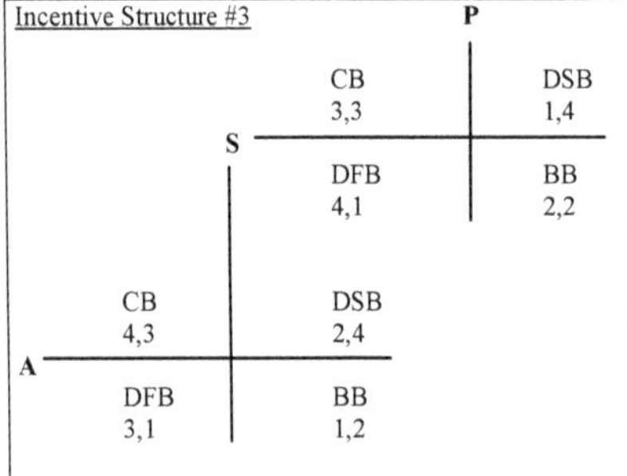

Collusion scenarios	No	**P-S**	S-A	Co
Upper budget				
Outcome:	BB	**CB**	BB	CB
Principal's Payoffs:	2	3	2	3
Supervisor's Payoffs:	2	**3**	2	3
Lower budget				
Outcome:	DSB	**DSB**	CB	CB
Supervisor's Payoffs:	4	**4**	3	3
Agent's Payoffs:	2	2	4	4
Agency Costs	12	11.5	11.5	6

Incentive Structure #4

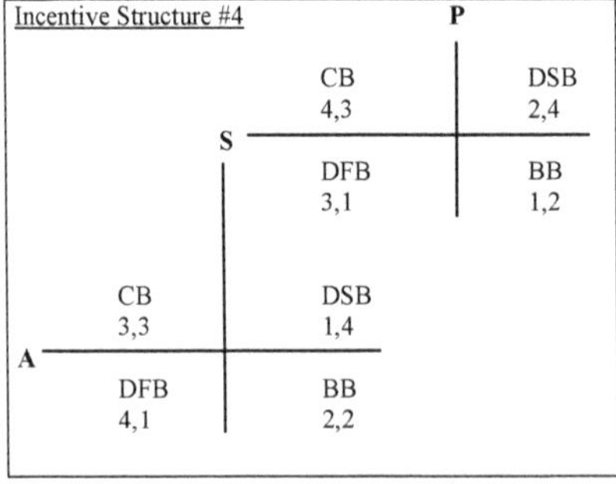

Collusion scenarios	No	P-S	S-A	**Co**
Upper budget				
Outcome:	DSB	CB	BB	**CB**
Principal's Payoffs:	4	3	2	3
Supervisor's Payoffs:	2	4	1	**4**
Lower budget				
Outcome:	BB	BB	CB	**CB**
Supervisor's Payoffs:	2	2	3	**3**
Agent's Payoffs:	2	2	3	3
Agency Costs	12	11.5	11.5	6

Note: Collusion scenarios: No: No collusion; P-S: Principal-Supervisor collusion; S-A: Supervisor-Agent collusion; Co: Collaboration.

Using the interval scales for each cost, it is easy to compute the relative agency costs of each outcome. Outcome BB, for example, which is the outcome of the simple game reported above in Figure 9.1, bears an information cost equal to 4, an efficiency cost equal to 3 and an incentive cost equal to 0, for a total agency cost of 7. The computation of agency costs resulting from complex structures (i.e. agency relationship with a supervisor), though a little more cumbersome, follows the same logic with the additional rule that information and incentive costs for upper and lower budgets are added whereas efficiency costs are averaged. This is to take into account the idea that information and incentive costs increase as additional layers of agency relationships are added, but that efficiency gains may be reached by additional delegations. Thus, for a type 1 incentive structure (IS1) and a 'no collusion' scenario, we have the cost structure given in Table 9.2.

Table 9.2 Computation of agency costs for a complex relationship with Incentive structure #1 and No collusion

	Upper Budget	**Lower Budget**	**Total**
Outcome	**BB**	**BB**	
Information costs	4	4	8
Efficiency costs	3	3	3
Incentive costs	0	0	0
Total agency costs	7	7	11

Applying these rules, one can compute the agency costs related to each outcome resulting from each collusion scenario and each incentive structure given in Table 9.1. This distribution of agency costs is displayed in Table 9.3, together with the agency costs related to the outcomes of the simple games analysed above. Two situations stand out as involving a cost level that is far below the others: simple agency relationship with long term interaction (Prisoner dilemma in a metagame), and Collaboration scenario without incentive. The lowest cost situation in simple games does not correspond to the outcome preferred by the principal on the basis of her payoffs. Indeed, the Nash equilibrium of game #21 is DSB, the principal's most preferred outcome, whereas the cost level is markedly higher than the lowest cost (5, as compared to 2). In complex games, the lowest cost outcome corresponds to the supervisor's most preferred outcome.

Table 9.3 Agency costs by type of agency relationship, incentive structure and collusion scenario

		Type of agency relationship				
		Simple	Complex (Collusion scenarios)			
Incentive structure	Game number*		No	P-S	S-A	Co
IS1 : None	#12	7	11	6,5	6,5	2**
	#12 (Metagame)	2				
IS2 : Both	#21	5	13	12,5	16,5	10
IS3 : Lower	Upper: #12; Lower: #21		12	7,5	10,5	6
IS4 : Upper	Upper: #21; Lower: #12		12	10,5	10,5	6

* Game number refers to Rapoport's and Guyer's taxonomy. #12: Prisoner dilemma; #21 budget game with built in incentives.
** Underscore indicates the outcome preferred by the supervisor in complex games, or by the principal in simple games, on the basis of her payoffs as given in table 9.1 or in figures 9.1 and 9.2.

Discussion and conclusion

The budget model described above has several normative and positive implications.

From a normative standpoint, the model helps answer at least three questions.

1. When is it rational for a principal to delegate responsibilities to a supervisor? Or, equivalently, can a principal improve her payoffs by moving from a simple to a complex budget relationship? The answer depends on the status quo position. It is clear from Table 9.4 that any move from RG#12 (simple relationship without incentive) pays: a principal can improve her situation from BB to at least CB by delegating to a supervisor. However if the status quo position is RG#21 (simple relationship with incentives) delegation deteriorates the principal's payoff. Therefore a rational principal should not delegate and should rather resort to incentives as a budget instrument. This is all the more true when we consider that delegation strips the principal from some of her power as it gives the supervisor a dominant role in determining the collusion scenario that is to prevail. Why, then, did the authorities in the university we analysed choose to delegate part of their budgeting responsibilities to the deans as supervisors? Because of an exogenous constraint. Indeed, the potential for resistance or outright opposition on the part of faculty members, support personnel, and students, was a serious threat to the political feasibility of the restrictive budgetary policy that the university wanted to implement in order to eliminate its budgetary deficit. One way to deal with this opposition was to

scatter the resistance points through delegation. This way, pressures against the university budgetary policy could be buffered through 60 departments and 16 faculties. In other words, the choice of a policy instrument is not always motivated by a single policy objective. Decision-makers simultaneously pursue several objectives. When facing a potentially strong political opposition, the principal may be willing to give up her most preferred budgetary outcome in order to secure the political benefits generated by delegation.

Table 9.4 Outcomes, principal's payoffs, and agency costs associated with incentive structures and types of agency relationship (extracted from tables 9.1 and 9.3)

	Simple relationship		Complex relationship							
			Upper Budget				Lower Budget			
	RG#12	RG#21	IS-1	IS-2	IS-3	IS-4	IS-1	IS-2	IS-3	IS-4
Outcome	BB	DSB	BB	CB	CB	CB	CB	DSB	DSB	BB
Principal's payoff	2	4	2	3	3	3	3	4	4	2
Agency costs	7	5	6.5	12.5	7.5	10.5	6.5	12.5	7.5	10.5

2. When, and with whom, is it rational for the supervisor to collude? The supervisor is in the unique position of choosing whether or not to collude and with whom. The analysis provided in Table 9.1 tells us that it is never to the supervisor's interest to let things go their own way nor to collude with agents against the principal.[3] Rather, the supervisor will prefer either a principal-supervisor collusion scenario or Collaboration, depending on the incentive structure in place. When there is no incentive in the lower budget, the supervisor prefers a scenario of collaboration. Otherwise, her preference goes for a scenario of collusion with the principal. My empirical observation of the university budget process is not detailed enough to provide a convincing confirmation of this hypothesis. However what I have observed so far seems to lead to that conclusion: there is no incentive structure in the university budget relationship and the collusion behaviour I have observed so far resembles a

3 Letting things go means allowing the budget outcome to be set only by the maximizing rationality of actors (i.e. a No collusion scenario).

collaboration scenario.

3. Given the collusion behaviour of the supervisor, when is it rational for the principal to change the incentive structure? Let us start with the situation where there is no incentive (IS-1) and where the supervisor chooses a scenario of collaboration. The principal cannot improve her payoff in the upper budget by modifying the incentive structure. But assuming that she shares the supervisor's preferences in the lower budget, she will get a better result in that budget if she implements incentives aimed at modifying the agent's preferences (IS-3). However, in doing that, the principal increases agency costs. Therefore, a principal who is insensitive to agency costs would try to implement incentives at least in the lower budget. A similar supervisor would pressure the principal for incentives in the upper budget as well. The result is the most costly situation, IS-2, with agency costs reaching 11.5 points. If we assume that agency costs enter the utility function of both the principal and the supervisor, an assumption that is coherent with our previous discussion about the importance of esteem in the utility function of budget actors, the best situation results from a scenario of collaboration without incentive neither in the upper nor in the lower budgets. In other words, the use of incentives in the budget process involving a supervisor is never the choice of a rational, well informed, principal. Incentive structure in the budget process may allow savings in agency costs but only in a simple structure process. With complex structures involving supervisors, it is cheaper to rely on individual's preferences and not to try to change the preference ordering of supervisors and agents through incentives. Higher agency costs are unavoidable for the most efficient budget outcome (DSB) to be possible.

From a positive standpoint, the model presented here also has important implications for overall spending and actors' behaviour. Indeed, agency costs end up in actual financial costs for the organisation. The time and energy invested in information search and in the implementation of incentives aimed at convincing supervisors and agents to be transparent, are resources that are deviated from the production of goods and services. Therefore, for a given output level, higher costs translate into higher spending, everything else being equal. Hence the following hypotheses concerning the level of aggregate spending:

H: Ceteris paribus, the level of aggregate spending is <u>lower</u> when an efficient incentive structure is at play in a <u>simple</u> organization (without supervisor).
H: Ceteris paribus, the level of aggregate spending is <u>higher</u> when an efficient incentive structure is at play in a <u>complex</u> organisation (with supervisor).

In addition to these two hypotheses that can be falsified through a quantitative analysis predicting the level of aggregate spending, several hypotheses predicting actors' choices can also be deduced in order to guide a qualitative analysis of the budgetary process in a given sector of government intervention.

H: A supervisor's collusion behaviour varies with the existing incentive structure: in the absence of incentives in the lower budget, she will tend to collaborate with both her principal and her agents; when there are incentives in the lower budget, the supervisor will collude with her principal.
H: A principal will resort to delegation as a budget instrument only if exogenous constraints makes it desirable. As soon as these constraints disappear, the process will be centralized again.

Transparency and opacity are two strategies in the hand of superiors and subordinates in the budgetary process of a bureaucratic organisation. The ideal world for the superior is one where she can be opaque while her subordinates are transparent. This is how she can get the most out of her interaction with them. However, their rationality tells them not to reveal the information they have, yielding a result that she could improve if she correctly used two policy instruments: incentives and delegation. Through incentives, a superior can alter her subordinates' preference scales thus making it more advantageous for them to be transparent. Through delegation, she can free herself from the dependence on her subordinates by making them responsible for the decision they make. For delegation to lead to her best outcome, incentives must be added, thus increasing costs.

There is an alternative instrument a superior may use to improve the outcome for both her and her subordinates while maintaining costs at their lowest level: trust. Acknowledging her personal interests and those of her subordinates, a superior may induce them to be more transparent through a long term relationship based on reciprocity: I will cooperate if you do, I will not if you do not. For this method to work, three conditions are essential: first, the superior must be willing to risk the uncooperative outcome where everybody is opaque; second, terms of office for both superiors and subordinates must be long enough to allow repeated interactions; third, the superior must give up her attempt to get her most preferred outcome and be content with her second best. Under these conditions, a cooperative solution may be stable.

When one looks at the new public management agenda for government bureaucracy, one can see that the preferred instruments are incentives and delegation rather than trust. The consequence may well be a stabilisation or a decrease in spending accompanied by a much sharper decrease in the quantity and quality of government services as most of the savings will have been absorbed by agency costs. And opponents to 'big governments' will comfort themselves, unaware that they created the real problem of diminishing efficiency by trying to solve the false problem of a benevolent superior facing malevolent subordinates.

References

Bendor, J. et al. (1985), 'Bureaucratic Expertise vs. Legislative Authority: A Model of Deception and Monitoring in Budgeting' *American Political Science Review* 79:4, 1041-60.

_______ (1987), 'Politicians, Bureaucrats, and Asymmetric Information' *American Journal of Political Science* 31:4, 796-828.

Bergman, T. et al. (2000), 'Introduction: Parliamentary democracy and the chain of delegation' *European Journal of Political Research* 37: 255-60.

Brams, S. (1975). *Game Theory and Politics.* (New York: The Free Press).

Breton, A. and Wintrobe, R (1982). *The Logic of Bureaucratic Conduct. An Economic Analysis of Competition, Exchange and Efficiency in Private and Public Organizations.* (New York: Cambridge University Press).

Dahl, R. (1967), *Pluralist Democracy in the United States: Conflict and Consent.* (Chicago: Rand McNally).

Eatwell, J., Milgate, M., and Newman, P. (eds.) (1987), *The New Palgrave: A Dictionary of Economics.* (London: Macmillan).

Gerth, H. and Mills, C. W. (eds.) (1946). *From Max Weber: Essays in Sociology.* (New York: Oxford University Press).

Gilardi, F. (2001), 'Principal-Agent Models Go to Europe: Independent Regulatory Agencies as Ultimate Step of Delegation' (Canterbury: ECPR General Conference).

Imbeau, L.M. (2004), 'Public Deficits and Surpluses in Federated States: A Review of the Public Choice Empirical Literature', *Journal of Public Finance and Public Choice 23*: 123-145.

Kopits, G. and Craig, J. (1998), *Transparency in Government Operations.* (Washington, DC: International Monetary Fund).

Lupia, A. and McCubbins, M. (2000), 'Representation or Abdication? How Citizens Use Institutions to Help Delegation Succeed', *European Journal of Political Research* 37: 291-307.

Michels, R. (1915), *Political Parties: A Sociological Study of the Oligarchical Tendencies of Modern Democracy.* (Glencoe, IL: Free Press).

Migué, J-L. and Bélanger, G. (1974), 'Towards a General Theory of Managerial Discretion', *Public Choice* 17: 27-43.

Rapoport, A. and M. Guyer, M. (1966), 'A Taxonomy of 2x2 Games' in Von Bertalanffy, L. and A. Rapoport, A. (eds.), 203-14.

Stiglitz, J. (1987), 'Principal and Agent' in Eatwell, J., Milgate, M., and Newman, P. (eds.), Vol. 3, 966-72.

Tirole, J. (1986), 'Hierarchies and Bureaucracies', *Journal of Law, Economics and Organization* 2, 181-214.

Von Bertalanffy, L. and A. Rapoport, A. (eds.) (1966), *General Systems: Yearbook of the Society for General Systems Research.* (Ann Arbor, MI: Society for General Systems Research).

Chapter 10

Redistribution, Decentralization and Constitutional Rules[1]

Federico Etro and Piero Giarda

Introduction

Policymaking at all levels faces a crucial trade-off between transparency of rules and efficiency. At the constitutional level, such an issue often emerges as a trade-off between a close control on the decision-makers and their autonomy.

An extreme degree of transparency is consistent with the possibility to check and balance the use and the abuse of political power. This balance is performed not only by the citizens-voters but also by the mass media and the opinion makers in general. Rules transparency is higher when the relationship between policymakers and their electoral basis is closer. Hence, there is naturally more transparency at the level of local governments than at the level of the central government. For this reason, federal states in which crucial powers are delegated from the central level to the local level are typically characterized by an high degree of transparency.

An extreme degree of independence and insulation of the politicians is a precondition to implement efficient policies and certain reforms which may be undermined by status quo biases. For instance, lobbies or unions representing a minority in the population may have strong tools to avoid reforms which make a majority of the people better off but make them worse off, however a high degree of insulation of a government can overcome this problem. Obviously, the cost of such a system is the excessive concentration of power at the central level. Paradoxically, a dictator has the easiest access to efficient reforms, but history is full of examples in which extensive power is abused.

This trade-off is at the basis of any problem of constitutional design. The horizontal allocation of executive, legislative and judiciary power and their separation is the classic example, but also the vertical allocation of power between local and central governments is a crucial example. The literature on fiscal federalism, for instance, has emphasized the trade-off emerging in problems of public good provision: uniform provision decided at the central level allows to internalise the spillovers between local districts, but it cannot adapt local provision to the local preferences and so it is optimal only when heterogeneity is low (Oates 1972; 1999).

---

1 We are grateful to Albert Breton, seminar participants, and the discussant for precious suggestions.

Other more specific constitutional rules are clearly based on the trade-off previously suggested: for instance, the period of time between one election and another at any level of government is an example: longer terms insulate more the policymakers and allow them to implement long term reform processes even though they also reduce the accountability of the politicians. A parliamentary privilege has a similar and even more delicate role. The choice of the degree of insulation of central bankers is a more important example from an economic point of view: more independent and conservative central bankers avoid the well known inflationary bias associated with the time-inconsistency problem of monetary policy. Moreover, a certain lack of transparency (in the sense of not revealing all information to the public), allows a certain flexibility in dealing with shocks to the economy without losing anti-inflationary reputation. Finally, simple tax rules are typically adopted for their simplicity even if more complex mechanisms may be optimal, while uniform tariff rates are often adopted to limit the influence of lobbying activity even though differentiated tariffs may be optimal.

From a normative point of view, this trade-off implies the existence of an optimal degree of transparency, which depends on the context to which it applies. In the real world such an optimum is difficult to realize and it is not even clear that there are the right incentives to realize it. The political economy literature has recently emphasized the trade-off between rules transparency and efficient reforms. In particular, Bordignon and Minelli (2001) have endogenized the choice between simple rules which allow to control the politicians in their application and complex rules which are more efficient but also more difficult to be monitored by the citizens and easy to be manipulated by the politicians. More recently, Aghion, Alesina, and Trebbi (2004) have developed a model where reforms are easier to implement when the government is more insulated from the voters and the choice of the degree of insulation is endogenized at a constitutional level. In both models, the trade-off between transparency and efficiency is clear, and more transparency is associated with a greater difficulty to implement efficient reforms.

This chapter belongs to this tradition and deals with the trade-off between transparency and efficiency in the constitutional design of a federal organization. In this context, transparency is synonymous with decentralization since delegation of power at the local level allows policies to be clearly adapted to local political preferences, and efficiency is synonymous with efficient allocation of resources between poor and rich regions (efficient redistribution) and between local public goods and private goods (efficient public goods provision). In our model of fiscal federalism, the trade-off between transparency and efficiency boils down to a *trade-off between decentralization and redistribution.*

We compare a centralized and a decentralized system in a two regions model with income inequality and local public good provision. The former achieves optimal income redistribution with an inefficient allocation of local public goods across the regions, while under decentralization there is limited redistribution and a tendency to generate overprovision of local public goods. Decentralization turns out to be preferred to centralization when inequality is high. Two other crucial results will also suggest a rationale for the trade-off between decentralization and redistribution: first, a transition from centralization to decentralization is supported by both regions if and only if the central government accepts incomplete redistribution; second, a decentralized system with a House of Regions, where the redistributive policy is decided by bargaining between regions, induces efficient policies but attains only partial redistribution.

The chapter is organized as follows. First, it provides an empirical discussion on the trade-off between decentralization and redistribution. It then presents the model. Following this, it studies the constitutional choice between a centralized and a decentralized system and provides some theoretical rationales for the existence of a trade-off between redistribution and decentralization. Afterwards, it discusses the relationship between transparency in politics and redistributive policies in a wider perspective and then concludes.

The trade-off between decentralization and redistribution

The distribution of powers and functions among different levels of government varies greatly among countries, ranging from the high centralization with complete redistribution and total lack of transparency of the old URSS and other communist countries to the high decentralization with low redistributive programs of the United States and other Anglo-Saxons countries. European continental countries are somewhere in the middle. The distribution of powers is also changing over time: while after World War II there has been a long tendency toward increasing centralization and social spending with the rise of the welfare state in most western countries, the last two decades have witnessed a discernible pattern of increasing decentralization of spending and taxing powers – which in certain cases is even going toward the last line – break up of nations in separate entities[2] – and a stop to the rise of redistributive efforts or even a decrease in them.

A widespread view claims that there is indeed a trade-off between redistribution and decentralization: a centralized state can implement a wider and more efficient redistribution of incomes among individuals and among regions than a decentralized state. In Table 1 we report some preliminary decentralization indexes for a number of OECD countries (built on the basis of the Fiscal Decentralization Indicators of the World Bank, based on Government Finance Statistics (GFS) data from the IMF)[3] ordered by social spending/GDP, which can be seen as an index of redistribution.

2 See Alesina (2003) for a related discussion.

3 We included all the OECD countries except for the smaller ones (Luxembourg, Cyprus, Iceland, Portugal, Greece, Israel and New Zealand) since the relevance (and even the same concept) of decentralization vanishes (or at least changes) for small countries. Developing countries were not considered because, despite they may also show a trade-off between decentralization and redistribution, they are characterized by less democratic and more centralized regimes, and hence they are not directly comparable with the developed countries. Ex Communist Countries were not considered since their process of decentralization was mainly developed through the break up of nations so that most of the subnational expenditures in the ex URSS, the ex Yugoslavia and the ex Czechoslovak became central expenditures in the new born countries. It would be interesting to verify that the trade-off between redistribution and decentralization holds for other homogeneous groups of countries.

Table 10.1 Decentralization Indexes

Countries ranked by increasing Social Spending/ GDP	Subnational Public Expenditures (percent of total – averages over 1972-2000)	Subnational Tax Revenue (percent of total revenues and grants – averages over 1972-2000)	Vertical Imbalance (in percentages)
USA	44.6	47.6	32.6
Australia	41.2	33.1	44.4
Japan	43.5	99.0	NA
Canada	57.4	56.0	26.4
Switzerland	51.9	52.6	22.8
Finland	38.1	49.3	31.5
UK	25.4	23.8	53.7
Ireland	25.1	8.8	66.8
Norway	34.6	45.6	32.3
Spain	20.0	41.5	40.4
Italy	21.2	19.1	65.4
Denmark	45.4	44.7	46.1
Germany	42.1	54.5	22.1
Austria	30.8	50.5	28.5
France	18.2	47.9	36.4
Sweden	37.7	62.6	22.8
Netherlands	25.0	7.1	75.1
Belgium	11.8	34.2	54.9

We adopt as a main Decentralization Index the *share of subnational (local, state and provincial) public expenditure on total public expenditure.* The main implication we want to draw from the table is that a preliminary look at these cross country data is in favour of a trade-off between decentralization and redistribution.

Notice that the variability of the Decentralization Index is very small in the OECD countries. Figure 10.1 illustrates its pattern for OECD countries and some other groups of countries in the period 1972-1997. Despite the lack of comprehensive data makes it difficult to evaluate these patterns, it emerges as a stable behaviour of the fraction of local public spending with at most a recent moderate upward trend.

Some problems with our index of decentralization should be emphasized. Defence and interest payments are rarely decentralized, and they can potentially distort measures of decentralization. For instance, the United States, despite being a much larger country, has a lower subnational share of expenditures than Switzerland. However, when defence and interest expenses are excluded from the subnational-to-total ratio, the United States has a higher subnational share of expenditures than Switzerland. While various expenditure patterns can be assessed by the GFS data, less can be said about expenditure autonomy. Expenditures that are mandated by the central government appear as subnational expenditures, even though subnational governments may have no autonomy in these spending decisions. Below, we also provide data on the *share of subnational (local, state and provincial) tax revenues on total tax revenue*, which is however a worst measure of fiscal decentralization. Indeed, a typical question asked in a decentralization context is how much autonomy do subnational governments have in raising revenue; for instance how much is collected through shared taxes versus piggybacked taxes versus locally determined taxes? Shared taxes appear as subnational revenue, although the subnational government has no autonomy in determining the revenue base or rate, since the GFS reports revenues based on which level of government ultimately receives the revenues. More qualitative information on legal and constitutional rules about fiscal decentralization is needed to build a better index based on all the available information. Finally, we provide an index of *vertical imbalance*, or the degree to which subnational governments rely on central government revenues to support their expenditures. This can be measured by intergovernmental transfers as a share of subnational expenditures. This measure does not distinguish what proportion of transfers is conditional versus general purpose, and the GFS data do not provide this information. Hence also this is not a good measure of fiscal decentralization. Finally we show in Figure 10.2 data on the Decentralization Index and the average *share of subnational (local, state and provincial) public expenditure on GDP* in the period 1972-2000 for the selected group of OECD countries. There is a high correlation between the two data sets (0.79) while the correlation between the Decentralization Index and the average *share of total public expenditure on GDP* is negative (– 0.25).

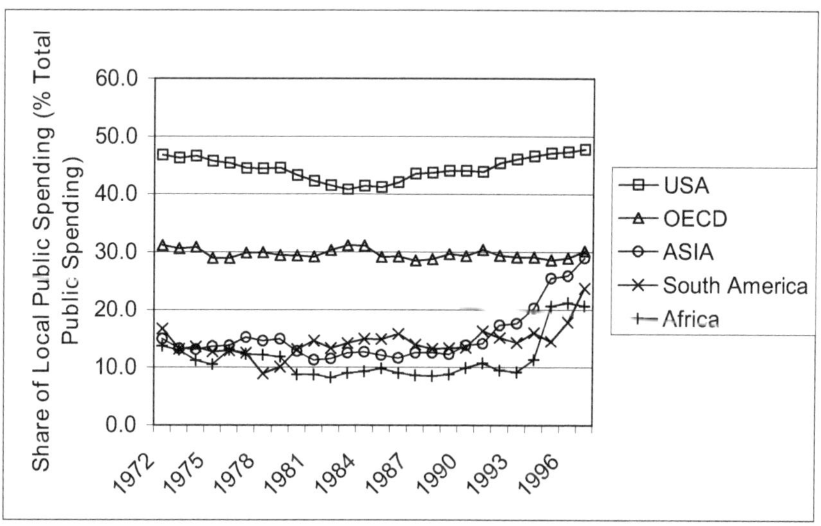

Figure 10.1 Patterns of Decentralization

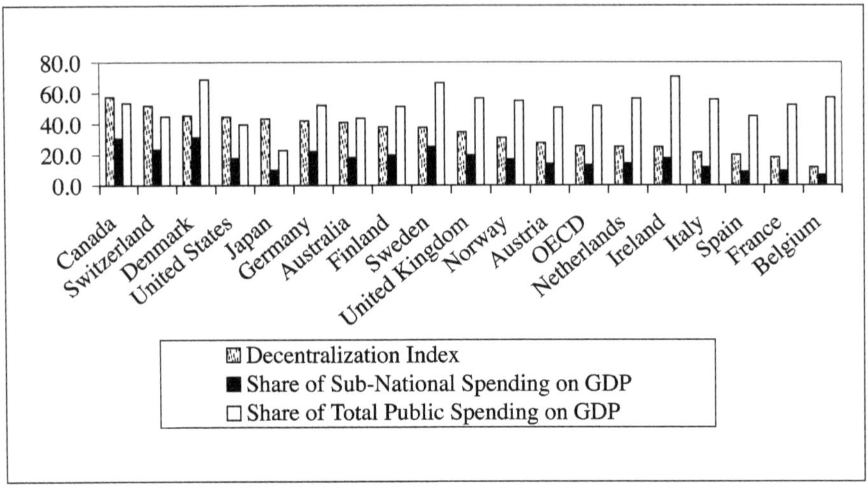

Figure 10.2 OECD Countries

Table 10.1 and Figure 10.1 suggest that public spending, as a proxy for redistribution spending, and decentralization are negatively correlated. Despite such a correlation may be spurious, since countries with high decentralization are also more liberal countries with stronger preferences for right wing policies and, hence, less redistribution, and also other factors (like social heterogeneity, national wealth, growth, labour market conditions affecting the distribution of earnings, size, openness) may affect both indexes, it is important to understand if and why such a correlation exists. A more accurate empirical research should try to disentangle the correct relationship between decentralization and redistribution controlling for other political, sociological and economic factors.

In the rest of the chapter we turn to the theory. It is not clear at all from a theoretical point of view why there should be a trade-off between redistribution and decentralization. A number of economic, sociological, cultural and political factors affect both variables and in many cases this happens in different directions. Some may well act against our suggested hypothesis. For instance, higher (regional) inequality may be associated with a stronger tendency toward decentralization but also toward more income redistribution for well known political economic reasons (Meltzer and Richard 1981): if this is true, the pure negative correlation between decentralization and redistribution may be even stronger than what is suggested by our previous data. In other words, we need a more accurate theoretical investigation of the relation between redistribution and decentralization.

A model of interregional redistribution

We will adopt a simple model of fiscal federalism between two regions. Since we want to relate redistribution and decentralization, we assume that the two regions are heterogeneous in income and have the same preferences.[4] In particular, let us consider a country composed of two regions, of equal population normalized to one, with different incomes, w for the poorer region B and kw with, $k \geq 1$, for the richer region A. Hence, the higher is the parameter k, the higher is inequality between the regions. Utility in region $i=A,B$ is given by:

$$U_i = u_i(c_i) + H_i(g_i)$$

where the sub-utilities of the two regions over net income (or private consumption) c_i and expenditure on a regional public good g_i are given by the same functions. For the moment we will not introduce spillovers from public good production in the other region.

For the sake of simplicity we will focus on the particular case in which $u_i(x) = H_i(x) = \log x$, so as to obtain closed form solutions. The public good is financed through a proportional income tax at rate t_i. We will always assume that the Constitution sets a social welfare function of the Bentham variety for the country as a all, that is an un-weighted sum of the regional utility functions:[5]

$$W = u_A(c_A) + H_B(g_A) + u_B(c_B) + H_B(g_B)$$

As a benchmark for our model, we establish what is the first best allocation of resources in this model. This could be implemented choosing the tax rates t_A and t_B and two local public expenditures g_A and g_B to maximize:

$$W = u_A\left[kw(1-t_A)\right] + u_B\left[w(1-t_B)\right] + H_A(g_A) + H_B(g_B)$$
$$s.v. kwt_A + wt_B = g_A + g_B$$

The first order conditions for the optimum centralized redistribution are:

$$u'_A(c_A) = u'_B(c_B) = H'_A(g_A) = H'_B(g_B)$$

which imply equalization of private consumption and public spending across the regions. In particular, under our functional form assumptions we obtain:

$$c_A^{FB} = c_B^{FB} = g_A^{FB} = g_B^{FB} = \frac{(k+1)w}{4}$$

and the utilities:

4 Income heterogeneity is also considered by Alesina, Angeloni and Etro (2005) and especially Bordignon, Manasse and Tabellini (2001) For models with heterogeneity in preferences see Alesina, Angeloni and Etro (2001; 2005) and Besley and Coate (2002). Persson and Tabellini (1996a; 1996b) are the classic references on risk sharing in fiscal federalist constitutions.

5 The earliest example of such a welfare function in the analysis of fiscal regional problems we are aware of is Pantaleoni (1891).

$$U_A^{FB} = U_B^{FB} = \log\left[\frac{(k+1)^2 w^2}{16}\right] \qquad W^{FB} = 2\log\left[\frac{(k+1)^2 w^2}{16}\right]$$

where *FB* clearly stands for first best.

If the two regions are completely separated in their decision making, region A would choose t_A to maximize $U_A = u_A[kw(1-t_A)] + H(kwt_A)$ and region B would choose t_B to maximize $U_B = u_B[w(1-t_B)] + H_B(wt_B)$, from which $t_A^I = t_B^I = 1/2$, which implies:

$$c_A^I = g_A^I = \frac{kw}{2} \qquad c_B^I = g_B^I = \frac{w}{2}$$

with utilities:

$$U_A^I = 2\log\left(\frac{kw}{2}\right) \quad U_B^I = 2\log\left(\frac{w}{2}\right) \quad W^I = 2\log\left(\frac{kw^2}{4}\right)$$

where *I* stands for independence (a possible bench-mark) situation with no inter-regional redistribution. Notice that $W^{FB} > W^I$ for any *k*, but also the independence outcome is Pareto-efficient, since any redistribution to the poorer region must hurt the richer one.

Let us now consider the two regions as members of a federal or unitary state country. The Constitution assigns the production of the public good to regions but the policy of taxes and transfers can follow a centralized system or a decentralized one.

Centralization

Under centralization, the Constitution requires a national and uniform income tax rate in all regions and no regional or central government deficit spending. Furthermore, it may entitle the central government: (i) to levy a lump sum tax on citizens in the rich regions to finance a negative tax program in favour of citizens in the poor regions *or* (ii) to set up a transfer programs by which rich regions are "forced" to transfer financial resources to poor regions. The parameter θ_1 represents the instrumental fiscal variable used to generate the rich citizen-to-poor citizen transfer; the parameter θ_2 represents a financial transfer from region A to region B required to ensure that regional spending on public goods is fully financed (by tax revenue and interregional transfer). We will assume that the Central Government cannot, at the same time, use both instruments: we assume that it can only redistribute income or transfer resources across regions. The first alternative being more interesting for our purposes we will focus on it, but comment also on the latter. In general such a constraint is well grounded on the limited availability of tax instruments of the government and it may be a short cut representation of its second best environment.

More formally, let us start considering the environment where the central government can choose the tax rate *t* and the lump-sum transfer θ_1 from rich to poor citizens. Local public expenditure is financed by each region through its own tax revenue as the central government does not have the power to enforce financial transfers from rich to poor Regions; in other words $\theta_2 = 0$. The objective function (where, for simplicity, θ stands for θ_1), is:

$$W = u_A[kw(1-t)-\theta\ ] + u_B[w(1-t)+\theta\ ] + H_A(kwt) + H_B(wt)$$

The first order conditions (with respect to t and θ) are:

$$u'_A[kw(1-t)-\theta\ ] = u'_B[w(1-t)+\theta\ ] = \frac{kH'_A(kwt) + H'_B(wt)}{k+1}$$

from which $t^C = 1/2$ and $\theta^C = (k-1)w/4$, where C stands for centralization. The allocation of resources is:

$$c_A^C = c_B^C = \frac{(k+1)w}{4} \qquad g_A^C = \frac{kw}{2} \qquad g_B^C = \frac{w}{2}$$

The outcome implies the right allocation of resources between private and public consumption in the country, but while we obtain perfect equalization of private consumption at the first best level for both regions – or optimal redistribution in our set up – there is no equalization of public expenditure, which is the same as in the independent regions case. This inefficiency is due to the lack of enough redistributive instruments which is constraining the central government. The utilities of the two regions are:[6]

$$U_A^C = \log\left(\frac{(k+1)kw^2}{8}\right) \quad U_B^C = \log\left(\frac{(k+1)w^2}{8}\right) \quad W^C = 2\log\left(\frac{(k+1)kw^2}{8\sqrt{k}}\right)$$

The alternative environment would be one where the central government can only choose the uniform tax rate and the inter-regional transfer directed to finance public expenditure in the poor region. In this case the situation is symmetric to the previous one with perfect equalization of public expenditure (at the first best level), but not of private consumption (which comes out equal to the value computed in the independent regions case).

Summarizing, *a centralized setting in which the central government can only redistribute personal incomes (or, alternatively, enforce interregional transfers) generates equalization of incomes after taxes (alternatively, equalization of local public expenditure) but differentiation in public good provisions (alternatively, incomes after-taxes).*

6 Of course, there is no reason why region A, if given the choice, should have chosen to sign a founding contract for a federation or an unification with region B. Nor that it should be glad to stay in the contract. In any case, the model has nothing to say on the birth or death of federations.

Decentralization

Consider now the case where the Constitution, while maintaining the same social welfare function, assigns tax autonomy to regional governments and assumes that private consumption and regional public goods production be regulated by lump-sum taxes or transfers.

The allocation of fiscal powers to regional and federal governments poses some problems of timing and of budgetary procedures. It is possible to envisage at least two alternatives. Remember that budgetary decisions by regional and central governments are interdependent. Somehow, one of the two levels of governments has to make a first step. Consequently, in our model it is possible to envisage at least two alternatives. In the first alternative, the central government chooses the redistributive policy first and the regions choose their regional tax rates afterwards. In the second alternative, the regions move first and choose their tax rates and the central government steps in a second stage to decide on the redistributive policy. These two different time sequences can be taken to describe two different budgetary procedures.

We will focus on the case in which regions are first movers and the central government cannot commit to a redistributive policy, since this is more realistic (indeed it is simple for the central government to operate transfers between regions, while tax rates are typically set in advance and require some time to be changed). This no-commitment case can be described by the following sequence of decisions:

1. each region chooses its own tax rate t_A and t_B : a) taking the choice of the other region as given; b) knowing that the central government is bound by the Constitutional objectives as defined in 2).
2. the tax-transfer θ is chosen that maximizes the social welfare function.

Each region knows that the government maximizes:

$$W^D = u_A[kw(1-t_A)-\theta]+u_B[w(1-t_B)+\theta]+H_A\left[kwt_A\right]+H_B\left[wt_B\right]$$

where D stands for decentralization. For given tax rates, the first order conditions imply:

$$u'_A[kw(1-t_A)-\theta]=u'_B[w(1-t_B)+\theta]$$

which generates equalization of private consumption in the two regions through the following transfer function:

$$\theta^D(t_A,t_B)=\frac{kw(1-t_A)-w(1-t_B)}{2}$$

Each region takes this in consideration so as to maximize:

$$U_A=u_A\left[kw(1-t_A)-\theta^D(t_A,t_B)\right]+H_A\left(kwt_A\right)=u_A\left[\frac{kw(1-t_A)+w(1-t_B)}{2}\right]+H_A\left(kwt_A\right)$$

and

$$U_B = u_B\left[w(1-t_B)+\theta^D(t_A,t_B)\right]+H_B\left(wt_B\right)=u_B\left[\frac{kw(1-t_A)+w(1-t_B)}{2}\right]+H_B\left(wt_B\right)$$

Taking into consideration the optimality condition for the central government tax-transfer, the first order conditions of the two regions imply:

$$u'_A\left[\frac{kw(1-t_A)+w(1-t_B)}{2}\right]=2H'_A\left(kwt_A\right)=u'_B\left[\frac{kw(1-t_A)+w(1-t_B)}{2}\right]=2H'_B\left(wt_B\right)$$

Given our functional form assumptions, Regions choose the tax rates:

$$t_A^D=\frac{k+1}{3k} \qquad t_B^D=\frac{k+1}{3}$$

which imply the transfer $\theta^D=(k-1)w/2$. Utilities are:

$$U_A^D=U_B^D=\log\left(\frac{(k+1)^2w^2}{18}\right) \qquad W^D=2\log\left(\frac{(k+1)^2w^2}{18}\right)$$

The allocation of resources is inefficient since public expenditure is now higher than in the first best while private consumption is lower than in the first best:

$$c_A^D=c_B^D=\frac{(k+1)w}{6} \qquad g_A^D=g_B^D=\frac{(k+1)w}{3}$$

Notice that income redistribution is less than optimal and less than under centralization ($c_i^D<c_i^C=c_i^{FB}$ for i=A,B). The nature of this inefficiency is interesting. Each region is now taking in consideration the effect of its own tax rate on the redistributive policy adopted by the nation state government. The higher is the taxation of the poorer region, the higher will be the negative tax assigned to this region. Hence, the incentive to set a higher tax rate. The opposite happens to the richer region, but the overall result is over-production of regional public goods, which is in contrast to the one derived by Bordignon et al. (2001), who find a tendency toward under-provision of regional public goods. It is to be noted that their result would be obtained if our model were constructed on a the central government with the possibility to enforce interregional transfers – θ_2 – to finance public goods production but without the possibility to apply the tax-transfer θ_1 on individuals of Regions A and B. Such a model would generate perfect equalization of public expenditure and private consumption, but with under-provision of public goods. Utilities would remain U_A^D and U_B^D as previously defined and country utility would remain W^D.[7]

7 Indeed, the Bordignon, Manasse and Tabellini model assumes that the central government can only force such an interregional financial transfer that equalizes public expenditure in both regions, thus proportional to the difference in tax revenues. As a consequence, both the rich and the poor regions have small incentives to tax: higher local taxes

Summarizing, *a decentralized setting in which the central government only controls its tax parameters (or, alternatively, can only enforce interregional financial transfers) obtains perfect redistribution of income and equalization of local public expenditure but generates over-provision (alternatively, under-provision) of public goods. It is important to remember that this result rests on the institutional assumption that regional governments are assigned a prominent role in the making of the economy-wide budgetary policy.* In later pages this solution will be referred to as a case of constrained decentralization.

As Bordignon et al. (2001) have shown, when the Central Government can commit to the redistributive policy, the first best outcome can be achieved. Moreover, if it could choose both a transfer of income and an inter-regional financial transfer, even without such a commitment, the first best allocation of resources could also be achieved. Once again the lack of a full set of policy instruments is crucial for the emergence of inefficiencies.

Discussion

In the real world, redistribution is implemented with different programs, with the central government involved primarily in personal income redistribution via taxation of income at differentiated rates and with richer regions forced to participate in equalization plans directed to the financing of local public goods in poorer regions.[8] If the redistributive activity is more relevant, we have shown that:
under centralization optimal income redistribution is achieved but the allocation of local public goods across the regions is suboptimal, while under decentralization there are limited redistribution and a tendency to generate overprovision of local public goods.[9]

---

for the rich region are lost in part to increase transfers to the poor one and higher local taxes in the poor region are lost in a partial reduction of the transfer from the rich region. Both regions reduce taxation – compared to the optimal level obtained under centralization – and public expenditure is sub-optimal. Our model, instead, focuses on redistribution of personal income, in the sense that the richer region finances, with the yield of the central government tax, part of the private consumption of the poor region. Hence, the central government chooses a tax-transfer so as to equalize private consumption in both regions (that is to implement a perfect redistribution) and it chooses a transfer which is proportional to the difference in net income. As a consequence, the two regions have now different incentives. For the poor region there is an incentive to increase local tax rates since this increases the net income differential between the regions, and hence it increases redistribution from the rich region. This effect determines the increase in local taxation and hence the overprovision of public goods in equilibrium.

8 Our result seems to be relevant not only for the constitutional design of fiscal federalism in countries, but also for the organization of unions of countries. For instance, the European Union is exactly characterized by a group of countries with large autonomy on their policies of taxation and expenditure in public goods, while a net of transfers between countries is managed at the union level with redistributive purposes: our model emphasizes that in this environment countries may engage in excessive expenditures on local public goods.

9 Such a result is more plausible than the under provision result from an empirical point of view. Indeed, the correlation of our index of decentralization with the average share of subnational public expenditure in GDP is highly positive; 0.87 worldwide and 0.9 for the

Clearly the tendency would be limited in case of spillovers between regions due to a well known free-riding problem.

Centralization versus decentralization

In this section we will deal with the choice between centralization and decentralization and the relationship between inequality and such a choice. It is interesting to investigate under what conditions the transition a) from the independent regions setting to a centralized or a decentralized system and b) from a centralized to a decentralized system will be accepted. Since the function of the central government in the model is to implement income redistribution, it is clear that the degree of inequality will play a crucial role in answering the question.

We start comparing centralization with independence. On the one side, the rich country always prefers a no-central government setting to a centralized system. Indeed $U_A^C - U_A^I = \log[(k+1)/2k] < 0$ for any k since under centralization the rich region redistributes income toward poor region. On the other side, the poorer region, that is benefiting from redistribution, is always in favour of centralization, no matter how inefficient. In fact $U_B^C - U_B^I = \log[(k+1)/2] \geq 0$ for any k.

The most important comparison is between the nation-wide utilities under independence and under centralization. It shows that a centralized system is always preferred to independence:

$$W^C - W^I = \log\left(\frac{(k+1)^2}{4k}\right) \geq 0 \text{ for any } k$$

Though the allocation of resources may be not perfectly efficient under centralization, a move from independence to centralization makes the poor region better off enough to compensate the losses of rich region: *centralized redistribution always makes the country better off compared to independence.*

Now let us move to decentralization. Again, the rich region always prefers the no-central government situation to this decentralized system. Indeed $U_A^D - U_A^I = \log[2(k+1)^2/9k^2] < 0$ for any k. More interestingly, the poor region, that is benefiting from redistribution, is not always in favour of decentralization, since this implies a considerable inefficiency. More exactly we have $U_B^D - U_B^I = \log[2(k+1)^2/9] \geq 0$ if and only if $k \geq [\sqrt{18}/2 - 1]$, that is, the poorer region prefers the decentralized structure if and only if income inequality is great enough. The reason is that under decentralization, only when inequality is very high are the benefits from inefficient redistribution are higher than those from the efficient allocation of resources under independence.

OECD countries. In other words, more decentralized countries tend to spend a higher fraction of their income in local goods than centralized countries. Notice that in our model there is no difference between local public expenditure in pure public goods or private goods, hence it is correct to look at data on local public expenditure without distinguishing between provision of public and private goods.

The comparison of the nation-wide utilities under independence and decentralization shows that:

$$W^D - W^I = \log\left(\frac{4(k+1)^4}{81k^2}\right) \geq 0 \text{ if and only if } k \geq 2$$

Again, *only a great enough degree of income inequality justifies a transition from regional independence to the inefficient decentralized redistribution.*

Finally let us compare the model of centralization with the model of decentralization. From the point of view of the rich region, centralization is always better:

$$U_A^C - U_A^D = \log\left(\frac{9k}{4(k+1)}\right) > 0 \text{ for any } k$$

the reason being that centralization allows to limit redistribution. Instead, the poor region prefers centralization if and only if the degree of inequality is low enough:

$$U_B^C - U_B^D = \log\left(\frac{9}{4(k+1)}\right) > 0 \text{ if and only if } k \in [1, 1.25]$$

Most important, centralization is the efficient choice if and only if the degree of inequality is low enough and decentralization is better when inequality is very high:

$$W^C - W^D = 2\log\left(\frac{9\sqrt{k}}{4(k+1)}\right) > 0 \text{ if and only if } k \in [1, (9+\sqrt{17}))^2/64]$$

Heterogeneity between the regions must be very high for the gains from decentralization to compensate the losses in efficiency associated with decentralized redistribution. Thus, there are some good reasons for a very heterogeneous country to be organized in a decentralized way, while the opposite holds for a relatively homogeneous country.

Notice that if we were going to introduce spillovers between local public goods (as in Alesina, Angeloni and Etro, 2001; 2005) a further tendency toward under provision of local public goods would emerge under decentralization. In such a model, decentralization would be socially preferred to centralization if and only if income inequality between the regions was great enough or if spillovers between local public goods were small enough.

In the rest of this section we will show other ways in which our simple model can rationalize the trade-off between redistribution and decentralization. First, we will show that a transition from a centralized system to an efficient decentralized one always implies giving up to some redistribution to be politically feasible. Later on, we will discuss a system of fiscal federalism with a House of Regions where an efficient outcome is realized with partial redistribution.

Transition from centralization to decentralization

Now we analyse an issue of transition. We consider a reform which moves the organization from a centralized setting to a decentralized one, as many countries have recently experienced or are experiencing. The question is: does a reform towards decentralization limit the extent to which the central government can redistribute income? We will show that for such a reform to be supported by the whole country, the level of redistribution must be lower than it would be required by the maximization of the social welfare function. This result shows that a trade-off between decentralization and redistribution emerges especially in transitions towards decentralization.

We assume that for the reform to be adopted, both regions must agree. Hence they must be both better off under decentralization than under centralization. However, we know that if the equilibrium decentralization is implemented, the rich region is worse off if inequality is great enough (and the poor region better off). Hence, the only way to implement decentralization is to limit redistribution in such a way that both regions benefit from it.

In particular the reform is feasible if the transfer between regions is limited by a cap on the redistributive tax-transfer $\bar{\theta}$. If this is binding, regions will consider $\bar{\theta}$ as not affected by their choices and will maximize:

$$U_A = u_A\left[kw(1-t_A)-\bar{\theta}\right]+H_A\left(kwt_A\right)$$

and

$$U_B = u_B\left[w(1-t_B)+\bar{\theta}\right]+H_B\left(wt_B\right)$$

from which we obtain the optimality conditions:

$$u'_A\left[kw(1-t_A)-\bar{\theta}\right]=H'_A\left(kwt_A\right)$$

$$u'_B\left[w(1-t_B)+\bar{\theta}\right]=H'_B\left(wt_B\right)$$

that is the functions $t_i = t_i(\bar{\theta})$ for $i=A,B$.

A credible value of the cut-off $\bar{\theta}$ is actually such that the rich region is just indifferent between centralization and decentralization. More precisely $\bar{\theta}$ is defined by the indifference relationship:

$$u_A\left[kw(1-t_A(\bar{\theta}))-\bar{\theta}\right]+H_A\left(kwt_A(\bar{\theta})\right)=u_A\left[kw(1-t)-\theta_1\right]+H_A\left(kwt\right)$$

Under our assumption regarding functional forms, we have:

$$\log\left(\frac{kw-\bar{\theta}}{2}\right)^2=\log\left[\frac{(k+1)kw^2}{8}\right] \Leftrightarrow \bar{\theta}=w\left[k-\sqrt{\frac{(k+1)k}{2}}\right]$$

To make sure that this is a right equilibrium we need to verify that also the poor region is always better off under such a form of partial decentralization, and that $\bar{\theta} < \theta^{DNC}$ so that the constraint is indeed binding; these two conditions can be easily verified to always hold.

Finally notice that this form of partial redistribution implies tax rates $t_A = \sqrt{\frac{(k+1)k}{8}}$ and $t_B = \frac{k+1}{2} - \sqrt{\frac{(k+1)k}{8}}$ from which we derive the allocations:

$$c_A = g_A = \frac{w}{2}\sqrt{\frac{(k+1)k}{2}} \qquad c_B = g_B = \frac{w}{2}\sqrt{\frac{(k+1)k}{8}}\left[\sqrt{\frac{2(k+1)}{k}} - 1\right]$$

This makes clear that an efficient allocation of resources is realized in each region, but redistribution from the rich to the poor is only partial. It is important to notice that the limit to redistribution is beneficial because it avoids the time-inconsistency problem emerging under decentralization: $\bar{\theta}$ is clearly independent from the tax rates chosen by the two regions. For this reason, despite the fact that best allocation of resources under constrained decentralization improves on constrained centralization only when inequality is high (as shown in the previous section), the feasible decentralization with partial redistribution always improves on centralization.

Summarizing, we have shown that *a transition from constrained centralization to a decentralization is supported by both regions if and only if the central government abandons the objective of complete redistribution.*

Fiscal federalism with a House of Regions

We now describe a system of fiscal federalism in which a House of Regions has the power to decide the redistributive parameter of the central government income tax (in previous notation, the parameter θ). Let us consider the decentralized system modified according to the following timing:

1. the regions decide on the redistributive transfer θ by bargaining;
2. each region chooses its own tax rate t_A and t_B a) taking the choice of the other region as given; b) knowing the transfer θ chosen in stage 1).

Given the transfer, the two regions maximize:

$$U_A = u_A\left[kw(1-t_A) - \theta\right] + H_A\left(kwt_A\right)$$

and

$$U_B = u_B\left[w(1-t_B) + \theta\right] + H_B\left(wt_B\right)$$

from which we obtain the optimality conditions:

$$u'_A\left[kw(1-t_A)-\theta\right]=H'_A\left(kwt_A\right)$$

$$u'_B\left[w(1-t_B)+\theta\right]=H'_B\left(wt_B\right)$$

that is the reaction functions $t_i=t_i(\theta)$ for *i=A,B*. This implies the utilities:

$$U_A\left(\theta\right)=u_A\left[kw(1-t_A(\theta))-\theta\right]+H_A\left(kwt_A(\theta)\right)$$

$$U_B\left(\theta\right)=u_B\left[w(1-t_B(\theta))-\theta\right]+H_B\left(kwt_B(\theta)\right)$$

We now assume that the redistributive policy is chosen by Generalized Nash Bargaining, assuming that the relative bargaining power of the rich region is η. Hence the equilibrium transfer solves the problem:

$$\max U_A\left(\theta\right)^{\eta}U_B\left(\theta\right)^{1-\eta}$$

Under our functional form assumptions, the problem becomes:

$$\max\eta\left[2\log\left(\frac{kw-\theta}{2}\right)\right]+(1-\eta)\left[2\log\left(\frac{w+\theta}{2}\right)\right]$$

whose solution is:

$$\theta(\eta)=w\left[(1-\eta)k-\eta\right]$$

Notice that when the bargaining power of the two regions is the same ($\eta=1/2$), the transfer obtained under unconstrained decentralization emerges and the first best solution follows; when the relative bargaining power of the two regions is k ($\eta=k/(k+1)$), the bargained transfer is zero and the independence outcome follows. The final utilities are:

$$U_A(\eta)=\log\left(\frac{(k+1)^2w^2\eta^2}{4}\right)\text{ and }U_B(\eta)=\log\left(\frac{(k+1)^2w^2(1-\eta)^2}{4}\right)$$

and they depict the set of efficient outcomes. The country's utility is:

$$W(\eta)=2\log\left(\frac{(k+1)^2w^2\eta(1-\eta)}{4}\right)$$

and it describes the welfare frontier.[10] The bargaining index is likely to range between the lower bound of η = ½ (equal regional power) and the upper bound

10 Notice that such a result is better than the result under constrained decentralization from the point of view of the social welfare if one of the two regions has not too much bargaining power (in particular $W(\text{h})\geq W^D$ if $\text{h}\in[1/3,2/3]$).

of $\eta = k/(k+1)$ (power proportional to income). The first case delivers the welfare of the full centralization case (the first best solution $W(\eta) = W^{FC}$); the second delivers the welfare of the independence situation $W(\eta) = W^{I}$ with no redistribution. Within the interval, values of η generate cases of partial redistribution.

Notice that this system of extreme budget decentralization solves the time inconsistency problem generated when the regions do not bargain. An extreme decentralization setting integrated by interregional bargaining (as it might happen if a House of Regions were in effect) induces efficient policies with redistribution outcomes depending upon distribution of powers among the bargaining agents. In a representative democracy, distribution of power in a House of Regions will depend on population size, electoral rules and, behind them, on the relative wealth of the regions.[11]

Regional cooperation as a reputational outcome

Another way in which decentralization can achieve an efficient allocation of resources is available in a dynamic setting or, in other words, when the budgetary "game" is repeatedly played over time. Under such circumstances, well known reputational arguments allow the regions to obtain any efficient outcome (as characterized in the previous subsection) if they are 'patient' enough. For simplicity we will just show how the first best allocation can be obtained if the discount factor δ is high enough. The important result is that, despite what one may think about the way inequality should affect the incentives of both regions to cooperate, in our example such a reputational argument works independently with the degree of inequality.

More precisely let us focus on an infinite periods extension of the model and on 'trigger strategies'. In equilibrium each region chooses the tax rates $t_A = (k+1)/4k$ and $t_B = (k+1)/4$ and the government implements the perfect redistributive scheme so as to guarantee the first best utilities in each period U_i^{FB} for $i = A,B$. To verify that this is indeed an equilibrium, imagine that one of the two regions deviates and chooses an alternative tax rate. It is easy to show that the best deviation generates the one-period utility:

$$U_i^{Dev} = \log\left(\frac{3}{8}\right)^2 \frac{(k+1)^2 w^2}{2}$$

for each one of the regions $i = A,B$. Now, such a deviation induces the other region to revert to the sub-optimal taxation strategy forever and so it induces the inefficient outcome with utilities U_i^D for $i = A,B$ in all the remaining periods. Hence, it is not profitable to deviate if and only if:

$$\frac{U_i^{FB}}{1-\delta} \geq U_i^{Dev} + \delta \frac{U_i^D}{1-\delta} \text{ for } i = A,B \Leftrightarrow \quad \delta \geq \delta_i{}^* \equiv \frac{U_i^{Dev} - U_i^{FC}}{U_i^{Dev} - U_i^D} \text{ for } i = A,B$$

11 For early discussions of such matters, see again Pantaleoni (1891).

Simple algebra establishes that:

$$\delta_A{}^* = \delta_B{}^* = \frac{1}{2}$$

hence, the first best allocation of resource can be achieved when the regions repeatedly decide on their local tax policy and care enough about the future and such a result is not affected by the extent of income inequality.

Transparency and redistribution once again

At the outset, we studied a model of decentralization with a central government in full control that uses only one policy instrument, a progressive income tax. We showed that redistribution is attained and that resource allocation is efficient. Efficient redistributional outcomes can be reached, more generally, by employing a linear combination of central government tax rate (θ_1) and interregional transfers (θ_2). In equilibrium $\theta_1 + \theta_2 = w(k-1)/2$. Depending upon central government choices on θ_1 and θ_2, different values of t_A and t_B are generated. If $\theta_1 = \theta_2$, each equals *w(k-1)/4* and $t_A = t_B = 1/2$. If $\theta_2 = 0$, the burden of equalization is put entirely on central government taxation which becomes $\theta_1 = w(k-1)/2$. If $\theta_1 = 0$ the burden of efficient equalization is put entirely on interregional transfer which becomes equal to $\theta_2 = w(k-1)/2$. This latter situation requires that regional governments adopt different tax rates from those they would choose in the two previous cases.

With $\theta_1 = 0$ the tax rate in the rich region would be higher than ½ and higher than in the case $\theta_2 = 0$. However, in the model, the three possible cases, implying the same allocation of resources, are welfare equivalent.

Abstracting from the model, one may try to evaluate the two polar situations from the point of view of the rich region: in one extreme case, taxes are low in the rich region and high in the poor region, with the central government raising positive taxes in the former and negative taxes in the latter. In the other extreme case, taxes are high in the rich region and low in the poor region, with high interregional transfers from the former to the latter. In the first case the Parliament of central government bears the burden of high taxes in the rich region; in the second case, the burden is on the Governor of the rich region.

Let us briefly consider a real world situation where politics and the public have a positive evaluation on a *quid-pro-quo* balance of regional taxes and regional public goods output. It is likely that the rich region will show stronger opposition to the interregional equalization program (that forces it to levy high regional taxes) than to the transfer of income via progressive taxation (that belongs to the powers of the central government).

In our model, the interregional equalization transfer (θ_2) can be thought of as an ideal representation of the so called "*horizontal equalization plans*" discussed in the literature on fiscal federalism (see Giarda, 2001). These plans require that the regions themselves decide on the extent of equalization by setting up the rules according to which money is going to be transferred from rich to poor regions.

In the model, the central government tax-transfer (θ_1) can be taken to represent the family of equalization plans that go under the heading of '*vertical equalization plans*', plans whereby the central government decides on the extent of equalization by raising taxes on rich region citizens to finance central transfers (grant programs) to poor regions.

Horizontal equalization plans are more transparent than vertical equalization plans. They are often considered to be better than vertical plans, because they impose a sort of peer control upon the way poor regions spend money that comes from interregional transfer programs. No-tax revenue is suspected to be used less efficiently than tax revenue. The incentive to use it efficiently is expected to be greater when the grant comes from the neighbour region than when it comes from a presumably distant central government. According to this view, transparency of the relationship between donor and recipient – via peer control – will improve technical efficiency, lower production costs of local public goods and produce more value for money in the execution of expenditure programs. At least according to this optimistic view, transparency promotes efficiency.

However, for the reasons outlined above, popular sentiments against equalization objectives are likely to be of bigger relevance under 'horizontal equalization plans' than under 'vertical equalization plans'. In the real world, it is rich regions that more loudly call for programs of interregional transfer to substitute for central government equalizing grants: they want to show that it is their generosity that makes solidarity rules working. It is rich regions that call attention to regional fiscal residua.

In intergovernmental fiscal relations, transparency (as it attained with horizontal equalization plans) may limit the scope of equalization as tax rates autonomously determined in rich region tend to be lower than optimal values as the donor region (a) will determine the size of the grant on unrealistic assumptions on the cost savings it expects the recipient region to generate and, (b) will resist levying the required taxes and not want to bear explicitly the full cost of equalization, though the same taxes might be imposed by the central government.

To our knowledge, no country involved in regional equalization plans relies entirely on horizontal equalization plans. Even where House of Regions exist (as in Germany), the Constitution provides strict rules for the concrete construction of equalization plans. *In practice, transparency and its offspring – horizontal equalization plans based on direct interregional transfers – have left the place to more obfuscated vertical equalization plans based on central government grants financed by (progressive) income taxes.*

Conclusions

This chapter has discussed the relationship between income redistribution and the organization of a system of intergovernmental fiscal relations. Here, we want to briefly mention the possible extensions of our simple model designed to tackle a variety of interesting questions.

The assumption of equal population in the two regions can easily be relaxed introducing a bias in the composition of public expenditure: indeed, in this case the production of the public good becomes more convenient in the region with higher population, because of greater scale economies.

The assumption of equal preferences in the two regions can also be relaxed: such a further heterogeneity would create a new advantage for decentralized systems compared to the centralized ones as long as decentralization allows the regions to adapt their policies to their preferences.

When a national public good is considered, the choice between independence, centralization and decentralization becomes more sophisticated: independence would generate benefits associated to the complete decisional autonomy, but also a cost associated to the loss of scale economies in the production of the public good (since independence would require the production of two separate public goods in each region). Between the extreme assumptions of two local public goods and a national public good there is a set of intermediate situations in which each public good is regional but exerts spillovers on the other region. In this more general case (in part investigated by Alesina, Angeloni and Etro, 2005) a further coordination issue emerges because independence and decentralization imply that the regions take their choices without considering the externalities induced on the other region.

The assumption that all regions have equal opportunity to participate in the economy-wide budget making may be substituted by the assumption that one of the two regions is a first mover. A substantial leadership of certain regions is often realistic. In our model of constrained decentralization such an hypothesis would shift the burden of the inefficiency on the follower region inducing higher public expenditure and higher utility in the leader region and lower welfare for the country than in the case of regional parity. In decentralized settings, care must thus be taken to preserve regional parity in the decision process and in budget making.

Finally, the assumption of non-distortive taxation can be relaxed by introducing endogenous labour supply or exogenous costs of tax collection, so that a second best solution becomes the benchmark to compare with the third best outcomes available under constrained centralization and decentralization. Bordignon, Manasse and Tabellini (2001) have already explored issues of optimal regional redistribution in a similar context, but the approach presented in this chapter will probably allow a more general treatment.

Altogether, a case can be made for analysing institutional rules of fiscal federalist systems in stylised models such as the one presented in the chapter. Forcing legal provisions into simple analytical models may provide fresh insights onto old questions. Equally important is empirical research on the relationship between the structure of nations between level of governments vertically related and policy choices. In this chapter we have advanced the hypothesis of a trade-off between decentralization and redistribution. The robustness of such a relation and the sense of causality remain to be carefully checked.

References

Aghion, P., Alesina, A. and Trebbi, F. (2004), 'Endogenous Political Institutions', *Quarterly Journal of Economics* 119:2, 565-611.

Alesina, A. (2003), 'The Size of Countries: Does it Matter?', *Journal of the European Economic Association*, 301-16.

_______, Angeloni, I. and Etro, F. (2001), 'Institutional Rules for Federations', *National Bureau of Economic Research Working Paper No. 8646.*

_______, (2005), 'International Unions', *American Economic Review* 95:3, 602-615.

Besley, T. and Coate, S. (2003), 'Centralized versus Decentralized Provision of Local Public Goods: A Political Economy Approach', *Journal of Public Economics* 87:12, 2611-37.

Bolton, P. and Roland, G. (1997), 'The Break up of Nations: A Political Economy Analysis', *Quarterly Journal of Economics* 112:4, 1057-90.

Bordignon, M. and Minelli, E. (2001), 'Rules Transparency and Political Accountability', *Journal of Public Economics.*

_______, Manasse P. and Tabellini, G. (2001), 'Optimal Regional Redistribution', *American Economic Review* 91:3, 709-23.

Giarda, P. (2001), 'Fiscal Federalism in the Italian Constitution', *Nation, Federalism and Democracy* (Bologna: Editrice Compositori), 105-118.

Meltzer, A. and Richard, S. (1981), 'A Rational Theory of the Size of Government', *Journal of Political Economy* 89:5, 914-927.

Oates, W. (1972), *Fiscal Federalism* (New York: Harcourt Brace Jovanovich).

_______, (1999), 'An Essay on Fiscal Federalism', *Journal of Economic Literature* 37:3, 1120-49.

Pantaleoni, M. (1891), 'Delle regioni d'Italia in ordine alla loro ricchezza ed al loro carico tributario', *Giornale degli Economisti*, Reprinted in Pantaleoni, M. (1938), *Studi di finanza e di statistica* (Bologna: Zanichelli).

Persson, T. and Tabellini, G. (1996a), 'Federal Fiscal Constitutions: Risk Sharing and Redistribution', *Journal of Political Economy* 104:5, 979-1009.

_______, (1996b), 'Federal Fiscal Constitutions: Risk Sharing and Moral Hazard', *Econometrica*, 64, 623-46.

Index

For Product Safety Concerns and Information please contact our EU
representative GPSR@taylorandfrancis.com
Taylor & Francis Verlag GmbH, Kaufingerstraße 24, 80331 München, Germany

www.ingramcontent.com/pod-product-compliance
Ingram Content Group UK Ltd.
Pitfield, Milton Keynes, MK11 3LW, UK
UKHW020009200926
475702UK00015B/2563
* 9 7 8 1 1 3 8 2 7 7 6 6 3 *